Old Scapes, New Maps

Old Scapes, New Maps

A Training Program for Psychotherapy Supervisors

Ludmila W. Hoffman, Ed.D.

MILUSIK PRESS
CAMBRIDGE, MASSACHUSETTS

Library of Congress Cataloging in Publication Data
Card Number 90-061678

Hoffman, Ludmila W.
Old Scapes, New Maps:
A Training Program for Psychotherapy Supervisors

Bibliography: p.
Includes index.
1. Psychotherapy supervision.
2. Training.
3. Professional psychology. I. Title. [DNLM:
1. Psychotherapy supervision training — Methods.]

Request for permission or further information should be addressed to:
Milusik Press, 457 Mt. Auburn Street #6, Cambridge, Massachusetts 02138.

Published by:
Milusik Press
457 Mt. Auburn Street #6,
Cambridge, Massachusetts 02138

Designed & Produced By: Good Graphics Group, Boston.
Set in Adobe Sabon on Macintosh II.

For information about our audio products, write us at:
Newbridge Book Clubs, 3000 Cindel Drive, Delran, NJ 08370

10 9 8 7 6 5 4 3 2 1

Printed in the United States of America

Dedicated to:
Herb, Barry and Kim

Acknowledgments

I extend my thanks to Dr. Dugald Arbuckle for having the wisdom to include in the doctoral program that he directed, and I attended, a seminar on supervision. The seminar left me with many ideas and curiosities about the process of supervision and the training of supervisors.

My appreciation is also extended to the Massachusetts School of Professional Psychology and especially to Dr. Haskel Cohen for supporting my selection to teach the seminar on Theory and Practice of Supervision. In that context my true learning about teaching supervisors began.

I thank Elisabeth Dodds, my wise, generous friend, for offering to me her valuable skill of editing.

I thank Dr. Louise Christian, my clear thinking, brilliant colleague for her good will and editorial advice.

I also thank Drs. Ed Nevis and Joe Melnick for their support and suggestions.

I thank my husband for his steadfast presence, patience, support, encouragement, caring and love; I thank him also for providing me with invaluable advice and for writing the final chapter of the book.

I thank most of all my daughter, Kim, who, once a precious baby, is now a grown up, exquisite woman. Steadfastly and patiently, she deciphered my handwritten manuscript and transferred it to a word processer. With infinite patience she listened to me, heard me and supported me through this project. No one, not even the closest of kin, can be asked for a greater gift and dedication.

Table Of Contents

Part II: Preparation For Supervising

Part III: Transition From Preparation To Practice

Part IV: Practice Of Supervising

Part V: Ethics And Supervision

Preface

A life extended in a thousand directions
risks depression and madness.

May Sarton

THIS IS THE age of information revolution, information explosion, information overload. As the information brings us closer to each other, the intensities of interactions magnify. Concurrently, we are burdened by contradictions and a paucity of clear values. The paradoxes of the past loom large again: be vulnerable to be strong; be grounded to transcend; be unique to feel integrity with the universe.

Socio-cultural institutions are changing. Mass media bombard us with depictions of violence and conflict. Our fears are fanned by ever increasing warnings of pollutants in the air, water and food. We hear daily reminders of drug wars, terrible diseases, homelessness, poverty, opulent wealth and mindless waste. The cacophony of messages is deafening. It renders us insensitive to the sounds of pain.

We witness the passing of old traditions as we encounter a void in their stead. Feelings of loss, alienation and anger distance us from each other; we long for new traditions, for myths congruent with our times, for new rituals, and most of all for meaningful relationships. Some of us, insensitive to the loss of old values and life purposes, become addicted to the rituals of work and the conditions of greed. Still others experience only depression, oppression and fear. Loneliness, dread of emptiness, alienation and tears in the social fabric are on the increase.

The effects of turmoil are multivaried, yet similar: conflict, confusion, inroads into self-esteem, denial, withdrawal, helplessness, anger, violence and depression. The scatter, splintering, polarizations and distress of our lives motivate an ever increasing number of people to enter into psychotherapy.[1]

The increased demand for and acceptance of psychotherapy has stimulated a burgeoning growth of this field. With growth comes differentiation. Institutions of learning offer increasingly varied programs for educating and training psychotherapists. The older, traditional schools of thought are enriched, revised, and built upon. The corresponding practices are modified and innovated.

Within the academic setting, learned men and women guide their students through mazes of histories, sciences, theories, and their own peculiarities of thought. In time (and frequently just in time), before the student's mind explodes into much smaller minds, the minds of insignifcance, the students, developing their role of scientist/practitioner, are introduced to a practice of a most peculiar and sacred nature. It is a practice that seems at once as simple as one's own breathing and yet as mysterious as the depths of the human spirit. As breathing reaches beyond that which is seen, so the effects of this special practice go beyond what is heard or said. Its existence has no proof of touch, taste, or smell. It is the practice of psychotherapy.

Throughout their years of training, the fledgling scholar-scientist practitioners of psychotherapy are assigned and trained by a series of psychotherapy supervisors. These supervisors play a pivotal role in the delivery of mental health services. Their functions interface with patients' expectations of good treatment and supervisees' hopes for good training; the training institutions depend on them and the professional accrediting bodies trust them. It seems reasonable to assume that these special teacher-guides are knowledgeable about and proficient in the art and skill of psychotherapy, and also trained in the skills and arts of psychotherapy supervision. Until recently, however, formal training programs for psychotherapy supervisors have been few and far between.

The views of the past need to be laid to rest. Psychotherapy supervisors do not spontaneously acquire skills for supervising. The experience of having been supervised is not adequate preparation for the practice of supervising; the experience and practice of psychotherapy is not sufficient preparation for assuming the role of supervisor.

1. Current statistics indicate that 1.5 million people in the United States enter into psychotherapy each year and one out of three families has at least one person attending therapy (Jacobson, 1988).

The scapes of the past need remapping. Currently, the field of supervision has the benefit of a sizable mass of information. This information, derived from many schools of thought and many points of view within each school, creates a tendency to extend the field in a "thousand directions". Formal, systematic training of psychotherapy supervisors will focus the knowledge gained thus far. It will advance the notion that psychotherapy supervision is rightfully a practice specialty. Serendipitously, it will effect an increase in research attention. Formal, systematic training for psychotherapy supervisors can have substantial and wide-reaching effects. It can advance the training of psychotherapists; it can provide improved treatment for their patients. Reciprocally, it can benefit the quality of the patients' lives, the lives of their families and society at large.

Echoes in a Cave
Introduction

We should so live and labor in our time that which came to us as seed may go to the next generation as blossom, and that which came to us as blossom may go to them as fruit.
Anonymous

THE DECADE OF the '80's ushered in a new, more profound interest in supervision of psychotherapy. The 1982 and 1983 *Counseling Psychologist*, volumes *10* and *11*, were devoted to the concerns of psychotherapy supervision. In 1983, the *Journal of Clinical Supervision* was launched. The June 1987 issue of *Professional Psychology: Research and Practice*, included an extensive section on Advances in Psychotherapy Supervision. These indications of the growing interest in psychotherapy supervision are supplemented by the publication of significant books (e.g., Alonso, 1985; Bernard, 1979; Bradley, 1989; Hart, 1982; Hess, 1980a; Stoltenberg & Delworth, 1987) and an increase in presentations at major professional meetings on the subject of psychotherapy supervision. The surge indicates that what Alonso (1985) referred to as a "quiet profession" has been gaining a voice that is more audible than ever before. Nevertheless, Hess (1987b) points out that "psychologists tend to take psychotherapy supervision for granted" (p.187), and

Bartlett (1983) concludes a review of papers on the topic by stating: "A final comment is needed about an important issue related to supervision...the training of supervisors. Unfortunately such training is often assumed and not specifically included in some training programs. It is a topic that is extensive in scope and warrants separate and specific discussion" (p. 16).

A Gap in Training

The number of doctoral programs in professional psychology have been increasing and many of the existing ones have been expanding. Practitioners of psychotherapy have grown in numbers and specialties; demand for practitioners of mental health services has continued to be high. However, training of the "core actor,"the psychotherapy supervisor, has been attended to sparsely, neglected, paid mere "lip service," or ignored. In many circumstances, training of psychotherapy supervisors has been subsumed under training of psychotherapists. Its differentiation from psychotherapy has been frequently unclear, its processes unsystematic, the thinking about it has been scattered and its parameters ill defined. Alonso's (1985) proclamation that supervisors "need to speak to one another, *to train new supervisors into their profession* [italics added]" (p. 4) calls for attention more imperatively now than ever before.

Although seasoned supervisors point out that psychotherapy supervision is a "profession with its own standards, theories, and practitioners who are well identified and legitimized" (Alonso, 1985, p. 4), it is unclear where, when or how these professionals have been trained in the practice of supervision, what the standards are and what the corresponding legitimizing authority is. Currently, only a minority of psychology graduate programs attend to training of psychotherapy supervisors and only a few training institutions offer regular and systematic training in the theory and practice of supervision. The relative lack of training for supervisors is a serious omission in the field (Leddick and Bernard, 1980). Corresponding to the relative lack of training is the paucity of psychological literature about the training of supervisors. As Loganbill, Hardy and Delworth (1982) have pointed out, it can still be stated that "literature in the area of training for supervisors is somewhat sparse" (p. 36).

Psychotherapist Turns Psychotherapy Supervisor

"It has been the tradition that once one finishes being trained as a psychotherapist, one is ready to begin supervising" (Alonso, 1985, p. 5).

Consequently, clinicians are often appointed to supervisory positions even though they lack competence in the duties demanded by the position. Peter and Hull (1969, p. 225) and Russell, Grimmings and Lent (1984) are among many others who question the often implicit assumption that an effective therapist will also be an effective supervisor.

The assumption that a trained psychotherapist can also function as psychotherapy supervisor is not unlike the notion that a patient who has completed a course of psychotherapy is now ready to deliver psychotherapy services to others. This premise is parodied by Collins (1962) in a story about a man who was looking at a skittish, seemingly undisciplined, harnessed horse. The man asked the owner if the horse had been broken to harness. The owner replied, "Oh, sure, he's been broken all right, he's watched the old horses work" (p. 671).

Hart (1982) notes, "The point is clear that longevity of service versus therapeutic expertise is not enough to qualify for a position as a supervisor nor to fulfill effectively the duties of that position..." (p. 225). The "Peter Principle" operates here as it does in other contexts. Those therapists who do rise to the level of their incompetence, when they supervise, influence not only the psychotherapists that they train but also the treatment of the psychotherapist's patients, their families and ultimately the community at large.

Without the benefit of systematic, specialized training, it is not surprising that many supervisors of psychotherapy practice "by the seat of their pants." Often the first supervisory experience that a psychotherapist engages in, is assigned to him/her at his/her workplace without any prior orientation about the practice of supervision. Having had no formal predoctoral or postdoctoral studies focused on this topic, the psychotherapist is expected not only to undertake supervising but to deliver that service in a manner which will satisfy the needs of the institution, supervisee and patient. The fledgling supervisor's nagging doubts about his/her ability to fulfill the necessary function and his/her feelings of incompetence are set aside in the service of his/her need to prove that the honor and implicit privilege of the supervisory assignment are not to be marred by insecurities.

"Resources available to new clinical supervisors are varied but *limited*. Generally, beginning supervisors are able to integrate into their new role skills and experiences from a number of previous professional roles, such as supervisee, teacher, therapist, researcher, colleague and consultant. These experiences are provided by most traditional clinical training programs but *are seldom taught for the purpose of developing supervisory skills*" (Styczynski, 1980, p. 29). The belief that learning to be an effective supervisor may demand skills beyond those used in being a supervisee, teacher, therapist, researcher or colleague has been growing in acceptance. However, the belief that training of psychotherapy supervisors is distinct from the training of psychotherapists is not axiomatic.

This latter point is illustrated by an experience I had at a recent professional conference during which I attended a panel presentation entitled *Teaching and Learning of Supervision.* The presenters were seasoned and senior professionals. Well into the presentation of the first panelist I began to wonder whether I had made a mistake in reading the title of the presentation and thus falsely assumed it to be about teaching and learning of supervision while the presentation was to be about teaching and learning of psychotherapy. Having misplaced the program, I inquired whether I had read and remembered the title of the program correctly. The chairperson confirmed my original understanding. Then, wondering aloud, I asked, why in contrast to the title, the presentation focus was on *training of psychotherapists.* With apparent confusion, which turned into indignation, the chairperson informed me that the processes and issues involved in supervision were not at all unlike those in psychotherapy, clearly implying that differentiation between the two was quite unnecessary. Later, the other two presenters explicitly and implicitly corroborated the chair's belief. The expressed thoughts and beliefs of those presenters are not uncommon. The belief that psychotherapy training is interchangeable with training of supervisors and that psychotherapists spontaneously evolve into supervisors has created serious barriers to the development of specialized training programs for psychotherapy supervisors.

Hess (1987b) supports the belief that psychotherapy supervision needs to go beyond training in psychotherapy as he points out that competence as a therapist is essential, but not sufficient, for the practice of psychotherapy supervision and that training processes for the two functions are not one and the same. Nevertheless, relatively few graduate psychology programs offer seminars and/or training in supervision of psychotherapy. Bernard (1981) refers to supervisor training as a "relatively new concept" (p. 74) and applauds the efforts of graduate programs that include courses in this area.

Lack of required and systematic training in psychotherapy supervision is paradoxical in view of the data indicating that 55% of academic clinicians spend between 10% and 20% of their time in supervision; another 7% claim to spend 30% of their time focused on supervision (Shemburg & Leventhal, 1978).

Effects of the Training Gap

As a result of poor psychotherapy supervision training practices, "many promising supervisors are so disheartened by finding themselves pressed into service with little or no supervisory training that they flee the role and are lost forever to the profession" (Alonso, 1985, p. 5).

As unfortunate as the data supporting Alonso's observation are, it is equally unfortunate to learn of the effects of untrained or poorly trained supervisors on fledgling psychotherapists. Most of us who have had any responsibility for the training of psychotherapists have heard reports about supervisors who were laissez-faire to the point of destruction, or of those who were judgmental, authoritarian, and demanding to the point of sadism. We have also heard of supervisors who were friendly, seductive, sexually abusive or otherwise nonobservant of appropriate professional boundaries. Many of the above behaviors tend to be responses of new, untrained supervisors to their need to "save face" or to defend their sense of worth in view of demands to perform in an area in which they have no direct training. Alonso (1985) corroborates this interpretation when she states, "If asked, new supervisors often will admit that they feel fraudulent and are terrified of being discovered as such" (p. 56). Meanwhile, as undertrained supervisors struggle to perform their role, the supervisees of such supervisors experience a sense of worthlessness, confusion, frustration, anger, or rage; and they may find what there is no room within the context of supervision for dealing with those feelings. "The unconscious silence about the supervisors' part of the process and its effect on him mitigates against the student finding reassuring guidelines around which to organize the expectations arising from this new venture" (Alonso, 1985, p. 59).

What is potentially the most damaging effect of these unhappy circumstances is the *modeling* which takes place in such unproductive supervisory relationships. These modeling experiences may reverberate in the student's professional life for years to come and may well be passed on to new generations of practitioners.

In time, however, even the untrained supervisors tend to mature. Some will have sought some formal supervisory training and consultation. Others learn from on-the-job experience and reading. At least some of the seasoned supervisors will tend to have mellowed out, become more gentle, more productively directive, more empathic and more capable of maintaining clear boundaries even as they become more personally engaging, spontaneous and able to use metaphor and humor.

Thus, I am cognizant that even without formal pre or post-doctoral training, some psychotherapy supervisors have developed and practice the skill of supervision to the benefit of their supervisees and the supervisees' patients. I propose, however, that those supervisors lacking specialized systematic training in the practice of supervision, though they function in their role comfortably and productively, can benefit from formal training in the practice of supervising.

When the desirable skills of supervision are allowed to develop unsystematically, without guidance of specific and direct training, their development is unnecessarily difficult, uneven in its outcome and in some instances incomplete or lacking scope. The above conditions can also result in psychotherapy supervisors, during their early years of supervising, reaching an asymptote of proficiency.

This belief is supported by Worthington's (1987) findings that supervisors overall do not become more competent as they gain experience. In concluding the findings of his research, Worthington points out: "Unwilling as we might be to accept it, most supervisors simply might *not improve with experience. One reason for this might be that supervisors have little training in how to supervise effectively and thus may perpetuate the mistakes of their own supervisors* [italics added]" (p. 206).

Ethical Implications of the Gap in Training

Aldrich and Hess (1983) conclude a research paper concerning the process of supervision by stating: "Supervision is a tremendously complex task that is far too often performed with no more preparation than the neophyte supervisor trying to recall his own supervisory experiences. The growing awareness of the difficulty of the task (Loganbill, Hardy and Delworth, 1982; Bartlett, Goodyear and Bradley, 1983) suggests the need for further recognition of supervision's crucial role in the training of competent service providers" (p. 8).

The lack of systematic and specialized training of psychotherapy supervisors remains a jarring gap. To be a family therapist, a psychologist needs to have specialized training in family therapy; to be a behavioral therapist, a psychologist needs to have had training in behavior therapy; and so it goes for group therapy, child therapy and other areas of professional practice. To be a supervisor of psychotherapy, however, a psychologist needs no specific or systematic training in supervision.

Stoltenberg and Delworth (1987) pose a serious and disturbing question: "In what other professional area would we allow trainees or professionals to practice without training?" (p. 160). In what other professional area are novices "at a loss when seeking ego-ideals, for although they exist in his/her own experience of being supervised, there has been little opportunity to learn explicitly about the process of supervision..." (Alonso, 1985, p. 59)? Stoltenberg and Delworth (1987) point out that "Principle 2 of the American Psychological Association (1981) ethics discusses the necessity of high standards of competence for all psychologists and mandates provision only of services for which psychologists are trained. Given the current lack of training in supervision...there appears to be a serious ethical issue in regard to competency to supervise. Just as we now consider it unethical to counsel without prior training, we may soon apply the same idea to supervision" (p. 171).

A Training Program for Psychotherapy Supervisors

Spurred by authors quoted above and my interest in professional psychology, I offer in this book a detailed description of a program designed for training psychotherapy supervisors. The program is designed to integrate experiential and didactic material. A major component of the program is an introduction to the practice of supervising. The scapes of knowledge past are remapped to provide new views. Views which will promote the emergence of new possibilities and new frames for integrating psychotherapy supervision.

The program is divided into four parts: Part I, survey of the training program; Part II, the first stage of training, preparation for supervising; Part III, the second stage of training, transition from preparation to practice of supervising; Part IV, the third stage of training, practice of supervising.

Part I consists of Chapter 1. The focus of this chapter is on introduction of the training program. It consists of an overview of the conceptual framework and its design.

Part II consists of Chapters 2 through 5. This part contains a detailed account of Stage One of the training, i.e., preparation for supervising. In Chapter 2, I describe the use of the Supervisory Life Line, a structure designed to review the trainees' experiences of being supervised. Based on this structure, trainees are led to consider how learning from experiences of being supervised might influence their own practice of supervising. In Chapter 3, I set out structures designed for facilitating the trainees differentiating psychotherapy supervision from psychotherapy, defining of psychotherapy supervision, processing these activities, and building working relationships. In Chapter 4, I describe a simulation structure which is designed to build on experiences gained during the preceding training sessions described in Chapters 2 and 3. This simulation provides the students with an opportunity to test out the role of supervisor and simultaneously continue developing mutual trust and working relationships. Chapter 4 concludes with abstracts of the didactic material related to the experiential component of the simulation session. In Chapter 5, the focus is on concepts which provide cognitive tools for organizing and recording experiences and observations that will be encountered during the stage of practice supervising. The concepts are also related to the experiential data gained during the stage of preparing for supervising.

Part III consists of Chapters 6 through 8. This part details Stage Two of the training, i.e., transition from preparing for to practice of supervising. In Chapter 6, I present the process of and issues in matching the student supervisors with supervisees. Related issues and concepts are detailed and discussed. Chapter 7 contains a description of the content and negotiation process of a supervisory contract. Chapter 8 consists of concepts to be used in assessing the supervisee, the supervisory relationship and how the supervisory relationship can be influenced by common defensive postures of both the supervisor in training and the supervisee.

Part IV, consisting of Chapters 9 through 11, provides an account of Stage Three of the training, i.e., the practice of supervising. Chapter 9 sets out the short, though significant, beginning phase of the student supervisor's practice. Chapter 10 sets out the middle, and by far the most extensive, phase of the practice. In this chapter I discuss a series of themes which frequently emerge during this phase. Although these themes are interrelated, for the purpose of brevity I have categorized them into 8 topics: 1. limit setting and related ethical issues; 2. use of confrontation; 3. coping with intra- and interpersonal conflict; 4. coping with resistance; 5. coping with power issues; 6. coping with gender, race and cultural differences; 7. differentiating between psychotherapy supervision and psychotherapy; 8. cognizance of professional standards and ethics. Chapter 11 is devoted to the end phase of practice and the related processes of termination, evaluation and celebration.

Part V consists of Chapter 12, contributed by Herbert J. Hoffman, Ph.D. In this chapter Hoffman addresses ethical issues and legal considerations encountered by the supervisor of psychotherapy.

The organization of this book reflects the sequence of activities and exposition of related concepts that were characteristic of the training program I have instructed. In an effort to weave experiential and didactic components of the training into a whole cloth, my presentations shuttle between experiments/structured experiences and theoretical/conceptual material. Thus, what is figure and what is ground has the quality of a woven fabric.

PART I

A Survey Of The Training Program

1

Aerial View
Ground And Scope Of The Program

Let knowledge grow from more to more.
Alfred Lord Tennyson

DURING THE PAST decade, a small, though increasing, number of authors have been attending to the supervision of psychotherapy as a distinct field of professional psychology. However, the authors of major publications in this field (Alonso, 1985; Ekstein & Wallerstein, 1978; Hart, 1982; Hess, 1980a; Stoltenberg & Delworth, 1987), continue to focus on and examine psychotherapy supervision as an established or a developmentally evolving entity, without an adequate examination of a process by means of which the supervisor of psychotherapy evolves his/her ability to function in that role. That is, in spite of the new attentiveness devoted to psychotherapy supervision in general, descriptions of programs designed to train psychotherapy supervisors have received only limited attention.

The noteworthy exceptions in this context are the papers and chapters of books by Bernard (1979), Hart (1982), Hess (1980b), Loganbill, Hardy & Delworth (1982), Loganbill & Hardy (1983) and

Stoltenberg & Delworth (1987). These authors offer significant, though only brief, outlines of the supervisor training programs. For example: Hart devotes only six out of 267 pages of his book to training of psychotherapy supervisors; Alonso devotes two pages of her 168-page book to the topic; Stoltenberg and Delworth devote six pages of their 223-page book to it. The outstanding papers offered by Bernard (1981), Loganbill, Hardy & Delworth (1982) and Henessey (1982) also devote only brief portions of their texts to the process and content of training programs for psychotherapy supervisors.

To supplement the literature available thus far, I present a description of a supervisor training program in much greater detail. Furthermore, the focus of the book is carefully steered to the vantage point of the supervision student, what needs s/he has, what skills s/he is expected to develop, and how these skills are introduced and practiced in the process of the training program. The needs and skills of the supervisees and how the supervisor attends to the training of the therapist is addressed only when inextricably linked to the competencies of the supervisor.

The training program consists of three major stages: I. Preparation for supervising; II. Transition from preparation to practice of supervising; III. Practice of supervising. Figure 1 represents an overall schema of these stages and approximate proportions of time devoted to each stage.

The description of each stage includes the presentation of corresponding training segments, identification and discussion of related issues and concepts, and relevant examples of processing the material during the training sessions.

The Goals of the Program

The program I set forth in this book is designed to enhance the supervision trainee's awareness of: what experiences and personal tendencies s/he brings to the process of supervising; how to increase his/her skills in managing the supervisory relationship to the benefit of the supervisee and their own professional development; and how to enrich his/her understanding of reciprocal meanings and concepts. Thus, participation in the program provides the nascent and/or more advanced mental health professional with: 1. basic skills and corresponding knowledge of psychotherapy supervision; 2. experience of practicing psychotherapy supervision; 3. information about which attitudes and behaviors in receiving and delivering supervisory service tend to be productive versus cumbersome and/or unproductive; 4. information which can be used in making decisions about further training in psychotherapy supervision; 5. information about whether to pursue a specialty in psychotherapy supervision.

Figure 1
Schematic Representation of the Training Program

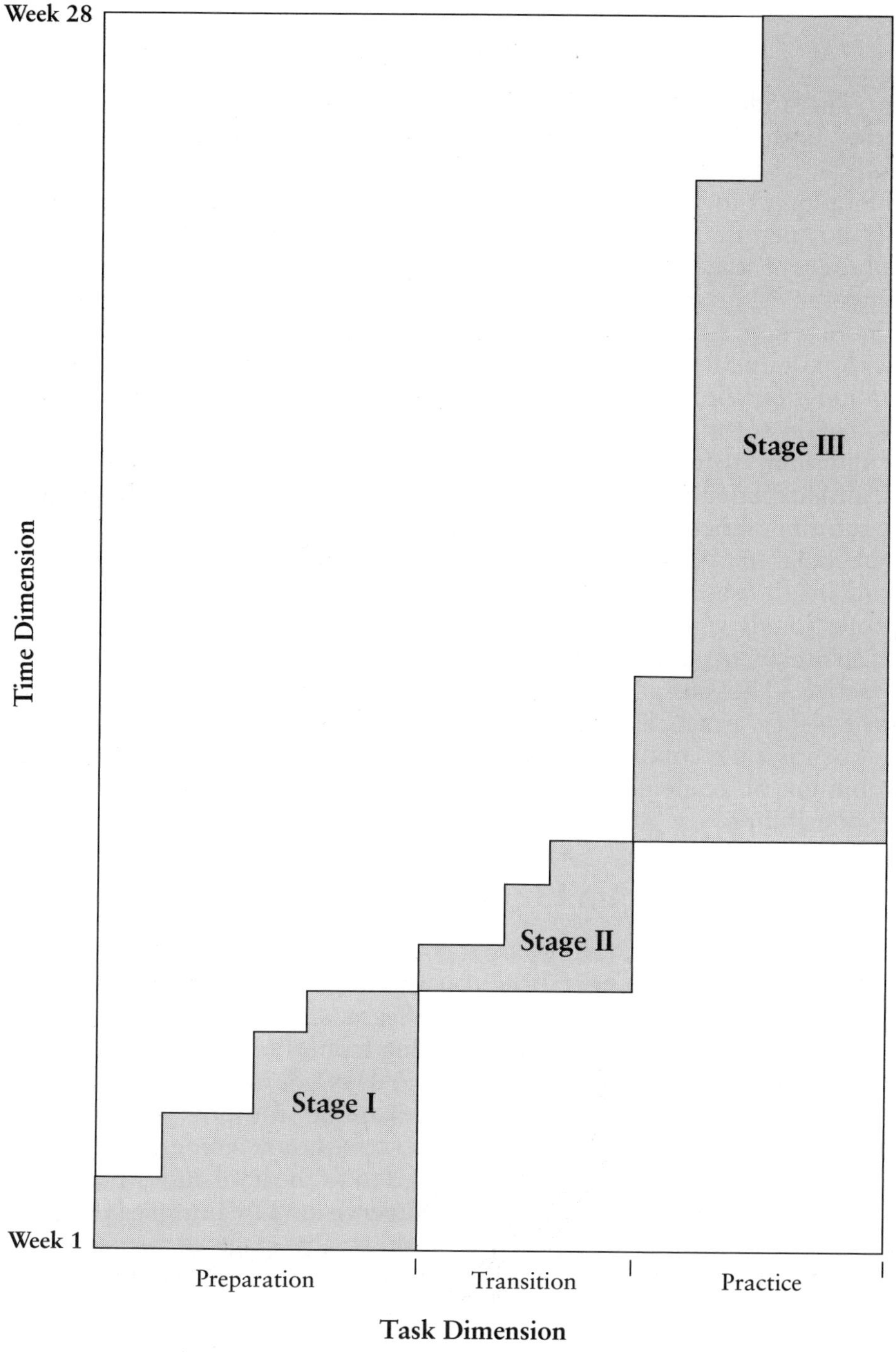

When the program is offered in part(s), the segments chosen for the workshop(s) will determine the expected goals of that learning experience.

Target Population

The student of psychotherapy supervision needs to have experienced being both a psychotherapist and a supervisee. Thus, the design and content of the program calls for all participants to have completed a minimum of forty supervised hours of psychotherapy practicum. Without a supervised practicum experience, neither preparatory stages nor subsequent stages of this program would have a meaningful or intended outcome. Many professional schools of psychology, as for example the school where I have instructed a program similar to the one described here, require all students to initiate a supervised part-time practicum in conjunction with the beginning of academic studies. Thus, at the conclusion of the second year in residence, these students will have accumulated a minimum of forty supervised hours of psychotherapy (or other practicum) experience. Doctoral programs in psychology which do not require a practicum component until the fourth or last year of a student's matriculation would not benefit by offering this training to predoctoral students. It would then be of special importance for the latter group of professionals, upon completion of their internships, to participate in this or a similar formal program designed to introduce them to supervisory practice. The basic acquaintance with the skill and knowledge of supervisory practice enables the new professional to step into the frequently called upon role of psychotherapy supervisor with at least the minimum of academic and practical background for discharging that responsibility.

Program in Form of Workshops

The program as a whole, or segments of it, can be offered in the context of continuing education in psychology and other disciplines at any level of professional development. Segments of the program can be offered in the form of workshops ranging from three hours in duration to a weekend (e.g., twelve hours over two days), or in an ongoing format of two to x number of sessions. For example, the preparatory stage can easily be divided into independent 3 to 4-hour seminars.

In addition, segments can be modified to fit the level and expertise of the audience. Thus, exploration of the Supervision Life Line (see Chapter 2) can be structured as a learning task at any stage of professional development. For example, in training advanced supervisors the focus of a segment organized around the Supervision Life Line can be changed from experiences of being supervised to experiences of supervising. Similarly, independent or sequential workshops can focus on issues inherent in early, middle and/or end stages of supervising: issues of gender; issues pertaining to managing conflict; ethical and legal issues raised in the context of supervising; application of Satir's positions to supervision; role playing and discussion of the "worst possible supervisor". On those occasions when the workshops are offered to advanced professionals, the structured portion of that workshop can be minimized and serve primarily as a common experience which lubricates discussion of the practitioner's current practice. The number and selection of segments would be a function of the time available, financial considerations, and the needs of group members enrolled or institutions undertaking the training.

Finally, as indicated above, the program, whole or in parts, can be offered to students and professionals in disciplines other than psychology; e.g., mental health counselors, psychiatric nurses, psychiatrists and/or social workers.

Conceptual Framework: An Overview

The program described in this book has general application and is atheoretical in its nature. That is, the program is not designed to follow any one theory or specific school of thought. Although some of the descriptive terminology is influenced by my orientation and theoretical persuasion, all components of the program can be used by instructors and students of any and all theoretical persuasions. Training psychotherapy supervisors within specific schools of thought – behavioral, psychoanalytic, person-centered – or training them to supervise specific skills, e.g., implosive therapy, strategic family therapy, couples therapy – should be introduced only when the practitioner has completed training in general processes of psychotherapy supervision.

The conceptual framework and design of the program is based on my experience of instructing students of supervision and on my knowledge and beliefs about psychotherapy supervision. Upon this foundation I have developed the following training principles.[1]

Principles

Psychotherapy supervision, not unlike the training for this activity, takes place in the context of *relationship(s).* The nature and parameters of this relationship can be defined by the content and process of the *supervisory contract. Communications* within the framework of the

1. Principles and Design of the Program can be offered to participants in the training program as a written supplement to the syllabus or workshop description.

supervisory contract provide the supervisor or student of supervision with *experience-based data.* These data, when organized and understood in context of the supervisory process, provide the ground for supervisory interventions.

The ongoing development of supervisory skills and the corresponding knowledge allows the supervisor or student of supervision to use his/her understanding of communications to address and cope effectively with an *increasingly complex comprehension* of supervisory tasks and issues.

Principle 1: Relationship

Psychotherapy supervision takes place in the context of a relationship between supervisor and supervisee. As Bernard (1989) has pointed out, "...the relationship between the supervisor and counselor will continue to be an important facet of supervision and must be given adequate attention while other experiences transpire" (p. 111). Accordingly, advancing the skills and enhancing knowledge of psychotherapy supervision takes place in the context of a series of relationships: relationships among the students of supervision; relationships between students of supervision and the instructor of the training program; and relationships between students of supervision and their supervisees.

The assumption that psychotherapy supervision is first and foremost a relationship process interfaces with the notion of "healing through meeting" and is complementary to Buber's "I-thou" phenomenon. As healing, from Buber's point of view, takes place "in the relationship between therapist and client" (Friedman, 1988, p. 2), so growth in supervision, I believe, emanates from a relationship between supervisor and supervisee. Viewing supervision through this lens, the supervisor's developmental process is "learning through meeting". New knowledge, in this view, does not emanate from the supervisor or from the supervisee, but from the "between" in the relationship between supervisor and supervisee.

Although it is both the supervisor's and supervisee's responsibility to attend to the supervisory relationship, the supervisor, following the supervision instructor's example, should lead in this activity and model to the supervisee how observations of the relationship yield information relevant to the content of supervision. A corollary to this principle is my belief and experience that satisfaction with and productivity of the supervisor-supervisee relationship correlate positively with each one's level of active participation, mutual trust, openness and authenticity. In context of the authenticity inherent in the I-thou relationship, the hierarchy of authority is diminished. Supervisor and supervisee both have the domain of their own authority.

Principle 2: Contract

Detailed articulation, negotiation and recording of a supervisory contract differentiates the supervisory relationship from other relationships and defines the parameters of each supervisory relationship and its goals. Accordingly, training of psychotherapy supervisors must include detailed attention to the development and maintenance of the supervisory contract.

All relationships proceed according to explicit or implicit, verbalized or not verbalized, assumptions and expectations which partners have of each other. Optimal conditions for a functioning relationship are established when the assumptions and expectations are conscious, explicit and verbalized (Sager, 1976).

In the context of the supervisory relationship, learning-training conditions are also optimized when both supervisor and supervisee are explicit and verbally expressive of their assumptions about or expectations of the supervisory parameters, processes and goals. Following articulation of these assumptions and expectations, a negotiation of encountered differences should produce a common ground or agreement which will then be referred to as a supervisory contract. Thus, both the general nature of the supervisory relationship and the unique nature of each supervisory relationship needs to be explicit, agreed upon, recorded, reviewed and, if at a later time found unsatisfactory, renegotiated. A corollary to this principle is my experience and belief that when contracts are created from and are based on the authenticity of the I-thou relationship, the arbitrary nature of interpersonal hierarchy is diminished. The path travelled by the supervisor and supervisee is wide enough for two. To this point, Rioch (1980) quotes Krishnamurti: "A disciple is one who learns all the time, and the word 'discipline' comes from the word 'disciple' – one who is learning. Now, if you are learning all the time, there is no need to conform, there is no need to follow any one. Therefore, the division ceases because both the teacher and the disciple are learning. Both are moving in the same direction at the same time..." (p. 77).

It is both the supervisor's and supervisee's responsibility to monitor their compliance with the contract and to confront and/or initiate renegotiation of those aspects of the contract that do not promote productive supervisory process.

Principle 3: Communication

The process of the supervisory relationship is based on a series of verbal and nonverbal communications between supervisor and supervisee. These communications include the messages emanating from or influenced by the personalities of supervisors and supervisees and by the dynamic established between them. Verbal and non-verbal communications provide an interactive mechanism and lubricate the learning process (Knowles, 1970). Verbal sharing of observations and experiences tends to order them, provides the student with an opportunity to learn about experiences of others, and presents opportunities to test reality for validation of their own experience (Stevens, 1971).

Maximizing opportunities for participating in and attending to a range of communications during psychotherapy supervision provides supervisors with optimal teaching opportunities and supervisees with optimal learning opportunities. Accordingly, training of psychotherapy supervisors should provide the students of supervision with a range of opportunities and ways to communicate.

Interpersonal verbal explorations of experiences, ideas and concepts promotes their understanding and integration with previous experience and previously or currently learned concepts and ideas. One-on-one relationships tend to limit the participant's reality testing and opportunities to experience a range of communications, reactions and/or opinions. Therefore, the program presented here is carried out in a group setting – a condition believed to maximize the varieties of communications, related experiences, opinions and ideas.

Principal 4: Experience

Psychotherapy supervision is, first and foremost, a process based on experience-based data. Accordingly, in the training of psychotherapy supervisors, experiential components of learning have essential value and when possible should precede consideration of didactic components of learning.

The position presented here overlaps Dewey's (1916) concept of "learning by doing". Therefore, it is not unlike the view of other Progressivism theorists of education who ascribe to the belief "that the key to reality is dynamic experience" (Brameld, 1959, p. 5). Based on that belief, Brameld elaborates on the centrality of experience in the learning process and he underscores that this notion stands in direct contrast to the passivity of "essentialist learning" (p. 180).

In concert with Progressivists, Knowles (1970), a pioneer in defining the process of adult education; i.e., "andragogy" also elaborates on the primacy of the experiential component to the process of andragogy. [My position, though closely related to Progressivist's views and Knowles' ideas of education, is supplemented by a belief that in the training of psychotherapy supervisors, data generated by interpersonal interactions arising out of the supervisory relationships, communications and the awareness of feelings generated by those interactions, are especially valuable.] Participation in the interaction designs incorporated into the program – the actual practice of supervision and its processing; i.e., interpersonal interaction with colleagues, instructor and supervisees, provides students of supervision with valuable experience-based data. These data, in the form of interactions, experiences, observations , feelings and opinions, can be examined, organized, related to corresponding concepts in literature and used for planning supervisory interventions. As the training instructor models the use of experiential data, so the supervisor in training should also model this process to his/her supervisee.

Principle 5: Development

As the skills and proficiency of the psychotherapy supervisor develop, s/he becomes capable of attending to and productively using data of increasing amounts and complexity. Accordingly, in training psychotherapy supervisors, it is important to order the presentation of learning tasks from lesser to greater complexity (Grater, 1985).

In general, the complexity of the communications does not vary according to the developmental levels of supervisor, supervisee or their relationship. However, the awareness, understanding and ability to use the complexity of phenomena and variables manifested in the process of supervisory communications reflects the developmental level of supervisor, supervisee and their relationship. Principle 5 accommodates this developmental progression.

In this training program, for example, understanding and using data necessary for experiments designed to order the trainee's experience of being a supervisee precede the experiments which facilitate the definition of psychotherapy supervision, and both precede the complexity of understanding and using data necessary in the practice of supervising.

A corollary to this principle is my experience and belief that it is the supervisor's responsibility to monitor the supervisee's readiness to be aware of, understand and use the level of complexity of his/her communications, and to adapt his/her interventions accordingly.

Design of the Program

The training program described in this book is designed to span two academic semesters, a total of 26 to 28 weeks, and consists of three major stages. The first stage is focused on *preparation* for supervising; the second stage is focused on *transition*, from preparation to practice of supervising; and the third stage is focused on the *practice* of supervising.

During all three stages of the training, trainees meet as a group weekly for a 2 hour session. At the onset of supervising practice, the group meetings are supplemented by regular meetings of the student supervisor with his/her supervisee.

Figure 2 presents an overview of the training program. Both axes, one representing the time dimension and the other representing the task dimension, are divided into three stages: preparation for supervising, transition, and practice of supervising. As indicated, tasks and time devoted to each stage can overlap. Time devoted to the practice of supervising is significantly longer in duration than the time devoted to the preparation and transition stages.

Stage I: Preparing for supervising

The preparation stage includes four segments. Each of the first three segments combine experiential and didactic components. The fourth segment is didactic in nature, though the data gained from the preceding segments of the program are useful in fleshing out and personalizing the concepts presented.

Segment One: Completion and examination of the Supervision Life Line. The Supervision Life Line (SLL) is a structure designed to provide an overview and experiential assessment of what the trainee has learned from experiences of being supervised and how this learning can be used in his/her practice of supervising. On the basis of completing the SLL and examining the data generated by that process, trainees have an opportunity to enhance their awareness about relationships they have experienced in having been supervised and how these experiences impact on current feelings, beliefs and goals related to the supervisory practice. Group discussions incorporate materials from the instructor's lecturettes and related readings.

In the process of examining data generated by the SLL, students frequently become aware that neither the supervisors nor they, themselves, have practiced according to a clear sense of differentiation between psychotherapy relationships, teaching or parenting relationships, and relationships of psychotherapy supervision. This awareness provides the basis for the second segment of the preparatory phase.

Segment Two: Defining psychotherapy supervision. This segment is designed to generate data for differentiating qualities of psychotherapy supervision from qualities descriptive of other similar relationships. To accomplish this objective the Core Quality Experiment (CQE) is introduced. Following the processing of that experiment, and on the basis of the data gained from the SLL as well as related readings, the students proceed to engage in a structured experiment designed to create cooperative and/or individual definition(s) of psychotherapy supervision. Discussion is supplemented with related readings and definitions offered by authors who have studied psychotherapy supervision.

The first two segments of the training program are designed to facilitate the understanding of psychotherapy supervision, and to maxi-

Figure 2

Schema of Time and Tasks Included in the Training Program

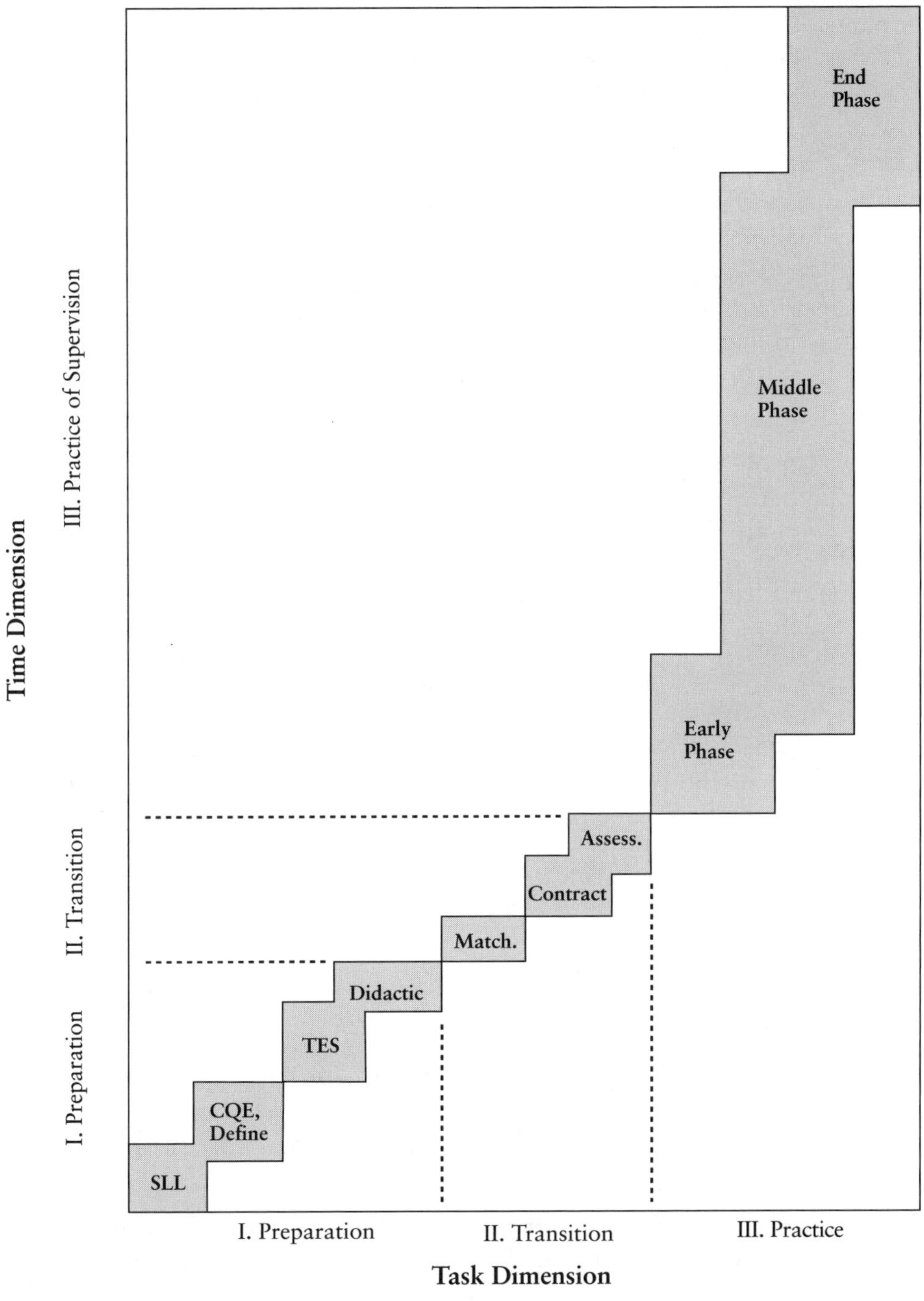

mize interpersonal contact and awareness of the nature of the relationships formed among the trainees. Thus, a by-product of the two initial segments of preparation is an increase in cohesion among the participants of training. The cohesion is accompanied by increasing growth in the trust level, a necessary component for meaningful participation in the third segment of this stage.

Segment Three: Triad Experiment Session. The third segment of preparation is based on an intensive simulation exercise which I refer to as the Triad Experiment Session (TES). The range of communications emerging from this simulation structure allows the trainees: 1. to test out their sensitivity to and awareness of non- verbal communications; 2. to explore the range of their observation skills; 3. to assume the position of supervisor; 4. to bring into the foreground the difference in manner of functioning as psychotherapist versus psychotherapy supervisor: 5. to build a learning community and a sense of trust. Here some of the data and meanings derived from the previous two segments (e.g., responses to questions such as: How might I function as supervisor? How do I demonstrate and experience the difference between supervision and psychotherapy? How applicable is our definition of supervision in this context?) are examined once again. The segment is concluded with an exploration of ideas about good supervision, an examination of supervision models and consideration of pertinent literature.

Segment Four: Concepts used to organize supervisory data. The fourth segment of preparation is of a didactic nature. Trainees have the opportunity to familiarize themselves with three constructs useful in the selection and organization of data emanating from the supervisory process. The constructs are examined and applied to the experience gained during the Triad Experiment Session. Completion of this segment concludes the first stage of training.

Stage II: Transition from preparation to practice of supervising

The transition sequence of the program consists of three segments: issues of matching a supervisee with a supervisor; introduction to elements of the supervisory contract; and introduction to concepts of supervisory assessment.

Segment One: Matching of supervisor and supervisee. This segment is devoted to matching supervisors-in-training with supervisees. Just prior to beginning of Stage III supervising, each trainee is assigned a junior colleague whom they will supervise. Although the assignments are made within unavoidable constraints, issues related to an ideal or productive match are examined.

Segment Two: Supervisory contract. During the period of time that the supervisors-in-training make the initial contact with their supervisees, the training sessions are focused on the elements of, parameters and processes involved in structuring a supervisory contract. The contract provides the student of supervision and his/her supervisee with a written set of agreements which will provide ground for the supervisory interactions and a frame for ongoing mutual assessments.

Segment Three: Supervisee assessment. The content covered in Segment Two overlaps with the content introduced during Segment Three. That is, in the process of determining items to be covered by the supervisory contract, the trainees are spontaneously alerted to the need for assessing the supervisee's learning style and professional development. Concepts and ideas which can help the assessment process are introduced and discussed.

Completion of these three segments concludes the second stage of the program.

Stage III: Practice of supervising

The third and most significant stage of this program is focused on the trainees' (at this stage referred to as Supervisors-In-Training, SITs) experiences of supervising a junior colleague. The three segments of the practice of supervision—beginning, middle and end—incorporate the SITs' developmental stages and related issues.

Segment One: Beginning phase of supervising. This segment consists of the SIT's initiation of a relationship with his/her supervisee, their negotiation of a supervisory contract, and the SIT's application of the assessment concepts learned earlier to the current task of assessing his/her supervisee.

Segment Two: Middle phase of supervising. This segment consists of the SIT delving into the process of supervising as s/he attends to his/her own and the supervisee's characteristic interpersonal defenses, relationship tendencies and developmental issues, and coping with issues which emerge out of this phase of the supervisory relationship.

Segment Three: End phase of supervising. This segment consists of the SIT preparing for and engaging in termination with his/her supervisee, and activities related to evaluation and celebration of completing the supervision experience.

Completion of Segment Three marks the end of the training program.

Process

As the SIT proceeds from the early to middle and then to the end phase of supervising, s/he encounters a range of phase related issues, changes in supervisory and colleagual relationships, as well as development in his/her ability to select, understand and use observations of progressively greater complexity. The SITs are invited to share issues and experiences pertaining to supervision during the group sessions. Trainees and the training instructor serve as consultants to the presenting SIT. Presentation and processing of the supervisory material may take the form of a monologue, dialogue, role play, feedback, reference to the relevant literature, or any combination of these teaching-learning tools. Supervisory data are ordered by using one or more of the organizing patterns which are discussed in Chapter 5.

In addition to their role as consultants, fellow trainees serve as built-in support systems. In consulting to, as well as in learning from, their colleagues the trainees have the opportunity to share their experiences and to test out meanings and concepts they derive from those experiences vis-a-vie their peers' feedback and understanding. In the process of and as a result of these communications, they also have an opportunity to compare and contrast the approaches and interventions which they have chosen to use in supervising with approaches and interventions used or suggested by their colleagues. Equally important is the opportunity for each SIT to become aware of the personal/professional impact they have on the other SITs and to compare and contrast that with the impact they have on their supervisee(s).

Ethical and Legal Issues

Throughout the seminar, and especially during the second stage of supervising, as supervisory issues are raised, a range of related ethical and legal issues are considered. When the participants enrolled in any part or all of the program identify with the discipline of psychology, the ethical issues are examined and dealt with in the context of and in accordance with American Psychological Association (APA) standards and the state's licensing or certification standards. However, when this program is offered to persons of other disciplines, corresponding ethical standards and licensing laws would provide the ground for discussion and/or action.

Use of Readings

The participants in the program are assigned readings pertinent to their training in psychotherapy supervision (see Appendix). The instructor invites the trainees to record their outlines of quotes from, and reactions to, the readings in a supervision journal. Trainees are also invited to use the group sessions to clarify topics from their readings which they found difficult to understand or which they found difficult to integrate with other learning. Similarly, trainees are invited to use the group sessions for discussing concepts which they have found to be enlightening or which have provided them with good organizing principles.

Trainees enrolled in the full sequence of this program are expected to have familiarized themselves with a major portion of the assigned readings during the initial 6-8 weeks of the training. I use the term "familiarized" advisedly. Clearly, for a majority of trainees, a careful study of the substantial amount of background material related to the task of supervising is not feasible. The instructor can be expected to facilitate the sequence of reading by matching the appropriate literature with the specific focus of each of the early sessions of the seminar. This coordination would be a component of the training.

Upon beginning the practice of supervising, the trainees are expected to have studied and be familiar with literature which is relevant to the questions and problems or discoveries they encounter in the process of supervising. That is, from the onset of the actual practice of supervision, literature will be used according to need or according to particular issues encountered and as reference material. For example, if an SIT encounters a gender-related issue, s/he might be directed to review the papers by Alonso and Rutan (1978) and Brodsky (1980). Earlier familiarization with a range of writings allows the trainee to select readings from books, chapters or papers most relevant to him or her at that time and in the context of the particular experience.

The instructor offers lecturettes summarizing some of the content of the assigned and/or other related literature, highlighting points which are applicable to the issues raised in the discussion. Trainees are encouraged to consider how the concepts, interventions and experiences recorded in the literature relate to their own practice of supervision.

Supervision Journal

A component of training which combines both the experiential and didactic aspects of the training is the recording of pertinent process and content in a learning journal. The instructor requests each trainee to record, at a minimum of once per week, his/her impressions and experiences of the content and process of training sessions and his/her reactions to personally selected concepts contained in the assigned readings. When supervision proper begins, it is suggested that the trainees use the journal to record their observations, impressions and ideas at least two times per week. One entry is focused on the experiences and thoughts emanating from the sessions with the supervisee, the other entry is focused on the experiences related to the material presented and/or discussed during the training sessions. Although the journal is intended to be the trainees's private resource, at times s/he may choose to share entries in the journal with colleagues during the group sessions. When training is offered in segments for post-doctoral students, participants can also be invited to write about their experiences and impressions in a journal. Time for writing these entries should be built into the workshop schedule.

Writing in the journal, as suggested above, has three objectives: 1. committing an experience of and learning gained from the training to written form—a process frequently effecting improvement in organization and understanding of the material; 2. collecting material to be used for the end of semester paper or for completing an evaluation questionnaire; 3. retaining the content of the new learning for future reference and training.

Supervision Papers

When the program is offered as a two-semester seminar to predoctoral students, the participants are required to write a 10-12 page paper at the end of each semester. The first semester paper consists of abstracted journal entries integrating the experiences encountered during the training group and in beginning to supervise with the material gained from readings. In completing the paper the trainees have the opportunity to demonstrate their ability in four categories: 1. selecting from the program's experiential sessions information which is pertinent to learning about the supervisory process; 2. demonstrating awareness of their own impact, or expected impact, on that process; 3. integrating their personal experiences with experiences of feedback received during the group sessions; 4. integrating their experiences with relevant concepts and literature.

The second semester paper also consists of selected portions of journal entries. In this assignment the focus of the paper is primarily the process of supervising, the relationships established during that process, and the manner of dealing with the range of issues raised during that process. Once again, the trainee has the opportunity to demonstrate his/her understanding of the process, to integrate that understanding with feedback received during the training sessions and concepts derived from relevant literature.

These two papers provide the instructor with significant information which is used in evaluating the development of the trainees. When the program is offered to postdoctoral students in segments, the instructor cannot expect the participants to deliver a written assignment. Evaluations in this case are based primarily on oral participation and written examination.

Trainee Evaluation

Trainees completing the two semester training are evaluated on the basis of competency demonstrated in their end-of-semester papers and on the quality of participation during the training sessions. Trainees enrolled in and completing one or more segments of the program are evaluated on the basis of completing a questionnaire or test.

Instructor and Program Evaluation

Formal (structured questionnaire) and informal (feedback and discussion) evaluations of the instructor and the program should take place on at least two occasions; 1. half way through the program and 2. at the completion of the program.

In summary, this training program combines experiential and didactic components of training to advance trainees' skills and knowledge of supervision. The design is geared to introducing trainees to sequentially more complex tasks. Participants are encouraged to communicate their reactions, experiences and the corresponding meanings and concepts in the group context with attentiveness to the process of relationships. A private recording of these experiences and attendant reactions is accomplished by maintaining a journal. The program consists of three stages: 1. Preparation for supervising; 2. Transition from preparation to practice of supervising; and 3. Practice of supervising. Literature relevant to the phenomena studied is examined and integrated with the experiential components of the program.

PART II

Preparation For Supervising

2

On The Road
Beginning Stage Of Training: Present Past, Growing Future

> *I try in the first meetings to develop a sense of fellowship and mutual service. An assortment of strangers may learn to speak directly to one another, turning gradually into a sensitively attuned body of men [sic], who have warmth of feeling and courageous discernment. They find how to learn and to teach. In them grows a relish for special qualities of individuals, so that any...may feel how it benefits by the presence of all. ...The interrelation of temperaments in a group of people is in itself highly educative.*
>
> M. C. Richards

Initial Meeting

OBVIOUS OR AXIOMATIC as it may seem, I want to underscore that prior to the training proper the instructor should facilitate the trainees getting acquainted with each other and the instructor. This earliest cultivation of trust forms the ground for further development of intellectual and interpersonal intimacy. Moreover, the evolution of intimacy builds a support structure upon which the participants feel safe to use mutual feedback and critique in a manner that is productive and creative. Concurrently, nourishing the attitude of trust models to the trainees the earliest task of supervising.

Thus, the program is initiated by inviting the sharing of experiences, both personal and professional, relevant to the focus of the training. Sharing of significant personal events such as, expecting a baby, family illness, a recent death in the family, as well as other events of current importance to the trainees is encouraged. In addition the trainees have the opportunity to express their reactions to the composition of the training group, to voice their expectations of the instructor and of each other, to share corresponding or related fantasies and fears. The time for processing these experiences, events and feelings is limited. Nevertheless, exchanges of this nature provide the trainees with exposure to each other's multidimensional, integral nature.

The process of building mutual trust should stay in the foreground of the early stage of training. Even as the instructor introduces the intended content, process, and parameters of the program (as described in Chapter One), the trainees should be invited to collaborate in the process by voicing their reactions to the instructor's beliefs and organization strategies. The process, infused with respect for others' views and with encouragement of a pro-active attitude, models to the participants a manner of dealing with some of the earliest and consistently the most important tasks they will encounter with their own supervisees.

The following description of an early interaction during a training session provides an illustration of the approach described above.

Instructor: One of the requirements of this course of training, as you might already know from having looked over your syllabus, is keeping a learning journal related to the training. You can initiate the journal by recording your impression of our beginning sessions and/or by recording some memorable experiences of having been supervised which might impact on your being a supervisor. At times these memorable moments are the difficult, angering or embarrassing encounters. Actually, it might be interesting to share some of those events, perhaps some of the embarrassing moments, right now.... Would anyone like to do so?
Participant: I am not aware of any embarrassing moments during the years of being supervised...and I certainly don't think that everybody has them.
Instructor: Yes, I agree with you, not all of us had them. But I think that if they did happen they usually are quite memorable.
Participant: Well, most of all I feel a bit surprised that you [directing himself to the instructor] would ask us to reveal something like that before we know each other well enough for such interchange.
Instructor: So, it seems that you and I have a different rhythm of getting close. I guess my invitation seemed sort of intrusive to you, is that so? [Student nods yes.] Right now some of us may want to get to know each other faster than others. I appreciate each one of us taking responsibility for setting limits about any difference in, or infringements on, our rhythm. In time I trust we will learn about these differences among us well enough not to make jarring or intrusive moves toward each other. On the other hand, the interjections or interventions which at times may seem to be, and indeed may be, mistakes, can provide us with excellent

and usually exciting opportunities to discover something new, to grow... I appreciate your pointing out to me the somewhat intrusive nature of what can be seen as poor timing of my invitation. I think that there might be others who did not want to share anything embarrassing as yet, and they might also be appreciating your intervention.

So let me turn to your colleagues and get feedback or a consultation...[Instructor turns to the group.] What is your reaction to this interaction? Or, taking on the role of consultants, what do you think can be a productive next step?

The instructor models to the participants an attitude and behavior which s/he believes in a parallel form will be repeated by the trainees when they begin supervising. Furthermore, the instructor in the above vignette introduces the trainees to the role of being consultants to each other and the instructor. It is important, I believe, to remind the trainees of this function and encourage them to assume the role of mutual consultation throughout the period of training. Finally, as illustrated in the above vignette, the message that setting personal limits or confronting the instructor can have a productive outcome should be communicated as early and as often as possible. In this manner the process and parameters of a supervisory encounter are modeled and the ground for honesty and spontaneity is prepared.

Present Past and Present Future: The Supervision Life Line

Following an initial introduction to the program, the instructor and each other, the instructor presents to the trainees a structure designed to elicit data based on their experiences as supervisees. The data gained from this structure will be, along with other materials, used as building blocks for developing the trainees' role as supervisor. "The heart of much learning for the supervisor remains, of course, the supervisory process with his or her own individual supervisor" (Stoltenberg & Delworth, 1987, p. 162).

The Supervision Life Line (SLL) is especially well tailored to organize the trainee's previous experiences in supervision. The examination of and derivation of meaning from these experiences provides a systematic process by which the impact of past learning in the role of supervisee can be applied to the trainees' current task of reorienting to the role of supervisor.

Completion of the SLL structure provides the trainees with ample data for heightening personal awareness and for sharing and discussing these data during the group sessions with the other trainees. Attending to other participants' experiences and observations, commenting on and comparing them, empathizing with each other about past encounters, enriches the trainee's experience base and at the same time builds additional ground for mutual support and trust. During the discussions, the instructor is responsible for facilitating the process of dialogue, providing opportunities for reluctant participants to engage in the process, and weaving in supervisory concepts and literature relevant to the subject being discussed.

Communication and discussion of the data gained from the the SLL structure, as well as from other structures and experiences, is one of the most important aspects of the teaching and learning presented in this book. Although time limits must be observed in all circumstances, within these limits the instructor should maximize opportunities for interactions, communications and derivations of corresponding meanings.

The structure of the Supervision Life Line consists of three parts: A. enumerating past supervisory relationships and recording selected materials corresponding to each one of those relationships; B. narrating selected descriptions of and reactions to past supervisory relationships; C. examining the impact of past supervisors and supervisory relationships on the trainee's development and on his/her current expectations of and goals for being a supervisor.

A. Past supervisory relationships

The first part of the SLL structure consists of drawing a vertical line and in chronological order marking off past supervision experiences. To the left and to the right of the line, participants will record in outline form selected descriptions of and reactions to those events. More specifically, the instructions are as follows:

A-1. Draw a vertical line in the middle of one or more (attached) sheets of paper.

A-2. Down the line arrange in chronological order each assignment/experience as a supervisee.

A-3. To the left of the line: a. assign a letter code to each supervisor (include all major supervisors of that training period), and b. identify each supervisor's discipline, age, gender.

A-4. To the right of the line: a. identify the year during which the supervision began, and the duration of that supervision, and b. assign a value of that supervision to your professional development using a scale of 1-10 where 1 represents the least value and 10 represents the most [see Figure 3]. [2]

Figure 3., *Example of Supervision Life Line,* illustrates a completed SLL, Part A.

Figure 3
Example of Supervision Life Line

G: psychologist, 50, F; N: psychiatrist, 32, F;	1984, 9 months, G was a 5 N was a 3
A: psychologist, 35+, M; S: psychologist, 40 ish, F;	1985, 12 months, (with a long vacation for S.) A was a 9+ S was a 5
L: psychologist, 30ish, F; M: social worker, 50, F; O: psychologist, early 40's, M;	1986, 10 months, except O. was 6 months, L was 8 M was 9 O was 7
B: psychologist, 50ish, M; other supervisors not yet assigned	1987, d.k. yet

B. Descriptions of and reactions to supervisors

The second part of the SLL structure consists of fleshing out each of the supervisions marked on the SLL. Trainees are invited to write brief descriptions of, and reactions to, their previous supervisory relationships. A time limit assigned for the completion of the narrative portion of the SLL provides the participants with an indication of how much detail to include. I suggest that the description of each supervisory experience be completed before proceeding to Section C. The narrative portion can also be assigned as homework following the completion of Section A of the SLL. If this portion is completed outside of the training

2. Descriptions and other entries corresponding to each mark on the SLL can be modified according to the interests and needs of the trainees, instructor or researcher using this tool.

session, the completed narratives are brought to the following training meeting for mutual sharing and discussion of the material in the group setting.

The second portion of the SLL is composed of seven sections.

> B-1. Write a brief description of the patient population served by you during each supervision. [Following each instruction, I like to provide the students with at least one example of possible responses.]
>
> For example: "During supervision with Dr. O, I worked with substance abusers. Sometimes I also met with a parent of the patient so I did a little family therapy."

The information from B-1 shared during the group meeting provides an opportunity to identify participants with special training experience who will be available as special resources. Later, when the trainees receive their supervisee assignments, this knowledge can be used to identify a fellow trainee as a potential consultant. The instructor, supportive of using such resources, though cognizant of the limitations, serves as an auxiliary consultant or as a resource for more appropriate consultants, e.g., colleagues who specialize in working with the population in question.

> B-2. Write a brief description of the supervisor's attitude or style, with special attention to the style in terms of the vertical power dimension (e.g., authoritarian, egalitarian, laissez-faire), and in terms of the proximity or intimacy dimension (e.g., distant, cool, warm, friendly). Include your reactions to that style.
>
> For example: "Dr. N had a very business-like attitude about her, she was a little cool, sometimes distant. I kept on waiting and hoping that in time she might warm up a little, but it never happened. I think she was quite authoritarian." Or, "Dr. S was the accepting type, she always had a little, shy smile on, and I always felt a bit protective of her; she was sort of laissez-faire or egalitarian and definitely friendly."

An invitation to focus on the supervisor's preference for a theory of psychotherapy which influenced the supervision is addressed by the following entry:

> B-3. Write a brief description of the theoretical stance and

source of teaching/supervisory style the supervisor appeared to use.

For example: "Dr. N was probably psychoanalytic. She never told me explicitly and it was not really clear to me what theory she functioned by. She did a lot of listening, said very little." Or, "Dr. A was definitely Rogerian; he told me that and I guess he acted accordingly."

Related to the supervisor's theoretical stance is his or her supervisory approach. The directions for this part of the experiment consist of the following item:

B-4. Write a brief description of the supervisor's approach to supervision.

For example: "Dr. N, the supervisor, focused almost exclusively on my work with my patient. She only asked what the patient's demands were, what effect I had on the patient, etc. There was zero focus on my feelings or on my relationship with this supervisor..." Or, "Dr. O was very attentive to my feelings, and sometimes to his feelings and really not all that interested in the patient's feelings."

In the context of processing this entry, the instructor can assist the trainees by providing a short lecturette and/or invite a discussion of supervisory approaches. I, for example, like to review a summary of Hart's (1982) characterization of supervisory approaches as didactic versus experiential.

In the didactic model "the supervisor helps supervisees acquire specific techniques of counseling or knowledge of client behavior. The focus of the supervision session is the behavior (skills, interventions, techniques, or strategies) of the supervisee with a client and/or on the supervisee's understanding of a client's behavior" (p. 31). This approach is sometimes referred to as "patient-focused".

The assumption of this model, especially when applied to a neophyte therapist, is "that supervisees are in need of specific professional skills. Supervisees who demonstrate these specific skills thus indicate their professional competence" (p. 31). For participants who are interested in pursuing this model or learning more about it, the following readings can be suggested: Matthews & Wineman (1953), Tarachow (1963), Dewald (1969), Semrad & Van Buskirk (1969), Windholz (1970), Spiegel & Grunebaum (1977); Krumbetz (1967), Delaney (1972, 1978), Butler & Hansen (1973), and Boyd (1978).

In the experiential model the focus is on the supervisee's attitudes and feelings. "The purpose of this supervisory behavior is to help supervisees understand and become sensitive to their own feelings as these feelings are displayed throughout interpersonal relationships" (p. 31). Others have referred to this approach as "supervisee-centered" or "supervisee-patient centered". Students interested in a more detailed study of the experiential model are guided to the works of D'Zmura (1964), Kaplowitz (1967), Ekstein & Wallerstein (1972), Arbuckle (1963, 1965), Patterson (1964), Lister (1966a, 1966b), and Altucher (1967).

However, the dichotomy of didactic vs. experiential models in current practices of supervision is not prominent. Indeed, I fully agree with Hart that the polarity of these models is not representative of the way many practitioners work in supervision. The models are frequently combined and other approaches, such as use of audio or video aids, are integrated, thus rendering the differentiation to be less clear.

The content of the lecturette and discussion of its content provides the trainees with tools for conceptualization of the data gained from the last part of the second section of the SLL.

Upon completion of the second part of the SLL, trainees should be aware of what styles, theoretical approaches and supervisory models they have learned from, how these variables affected their learning, and on the basis of that awareness project what corresponding methods and procedures they will prefer to use when they begin to supervise.

The SLL structure continues with the completion of the following sections:

B-5. Summarize and write a brief description of the most salient aspect of what you learned in that supervision.

For example: "In supervision with Dr. L I learned how to set limits—the supervisor was good at modeling it to me". Or, "In supervision with Ms. M, I learned about my tendency to give either glowing or very negative feedback to my patients. So I was learning to balance the two."

B-6. Identify and write a brief description of those aspects of each supervisory relationship which were easy and/or productive, and which were difficult and/or unproductive.

For example: "In supervision with Dr. G the boundaries were very clear and I felt quite safe, but at times the supervisor was too authoritarian and it would make me angry or more resistant to her perceptions.

B-7. Identify and write a brief description of what, if anything, was missing in the supervisory experience.

For example: "In supervision with Dr. N the supervisor seemed to lack any awareness of my feelings and my need for concrete guidance." Or, "In supervision with Dr. S I was unable to articulate what I expected or what I experienced."

B-8. What awareness have you gained from the discussion of SLL material produced by the other trainees?

For example: It was reassuring to hear of the confusion or difficulties that others experienced in their past supervisions. I also became aware of some things that I will be careful about when I begin supervising, such as checking in about the supervisee's understanding my suggestions.

Completing and examining parts A and B of the SLL structure provides the trainees with many potentially valuable insights about: their relational and learning patterns as supervisees; the relational and teaching patterns of their past supervisors; the effects of both sets of these patterns on the learning of psychotherapy and on opinions about supervision. Furthermore, the value of this part of the SLL exercise lies not only in each participant's examining and learning once again from past supervisory relationships, but in gaining new awareness and information from listening to the presentations of and participating in discussions about the SLLs of the other participants.

C. Trainee's professional development

The purpose of the third part of the SLL is to help the trainees continue expanding their awareness of their own professional development and to feature the impact of past experience on the soon-to-be practiced role of supervisor. In this way the trainees are expected to continue integrating past experience with their future expectations and goals of being a supervisor.

This part of SLL is composed of eight sections.

C-1. In examining the SLL, parts A and B, do you become aware of any changes over time regarding what you learned and how you learned? If so, describe these changes.

For example, do you notice differences in your appreciation of or preference for didactic versus experiential approaches; changes in preference of different qualities in supervisor or supervisory approach; differences in preference for closer or more distant supervisory relationship; etc.? If you observe no change, to what do you attribute this lack of change?

C-2. Have you become aware of your current preferred style of learning? For example, do you experience more or less tolerance of informational ambiguity? If aware of the current style, what is this style and how, if at all, has it changed over time? How will this knowledge influence your supervisory style?

C-3. Have you increased your awareness of your characteristic barriers to learning? For example, do you withhold instances of experienced failure? If aware of their barriers, what are they and how, if at all, have they changed over time? How do you imagine they will influence the process of your supervising?

C-4. Have you changed in the manner you handle conflict in supervision? For example, do you confront it more or less rapidly, if at all? If aware of changes, what are these changes? What impact may these changes have on your supervising?

C-5. Have you enhanced your awareness of qualities you want to nurture or avoid in your role as a supervisor? For example, have a sense of humor, avoid exaggeration of supervisee's mistakes. If aware of the enhancement, specify what it is.

C-6. Have you enhanced your awareness of the components of the supervisory process you will want to maximize or minimize in your role as a supervisor? For example, I want to maximize my attentiveness to supervisee's discouragement. If aware of this enhancement, specify the particulars.

C-7. Have you become aware of your preference and/or change in preference for the gender of your supervisor? If so, what is your current preference and reasons for it? How does this influence your preference for the gender of your supervisee?

C-8. What awareness have you gained from participating in discussions of SLL material produced by the other trainees?

Once again, *sharing* and *processing* the awareness gained from the SLL structure provides the trainees with some of the most important components of the total learning potentiated by completion of the SLL. For example, a woman trainee says, "In looking over my SLL I became aware that I had predominantly female supervisors, and actually I am sort of pleased about it. Now I'd welcome working with a few more male supervisors. Except for a few of my supervisors, I think their tendency was to use both didactic and experiential approaches which I appreciated, although now I am more into examining and learning from my countertransference. In the beginning I was more uncertain, scared, and I kept more of a distance from my supervisors. I think that presented some of the barriers to my learning. Now I appreciate a greater intimacy; I like my supervisors' interest in at least some of the most important events in my life outside the clinic. It makes me feel more of a whole person when I'm with them. I also appreciate their sharing something private about themselves. So I think I will apply this awareness to my supervising. Although I also think it's important not to overstep the supervisee's needs for distance and privacy."

Another trainee may resonate, "My development in supervision was sort of similar to yours. I started kind of cautiously, I was scared, I really wasn't certain what to do or how to handle myself in supervision. Neither one of my two supervisors during that placement were too helpful. But one of them was very friendly, a bit too friendly—that confused matters even more. When I begin to supervise I hope I will always guard against my supervisee being confused by a nonchalant, buddy-buddy attitude..."

Another participant summarized the salient aspects of her SLL: "I also like to start into the process slowly, I am basically shy, cautious, but when my cautious approach is allowed it helps me to feel trusting. I can even explore the darker sides of myself, take negative feedback quite well, and lately I have noticed that I can even take conflict—use it more productively, or at least it does not seem to be the end of the world the way it did before. I know I'll have to work on that more and to be cautious not to avoid it when I begin to work with my supervisee. I hope I will be warm, understanding, bright, all those good things. But when I am anxious or feel I might be judged harshly, I tend to withdraw, so that might be a pitfall for me to watch out for. Most of all I hope I can tune in, listen well to my supervisee..."

Of course not all trainees speak easily about their perceptions of self and the qualities included in the above examples. For many trainees it is easier to focus on each issue in A-1 through C-8 in sequence and/or to share with the other participants only some of the awareness they have gained from completion of the SLL experiment. The instructor's function is to facilitate the discussion and to validate the participants' choices, individual rhythms and learning styles. I also remind the participants to record their responses and other data gained from the SLL experience and related processing in their supervisory journals.

Upon completion of the full SLL structure, most trainees report their awareness of many changes in the preferences and attitudes they have experienced over the time of having been supervised. They also tend to become more discriminating about their learning needs at successive stages of professional development and aware of differences in supervisory skills or special talents of their supervisors.

Developmental Phenomena

Awareness of the developmental phenomena inherent in discussions and processing of the data gained from completion of the SLL provides the instructor with opportunities to offer a lecturette or weave in some corresponding didactic material. I like to use resources offered by Hess (1986) and Stoltenberg and Delworth (1987).

Hess (1986) points out that, due to the lack of supervision training, the beginning supervisor, i.e., Stage A supervisor, tends to use psychotherapy skills more than supervisory skills. Hence, the inexperienced supervisor might do more psychotherapy in the process of supervising than s/he is aware of doing (Hess and Aldrich, 1986). For somewhat different reasons, which are discussed in a subsequent chapter of this book [Chapter 3], Ekstein and Wallerstein (1978) also perceive the new supervisor of psychotherapy as tending to step into the role of psychotherapist. The Stage A supervisor, Hess (1986) notes, may also be unaware of such supervisory issues as structuring of the supervisory process. McColley and Baker (1982) enumerate major difficulties experienced by new supervisors: trainee [supervisee] resistance to supervision (26.7%); not knowing how to intervene (21.3%); not understanding the case (21.3%); and lack of knowledge of techniques and research (15.2%).

Participants in the program I have instructed are forewarned of the tendencies noted above. However, they are cautioned not to adopt this knowledge as a self-fulfilling prophecy and in this context I emphasize my experience with student supervisors. In my experience supervision trainees, though professionally less senior and contextually less powerful than staff supervisors, have a number of special advantages: 1. no responsibility for formal evaluation of their supervisee; 2. no legal responsibility with respect to the case supervised; 3. participation in systematic, specialized training; 4. ample opportunities to process their supervisor/supervisee relationship and get feedback and consultation from the resources available in the training group.

Perhaps as a consequence of the advantages listed above, I have encountered infrequent and then only limited resistance by the supervisee to the supervisor in training. Interventions, case understanding, knowledge of techniques and research are amply enriched by assigned readings, in-class discussions, consultations with colleagues and the instructor of the program.

Finally, I carefully prepare the trainee for a somewhat tedious, though essential, component of their training which is devoted to the elements of structuring the frame and dimensions of the supervisory process [see Chapter 7].

Stoltenberg and Delworth (1987) offer a detailed review of the developmental model of psychotherapy as well as their own developmental model of supervision. The trainees are encouraged to become familiar with and at appropriate times study the contents of Stoltenberg and Delworth's book. Many of the concepts and findings contained in that book will become useful as the trainee progresses and eventually engages in the process of supervising. At this preparatory stage, however, I like to review with the trainees a relatively small, though significant, portion of Stoltenberg and Delworth's work which is focussed on the phenomena manifested by a beginning supervisor.

Stoltenberg and Delworth (1987) describe supervisors at Level 1, the level most akin to the students in the supervision seminar, as "...highly anxious or somewhat naive....anxious to do the 'right' thing and be effective in the role. They often tend toward a fairly mechanistic approach to supervisory tasks and may play a strong 'expert' role with the supervisee....they are highly motivated, fairly dependent on their own supervisor for help...and generally more aware of their own reactions than of their supervisees'.... [they] take real pride in coming up with appropriate conceptualizations or interventions for supervisees to use.... [and have] real investment in getting the trainee to adopt their therapeutic orientation and techniques"(p. 154-155).

It is well for the student of supervision to be cognizant of Stoltenberg and Delworth's experience described in the above passage. However, in view of significantly different attitudes I have perceived among beginning supervisors participating in this training, I like to caution these beginners that they might witness each other and themselves as being unlike the beginner supervisors encountered by Stoltenberg and Delworth.

For example, in contrast to Stoltenberg and Delworth's (1987) description of a Level 1 supervisor, the student supervisors I have instructed were not overly anxious. This contrast, I believe, is due not only to the context in which these trainees begin to supervise, but also to their having systematic preparation for the practice of supervising. By the time a trainee begins supervising, s/he will have been prepared for that function by means of experiential and didactic learning opportunities. Further, a support system of other trainees and the instructor tends to ameliorate much of the potential anxiety. Thus, though trainees tend to have moderate anxiety just prior to or at the very onset of supervising, it is unusual for them to be highly anxious or to remain anxious for an extended period (more than three weeks) of time.

Similarly, perhaps because of the reasons enumerated above, the student supervisor does not tend to manifest naivete about the tasks of supervision or how to perform them. S/he might experience at times a temporary confusion, e.g., "How am I to intervene into my supervisee's countertransference with her patient without assuming a therapist role?", or temporary frustration, e.g., "My supervisee just does not seem to understand the importance of the supervisory contract." However, presenting and processing confusion or other difficulties during the training sessions usually resolves them and it is only in the most exceptional cases that the trainee experiences an extended sense of impasse or discouragement.

Stoltenberg and Delworth (1987) further see the beginning supervisor as having a mechanistic approach to the task of supervising. My experiences with student supervisors differs. The novice supervisor in the context of this training is often surprisingly creative and capable of impressive interventions with supervisees. S/he also tends to be attentive to, and use productively, even the most subtle messages from supervisees and other trainees. Although the student supervisor, just as the Level 1 supervisor described by Stoltenberg and Delworth, is ambitious about doing things right and takes pride in achieving a productive supervisory relationship, a learning alliance, and effective interventions, s/he is not often overly invested in having the supervisee adopt his/her theoretical or therapeutic orientation. Instead, I have encountered a range of attitudes. Some student supervisors are most accepting of their supervisees' preference for any theory or approach. Others are quite attached to their own views and are disappointed or judgmental when their supervisee has other preferences. Many are quite willing, when encountering a theoretical difference, to combine the two interests and explore how to view the same phenomena from different points of view. More often than not, however, the supervisees do not have an established or strong preference of their own and are more than pleased to adopt the theoretical approach of their supervisor.

My experience of student supervisors also diverges from Stoltenberg and Delworth's (1987) observation that new supervisors are more aware of their own reactions than of their supervisee's. Indeed, it has been at times difficult and a bit of a struggle for me , as instructor, to redirect the trainee's attention from their supervisee, from the supervisee's patient and from the relationship of that pair, to the supervisor's own reactions and experiences and to the relationship with their supervisee.

Thus, even a minimal training experience and systematic preparation for the role of supervisor appears to diminish significantly the new supervisor's anxiety and naivete about the supervisory role. It also tends to diminish mechanistic approaches to supervisory tasks or rigid insistence that the supervisee adopt a supervisor-preferred theoretical stance. It is unclear, however, whether the trainees I have encountered had a tendency to be more attentive to the supervisee than the Level 1 supervisor described by Stoltenberg and Delworth. This attentiveness might be attributable to a general tendency for beginners to do what they have learned before, rather than to practice a new skill.

Like the Level 1 supervisor, the student of supervision is fairly dependent on whatever source of processing or support s/he uses. Hence, after the trainee begins supervising, it is of utmost importance for the instructor to facilitate opportunities for participants of the training to present the supervision experiences during the group sessions and to get feedback, consultation and support.

Selectively, and when appropriate, I present the contrasts elaborated above to the trainees and invite them to collect their own data which is descriptive of experiences they and their colleagues will have when they engage in supervising.

Thus, the first part in the preparation of the trainee for the role of supervisor begins with mutual introductions, then his/her completion and examination of the SLL. Completing and processing the SLL stimulates the trainees' review of their past experiences of supervision. "It is a rare and blessed clinician who can look back on the training experience with totally benevolent memories of supervision. Most had a range of supervisors, some of whom were inspiring, but a few of whom may have left the neophyte with some distress and a bruised self esteem. The whole range of affective memories is awakened, and the young supervisor's initial identity emerges in the shadow of these 'supervisory introjects'" (Alonso, 1985, p. 57). Reviewing past supervisory experiences frequently facilitates a range of insights relevant to the supervisory process and presents trainees with an opportunity to cleanse themselves of unwanted introjects.

3

Lay Of The Land Boundaries And Parameters Of Supervision

All knowledge about reality begins with experience and terminates in it.
Albert Einstein

I think I think; therefore, I think I am.
Ambrose Bierce

IN CHAPTER TWO, the use of the SLL was introduced as a tool to be used in examining the trainees' past supervision experiences. In this chapter, building on the ground of the SLL, parameters which determine and define the process of psychotherapy supervision and variables which differentiate psychotherapy supervision from other relationships, become the focus of discourse. At the conclusion of this segment of the training, it is expected that the trainees will have created for themselves boundaries and a working definition(s) of psychotherapy supervision.

Differentiation of Psychotherapy Supervision from Psychotherapy

The issues raised in discussing and integrating a definition of psychotherapy supervision parallel the issues involved in differentiating psychotherapy from psychotherapy supervision. Discussions covering the comparison and contrast between psychotherapy and psychotherapy supervision reoccur throughout the period of supervisory training. During this early phase of training, inviting the trainees to examine and discuss their thoughts about this differentiation produces a wealth of data to be used in later sessions and especially during sessions devoted to processing of the trainees' practice of supervising.

The most salient aspect of the differentiation, awareness of which the trainees readily articulate, is the difference in intent or purpose of the two relationships and corresponding activities. That is, the primary goals of psychotherapy are resolution of the patient's conflicts and reduction of barriers to personal growth. Concomitant effects of psychotherapy include an increase in the patient's awareness of available options in feeling, thinking, doing, and a sense of overall satisfaction with life. The primary goals of psychotherapy supervision are sharpening the supervisee's psychotherapeutic skills and knowledge and development of the supervisee's professional identity. A concomitant focus is the effective treatment of the therapist's patient. Differentation of psychotherapy supervision from psychotherapy is therefore inherent in the intents and foci of each function.

The next most frequently attended to aspect of the differentiation between psychotherapy and psychotherapy supervision is focussed on the assumption that the supervisor will tend to have an investment in the supervisee changing in a particular way or direction, e.g., increased ability in limit setting, forming rapport or learning to identify phenomena attended to by a specific school of thought. The therapist, on the other hand, ideally has either very little or no investment in a patient's changing in a particular manner or direction, e.g., if the patient chooses to dress in black leather and ride motorcycles, most therapists will refrain from directing the patient to do otherwise. However, this point of differentiation is a relatively weak one. In significant relationships, no matter how impartial we might intend to be, our basic beliefs and values influence our personal and professional interactions. Thus, although an overt, verbal message might communicate one type of information, the covert and non-verbal messages may communicate an entirely different intention. The therapist, empathizing with the patient's pain or suffering, is likely to have at least some vested interest in how and in which direction the patient might change. In the context of supervision, the supervisor, no less than the therapist in the context of therapy, should do his/her utmost to listen for and follow the supervisee's growing edge and developmental needs.

A stronger and more valuable aspect of differentiation, awareness of which also tends to emerge rapidly and spontaneously from the trainees during the discussion of this subject, is the issue of supervisor's evaluations and/or recommendation(s). Indeed, the issue of evaluation and its effects on the new supervisee's professional future are at the core of the complications inherent in supervisory relationships. A similar complication is not likely to emerge in the relationship between therapist and patient. That is, most patients do not enter therapy with an assumption that their professional or occupational skills will be evaluated by the therapist.

Overall, however, the differentiation between therapy and supervision remains murky. The gray areas are further complicated by the fact that many of the attitudes, personal qualities and behaviors characteristic of psychotherapists are expected from and practiced by psychotherapy supervisors. Thus, the differentiation between the two practices poses a serious challenge.

The significant overlap between the desirable qualities of psychotherapists and the qualities of psychotherapy supervisors is featured by Carifio and Hess (1987) when they point out that some authors, i.e., Peirce, Carkhuff, and Berenson (1967), frequently assume that "the ideal supervisor seems to embody the same personal characteristics as the ideal psychotherapist" (p. 244).

According to Carifio and Hess (1987), some theoreticians such as Albott (1984), Aldrich (1982), and Gitterman and Miller (1977), intuitively described factors important to supervisory function which differ from factors important to psychotherapy. "These investigators suggested that positive supervisor characteristics include flexibility, concern, attention, investment, curiosity and openness" (p. 245). It is not clear, however, that the above characteristics may be differentially preferred by patients versus supervisees.

Competent supervisors are viewed as capable of creating a trusting and open environment in which two-way communication and collaboration are emphasized (Bruch, 1974). In considering this notion I again pose the question, "Are these conditions differentially preferred by supervisees in supervision versus patients in psychotherapy?" Some trainees report positive experiences with supervisors who are more supportive, instructional, and interpretive (Kennard, Stewart & Gluck, 1987). Once again I ask, "Do not many patients prefer similar qualitites in their psychotherapists?" These murky aspects of differentiating preferred and productive conditions of psychotherapy supervision versus preferred and productive conditions of psychotherapy provide a rich topic of discussion. Discourse on and study of the topic lead the trainees to the three clearly tenable points of differentiation between the conduct of psychotherapy supervision and psychotherapy: 1. inherent expectation of evaluation; 2. intent of the supervisor's communications; 3. focus of the supervisory relationship.

Most of the qualities, exclusive of specialized skills and knowledge, found to improve the process of supervision are qualities of any person skilled in forming successful relationships in other contexts. This essential quality of the supervisory process anoints it with special power and complicates our ability to differentiate it from other significant relationships.

Relationships as a Process

At this juncture I invite the program participants to consider the core phenomenon of human interaction, i.e., relationship. I review the entomology of the term "relationship": 're' (from Greek) means "again"; 'lation' (from Latin) means "connect"; 'ship' (from English) means 'ability' bestowed, as in lordship, or earned, as in friendship. Integrated, the phrase becomes "ability to connect again". More a verb than a noun, "relationship" should be considered a process of *connecting*. In all interactions which are based on a relationship, connection is made again and again. This is a *process of being* rather than a *state of being*. In this kind of contact, the two parties need to attend to each other's beingness as much as to the meaning of the content they are to deal with and to the ever new and not fully predictable outcomes which they both influence. The supervisory relationship, as other relationships, when considered with the above awareness, promotes the potential for being a journey of adventure, risk and promise. Supervisor and supervisee are ever changing and, according to the rhythm of the dyad, connecting and reconnecting again and again. The basic currency of such conscious relationships is trust; trust that even when disconnection is experienced, reconnection is possible and will occur. This phenomenon is based on attentiveness to change, i.e., when we reconnect, you and I are new and I must do my utmost to attend to what is now and not be attached to what was in the past or is expected to happen in the future. The training instructor models this relationship process and thus promotes the student supervisors' modeling of the process to their supervisees.

Supervisor's Mind Set

The direction of the supervisory relationship, however, is supported by a specific mind set. This mind set guides the supervisor's attention to those aspects of relating which enhance psychotherapeutic functions and professional development of the supervisee.

Emanating from the supervisor's cognitive change from "thinking like therapist to thinking like supervisor" (Heath and Storm, 1983, p. 36), this mind set is at the very core of supervisory functioning. Thus, although the supervisors can manifest personal qualities and interpersonal attitudes similar and/or identical to the qualities and attitudes of the psychotherapist, the thinking related to the goals of his/her task as supervisor are distinctly different from those of a psychotherapist. Borders (1989) in her paper, *Learning to think like a supervisor*, points out that although the conceptual shift may seem to be a relatively simple process, it requires unmitigated effort and specific training.

The training program I present has been designed with the awareness that the process of psychotherapy supervision is distinct from the process of psychotherapy; that the mindlessly practiced overlap of attitudes and skills between the two processes can threaten the clarity of the supervisory stance and have a negative effect on the supervisory outcome. This chapter, along with Chapters 4 and 7, describes the content and process of training specifically focused on differentiating variables related to psychotherapy supervision from those specific to psychotherapy.

It is important to underscore, however, that although the definition of the supervisory task and the focus of the supervisor's intent may be clear to him or her, the supervisor's ability to perform accordingly may still fail. The efforts, especially among the new, inexperienced and/or untrained supervisors, to reduce personal anxiety and limit the threat of entering uncharted territory may unconsciously motivate them to shift into the more familiar role of therapist. Furthermore, although it is usually assumed that advanced or senior supervisors are more likely to stay on the track of supervision, there are no clear data to support that view.

Core Quality Experiment

To personalize and enliven further discussion about differentiating psychotherapy supervision from other dyadic relationships and especially differentiating it from psychotherapy, I introduce the trainees to the Core Quality Experiment.

To carry out this experiment, each participant is invited to engage in the following sequence:

1. Divide a page of paper into four columns. Label the columns Parent, Teacher, Therapist and Supervisor. In each column, respectively, enumerate eight qualities which you consider to be most important and most descriptive of that role.

2. Rank the qualities within each category in order of their importance (using Roman Numerals for logistic clarity), so that number (I) will correspond to the most important quality and number (VIII) will correspond to the least important one.

3. Cross out the qualities numbered (VIII), (VII), and (VI).

4. Examine the remaining list and be aware of how the role is or is not changed by paring the list down to five qualities.

5. Record the impressions/observations based on awareness gained from step 4.

6. Upon completion of step 5, eliminate qualities (V) and (IV).

7. Repeat steps 4 and 5.

8. Upon completion of examination of the new list, record the corresponding impressions/observations and eliminate quality (III).

9. Repeat steps 4 and 5.

10. Upon completion of examination of the new list, record the corresponding impressions/observations and eliminate quality (II).

11. Repeat steps 4 and 5.

12. Share with the group participants and the instructor the remaining quality (I) in each of the columns. Share your experience of the process of eliminating the qualities, how it felt and how it changed the meaning of each relationship. Share how representative this last quality is of each role and how it helps or hinders differentiation of these roles.

In those cases where the core quality of the corresponding role seems to be inadequate for performance of that role, the group is invited to discuss why that is so and which of the other qualities, though crossed out for the purpose of the experiment, seem to be necessary for functioning of the role in question.

For example, a trainee might end the experiment with this set:

The most important parent quality is nurturing.
The most important teacher quality is understanding of the subject and student.
The most important psychotherapist quality is listening with the third ear.

> The most important psychotherapy supervisor quality is meeting the supervisee at the level of supervisee development.

However, the trainee might point out the following:

> For a parent, nurturing, as a core quality, is not enough. It is also important to have the ability to set limits; at the core, a teacher should have at least two other qualities, ability to communicate and to set limits; in the case of the psychotherapist many more qualities are necessary, but I am unable to choose which qualities in addition to number (I). For the supervisor, the trainee believes that the most important quality is indeed the core, i.e., meeting the supervisee at the level of the supervisee's development.

Others have the opportunity to compare their responses, agree, disagree and build on their initial responses. Since the trainees produce different core qualities which define each of the roles, the differences provide rich material for discussion. Usually it is possible to arrive at a closure about the core qualities of psychotherapists as differentiated from those of psychotherapy supervisors. The questions that remain unanswered and the differences in the points of view, create the productive tension which motivates future exploration and potentiates creativity.

The experiment is introduced and processed not only to gain data contrasting each participant's ideas about core qualities of the roles in question, but also to prepare them for the process of defining and adopting a working definition of psychotherapy supervision.

Forming a Definition of Psychotherapy Supervision

To begin the process of defining psychotherapy supervision, the program participants are invited to spend a few minutes thinking about and then articulating in written form their own definition of supervision. They are reminded to draw on the discussion of the preceding experiment, pertinent literature and awareness gained from the Supervision Life Line exploration.

At the conclusion of the above task, each participant pairs off with another trainee and engages in a ten-minute discussion of their definitions. The participants are also instructed to take note of the special skills or strengths that each one of them contributes to the process of their dialogue and communication, e.g., one member of the dyad might be creative in reframing a difference, the other member might be especially adept at focusing on the essence of a communication. Following this phase of the dialogue, the participants are instructed to continue the dialogue for five minutes during which they are to consider integrating the two definitions into one. At the conclusion of the encounter, each dyad will present to the other participants either one combined definition and a summary of the process which lead to it, or two definitions, accompanied by reasons for keeping the definitions separate.

The process described above is introduced, in part, as an opportunity to experience the *collaborative aspect of supervisory interaction*. Intrinsic to a productive process of supervision is the supervisee's and supervisor's experience of coordinating their knowledge, experience, awareness, and skill. No matter how much of a beginner the supervisee might be, s/he comes to perform this role with his/her unique set of past and current experiences and his/her knowledge. The supervisor must be open to and make use of the contribution of the supervisee. At the same time, to achieve a productive outcome of supervisory encounters, the supervisee needs to be open to and judiciously make use of what the supervisor has to offer. It is out of such collaboration that the best results of this special kind of learning are realized.

When the attempt at combining two definitions fails, the trainees, as instructed earlier, come back to the group with two separate definitions. In this case one does not need to assume that the collaboration failed. The dyad might have had a great deal of mutually enriching dialogue, respect for each other's point of view and yet came to no agreement about the end product. Likewise, the supervisor and supervisee do not need to agree at all times. The exceptions to this latter point are cases in which the supervisor perceives an impending crisis, e.g., homicide, suicide, or the potentially destructive impact of the supervisee's attitude or behavior on the patient, e.g., sexual acting out. Barring the unusual misjudgments, the differences experienced and confronted during the supervisory process can be viewed as opportunities for discovering personal or professional boundaries, uniqueness of thinking and approach.

Of course, there can indeed be failures in actualizing the collaborative spirit of the encounters. Conflict or discord warrant a careful examination. Emergence of even a slight conflict in these early encounters might indicate that similar stimuli will arouse future conflict. The instructor, just as later the student supervisors with their supervisees, should have maximal awareness about what sort of stimuli the participants are especially sensitive to and thus arouse conflict, resentment or anger. Furthermore, the instructor should be ready to manage these occurrences in such a way as to produce maximal learning benefits.

An illustration of three different outcomes of a discussion between trainees Sally and Sam follows:

Sally: My definition reads, supervising of psychotherapists is a process of regularly scheduled meetings between two or more persons for purposes of learning and increasing their professional competence.
Sam: In my definition I said, supervision of psychotherapists is a process where one person, senior and more experienced than the other person, instructs the junior therapist in observations, understandings, and techniques of psychotherapy.

In the discussion between Sally and Sam, Sam apparently felt Sally's definition lacked recognition of differential in seniority or hierarchy between supervisor and supervisee. Sally on the other hand felt that not all supervision needed to have one person be senior to the other; that there was no need for a hierarchical structure and that she valued those supervisors with whom she did not feel in a "one down" position. Sam, however, felt insecure and too readily critical of his supervisor when the hierarchy was unclear. After a bit of discussion, they decided to combine their definitions to read: "Supervision of psychotherapists is a process where usually, but not necessarily, a senior and more experienced person offers his/her skills of observation, understanding and techniques of psychotherapy to a person who is in a process of learning those skills." Sally and Sam of course did not need to agree to combine their definitions, though as a result of discussion both would have learned what is, at this time in the context of supervision, non-negotiably important to them. If sufficiently open, the dialogue will guide them to the very point of their growing edge. For example, Sam says, "I really tend to be quite dependent in learning situations so I like the supervisor to know more than I, and to tell me what's going on and what to do. Perhaps as I become more experienced I'll be more assertive about my opinions. I am not sure as yet how this is going to influence my work with the supervisee."

It is also possible that during the discussion between Sally and Sam the difference becomes angering to one or both of them. For example, Sally implies that she is pleased that she does not have Sam's dependency needs. Sam in turn insinuates that Sally needs to attend to her difficulties with authorities. These uncontracted-for and thus invasive interpretations (even though perhaps correct) aggravate both Sally and Sam. They want to keep their definitions separate and themselves at a distance from each other. Sally's and Sam's covert or overt conflict needs to be addressed during the training session. With the help of colleagues and instructor the conflict can be reframed, resolved and viewed as a learning opportunity. The instructor, for example, may solicit positive feedback to be offered to Sally or Sam. Susan, one of the participants, may accomodate by saying:

Susan: Sally, it seems to me that you are coming out of the discussion, with Sam, feeling accused or blamed for being independent, but that is exactly what I love about you, your 'guts', your courage and independent spirit.

Sam [clarifies]: I didn't mean to say that Sally's independence is bad. I was just wondering whether she had some difficulty with authorities.

Instructor: True, independence and problems with authorities don't have to be one and the same. You know, however, I usually am especially sensitive of another person's growing edge when I experience the very same challenge from within me. Whenever my dependency need rears its head, I tend to play the other side and *here come my difficulties with authority...* Hopefully a short visit, but...

Sam: Well, I know that I am very sensitive to being called dependent. I really think of myself more as conscientious or ambitious. Still, I suppose when one's dependency on authority becomes prominent, it becomes easy to identify with the aggressor. Sally on the other hand may act out by becoming oppositional.

Instructor: Here, if we don't watch it, we could get into the jargon and then lock ourselves into a no-exit set up. What is important, however, is that it seems, Sally, you and Sam might have more in common then it appeared a while ago.

Other participants can be invited to share their experiences of dependence, independence and related defensive needs. If this process dissipates the tension between Sally and Sam, the instructor can invite both Sally and Sam to share their perceptions of each other's strengths.

Time permitting, upon completing the group discussion of supervision definitions, the whole group is encouraged to collaborate in creating one integrated or two contrasting definitions to guide their soon to commence practice of supervising. The definition(s) is prominently posted and serve(s) as a reminder of the parameters of supervision. Later, when the practice of supervising is in process, the definition(s) can be revised, modified and enhanced. Until that time, however, the full group discussion of the content and experience of the dyadic process provides the participants with ideas about psychotherapy supervision, as well as data, which can be used to supply feedback to the dyads about their process. This same data gained from the experience can be useful during future group consultations. Meanwhile, the interactions provide trainees with opportunities to increase their familiarity with each other's vulnerabilities and strengths and to continue the process of building mutual trust. These conditions will, in time promote the student supervisor's willingness to be authentic and non-defensive in his/her interactions with, as well as supportive of, his/her colleagues. This same or similar attitude in the form of parallel process is then modeled to the supervisees.

Some Relevant Literature

As the instructor of the training program, I not only assume the responsibility of facilitating the interactive process and the cross fertilization of relevant ideas and/or feelings regarding psychotherapy supervision, but also weaving-in definitions of supervision that have been cited by authors and researchers concerned with psychotherapy supervision. For example, I remind the trainees that"after the large body of research in the area of psychotherapy supervision over the last ten years is examined, it seems somewhat difficult to formulate a broad set of guidelines for 'ideal' therapy supervision that is applicable to a wide variety of different clinical settings. However, it does appear that authors of some more general articles have proposed broad guidelines to help supervisors to function in different situations" (Carifio & Hess, 1987 p. 244).

Time permitting, I might continue with a lecturette focussed on the range of definitions articulated by authors well recognized in the field of psychotherapy supervision. Hart (1982) points out, "Authors in all mental health fields have attempted to define supervision. Authors from psychiatry (Ekstein & Wallerstein, 1958, 1972; Fleming & Benedek, 1966; Schuster, Sandt & Thaler, 1972), from psychology (Kell & Mueller, 1966; Mueller & Kell, 1972), and from education (Goldhammer, 1969) have described" (p. 11) what they consider to be the parameters of supervision. Hart offers his own definition of supervision as "an ongoing educational process in which one person in the role of supervisor helps another person in the role of the supervisee acquire appropriate professional behavior through an examination of the supervisee's professional activities" (p. 12). This definition encompasses a wider sense of psychotherapy supervision than many of the other authors have included in their definitions. Indeed, Hart states that his definition is based at least in part on some of the definitions he had examined earlier: "Supervision is the conceptualization, implementation, control, and management of training in applied circumstances and conditions" (Kurpius , Baher & Thomas, 1977, p. 224); "Supervision is the assignment of an experienced person to help a beginning student to learn counseling through the use of the student's own case material" (Brammer and Wassmer, 1977, p. 44); [Supervision is a] "continuous relationship of an organizational superior and subordinate – supervisor and supervisee, respectively – in which the latter is required to report regularly to the former on the state of his or her work and the supervisor provides direction that the supervisee is bound to follow" (Kutzik, 1977, p. 5).

Interestingly, out of some of the major works on supervision such as Alonso (1985), Fleming and Benedek (1966), Ekstein and Wallerstein (1978), Hess (1980a), or Stoltenberg and Delworth (1987), only Hart (1982) includes a "definition" in his subject index. It is as if some of the other authors assume the definition of psychotherapy supervision to be a given.

Indeed, it is difficult to distill from Fleming and Benedek's book (1966) exactly how they do define supervision. This might have been intentional. Perhaps this lack of basic definition is most appropriate to the understanding of psychotherapy supervision. Any definition tends to have a limiting effect on the subject it is representing. Fleming and Benedek's thinking, on the other hand indicates their understanding of psychotherapy supervision to be an ever changing process. "Supervision is 'post facto' teaching, a retrospective scrutiny of interactions and their reciprocal effects. What the student learns in one supervisory session about his patient and/or about himself, he can apply only in the future to situations which are similar but never identical with the one on which the supervisor's intervention was based. The 'experience' itself can not be repeated" (p. 238).

Similarly, Ekstein and Wallerstein's (1972) descriptive style of examining the process of supervisory encounters seems to override their attention to a concise definition. Alonso (1985) precludes the limiting aspect of definition by offering perhaps the broadest general definition regarding psychotherapy supervision, "Supervision is the primary professional training model for mental health clinicians" (p. 12). She elaborates by discussing a "cognitive definition" (p. 14) versus "an emotional definition" (p. 17) of supervision. In concert with Ekstein and Wallerstein (1978), Alonso considers the supervisory system to include therapist, patient, administrator and supervisor. According to Ekstein and Wallerstein, the system can be visualized as a rhombus where lines of communication and influence move between all of the participants: administrators, supervisors, therapists and patients.

I draw the trainees' attention to the fact that although the authors cited above devote their books to a range of supervisory topics and explorations of many components and processes of supervision, they do not spend their energies on further refining a definition of psychotherapy supervision. I challenge the trainees to speculate on why this is the case.

Hess (1980a), in what to date seems to be the most extensive book on the subject of psychotherapy supervision, is very cautious in defining supervision. No definition, he believes, can be adequately inclusive to: satisfy all schools of therapy, each of which has adopted its own model of supervision; to cut through the abstract amorphous nature of supervision; to differentiate it from other learning relationships or to differentiate it from psychotherapy in view of the fact that "none of the skills to be acquired or techniques of acquisition are *unique to supervision*" (p. 527). At the conclusion of these disclaimers, "mindful of the pitfalls attendant on defining such an abstract activity" (p. 528), Hess forms a tentative definition. "Psychotherapy supervision is: a relationship where one or more person's skills in conducting psychotherapy or mental health services are intentionally and potentially enhanced by the interaction with another person" (p. 528). Hess then continues his disclaimer a bit further as he quotes C. K. Chesterton, "I like getting into hot water, it keeps me clean."

In a recent publication, Stoltenberg and Delworth (1987) offer an extensive theoretical statement and discussion of supervision from a developmental approach. This in-depth study is based on a definition offered some years earlier by Loganbill, Hardy, and Delworth (1982) and cited by Stoltenberg and Delworth (1987). "An intensive, interpersonally focused, one-to-one relationship in which one person is designated to facilitate the development of therapeutic competence in the other person"(p. 34). This definition has a striking resemblance to the definition offered by Hess (1980a) and both definitions might invite similar discussion and/or criticism. Though Hess has covered himself more thoroughly by pointing out that in the psychotherapy supervision relationship "one or more person's skills"[3] are considered and that although intent of the supervisory process is usually clear, the effect of the process is not fully predictable; thus skills are "intentionally" and only "potentially" enhanced. In my understanding, Hess, at least by implication, indicates that in the process of psychotherapy supervision, the supervisors' psychotherapy skills can also be enhanced, i.e., he merely points out that the skills are "intentionally and potentially enhanced by interaction with another person" without specifying the persons to whom he refers.

Once again, it seems noteworthy that although Stoltenberg and Delworth have presented us with a thorough, scholarly, well-developed theory of and book about psychotherapy supervision, they chose not to offer an original definition of psychotherapy supervision and instead used a definition that had been developed five years earlier. This might indicate either the difficult nature of defining supervision or, that in spite of increasing advances in understanding psychotherapy supervision, the basic definitions have not warranted modification and change.

The participants in the training program, having been exposed to discussion regarding the definitions of psychotherapy supervision, feel relieved and encouraged in knowing that the task of defining psycho-

3. It is not clear when Hess says "one or more person's skills" whether the inference to persons refers to other supervisees in a group setting or to joint efforts of supervisor and supervisee.

therapy supervision is indeed a formidable one. In inviting original definitions of supervision, I disclaim the similarity of my intent from the professor who, for an end of the year exam, gave his students a well known passage from one of Shakespeare's major plays and instructed them to "Improve on this!" I do, however, claim to challenge the trainees with a difficult task. I make my belief known that an all inclusive definition of psychotherapy supervision is neither necessary nor possible. The wider range of definitions that we have, the more possibility that one of them – for at least a short time – will enlighten us and facilitate our work.

Each supervisor, as indeed each person in all other contexts of life, can apply a definition and live creatively by that definition only part of the time or only partially. This observation I share with the trainees to emphasize that, intrinsic to the human condition, is a process of change; no matter how desperately we may try to hold on to a comfortable perception, definition or organizing principle, it can fit us only at some time, only in some places, only for short periods of time, or for a long long time and everywhere when using a heavy set of blinders. As ever new stimuli present themselves to us, as new gestalts are formed, we are challenged to new meanings. Definitions of yesterday fall short of incorporating the experiences of today or integrating the corresponding new realities. The definitions of any human interactions are either so general that they can hardly be useful in guiding our conduct, or if specific enough they guide us for a mere wisp of time. This understanding is an important one to communicate to the students of supervision, for it is precisely this understanding that will give them the freedom to be both knowledgeable and inventive while inviting their supervisees to excellence and creativity.

For example, one or more of the participants believe that a core quality of a good supervisor, just as a core quality of a psychotherapist, should change according to the needs of a supervisee or a patient. Thus, the core quality, at which they have arrived in concluding the experiment, is the outcome of a forced choice and therefore of very limited utility. In contrast, another trainee or group of trainees believe that the core quality of a psychotherapist, such as creative listening or empathy, and the core quality of a psychotherapy supervisor, such as ability to convert parallel process to productive instruction, are immutable. The differences between the views offers the trainees with an opportunity to devise an experiment. The data for that experiment will be collected during the third phase of the program when the trainees engage in the practice of supervising. This data can provide the trainees with road maps for arriving at clarifications, conclusions and/or direction for further research.

In summary, the design of this portion of the training program calls for participants to do some hard thinking about the parameters of the journey they are to undertake in the practice of supervising. However, the manifest content of the discussions is of no greater value than the process of the discussions; a process which reveals the trainees' learning/teaching styles, builds trust and leads to realizations of ever-changing views and realities.

4

Varieties of Scapes The Triad Experiment Session

The authentic person, rooted in himself and not imprisoned in a system of fixed procedures, policies and regulations, does not analyze and explain reality, he engages in it freely, openly, immediately, spontaneously. In this way he achieves new integrations, new meanings and growing actualization of his identity.

Clarke Moustakas

We must be aware that everything we do in silence, movement and presence speaks to the nature of things...

Clarke Moustakas

INFORMATION ACQUIRED FROM the earlier segments of training, i.e., the Supervisory Life Line and the defining of psychotherapy supervision, forms the ground for the third segment of training. This segment consists of trainees' participation in and processing of a simulation exercise, i.e., the Triad Experiment. The simulation activities are followed by discussion of didactic material related to the data gained from the experiment. The exercise is designed to: 1. enhance trainees' awareness of their observation skills; 2. expose trainees to functioning in the role of supervisor; 3. provide trainees with an experience of differentiating between the functions of psychotherapist and psychotherapy supervisor; 4. provide the trainees with an opportunity to enhance mutual trust and build a support system. Finally, participation in and processing of the simulation exercise also provides the trainees with the data they will use in fleshing out their understanding of the three organizing principles studied during the following segment of training.

Triad Experiment

The instructor introduces the experiment to the trainees by stating the major intent of its design. However, following the presentation of the purposes of the experiment as specified above, the trainees are alerted to an inherent paradox related to the stated intent: to gain the most from the experience, they need to let go of their preconceptions about its inherent outcome as much as possible. That is, gains from participating in the Triad Experiment Session (TES) are maximized by bracketing the knowledge of its goals and by entering into it without expectations or prejudgments. Previously gained knowledge, experience and expectations will now serve only as a backdrop to the experience of interaction in the here and now.

Instructions

The participants are invited to form triads with an accompanying suggestion to select those whom they have known the least, thus minimizing personal preconceptions. Having formed the triads, the trainees receive the next set of instructions.

The full experiment consists of three sets. During each set, each participant of each triad has an assigned role to be either Patient, Therapist, or Supervisor. When all three sets have been completed, all participants will have experienced being in the role of a Patient, Therapist and Supervisor.

To facilitate the process of role assignment the trainees from each triad draw at random letter A, B or C. Then, by referring to the chart (see Figure 4), all those who have drawn letter A will follow a sequence of being Patient during set 1, Therapist during set 2, and Supervisor during set 3. Those who have drawn letter B will assume the role of Therapist during set 1, Supervisor during set 2, and Patient during set 3. Those who have drawn letter C will assume the role of Supervisor during set 1, Patient during set 2 and Therapist during set 3.

Figure 4
Chart of Role Assignments

Set	Sequence of Assignments		
	A	B	C
1	patient	therapist	supervisor
2	therapist	supervisor	patient
3	supervisor	patient	therapist

The instructor proceeds with outlining the responsibilities and tasks of being Patient, Therapist and Supervisor in the context of this experiment:

Patient: The trainee as the patient assumes the role of a severely disturbed and regressed, or autistic person. In either case the "patient" is to present him/herself, initially, as unavailable for, or extremely fearful, of contact with the therapist. The patient, within the limits of his/her role, is invited to be attentive to his/her feelings, images, reactions to the therapist and other stimuli.[4]

Therapist: The trainee as the therapist is to establish at least minimal contact and/or teach the patient a simple task. While interacting or doing his/her best to do so, the therapist is to be attentive to his/her own feelings, thoughts, fantasies and personal or interpersonal barriers to his/her interventions.

Supervisor: The trainee as the supervisor does not interact with either the therapist or the patient. S/He observes the interactions between Patient and Therapist as if through a one-way mirror, moving from the assumed sitting or standing position only when it is necessary to change his/her view of the Patient-Therapist dyad or to improve the opportunity for better observation. His/Her focus is on observing the interactions/ reactions of both therapist and patient and recording these observations as well as his/her own feelings and thoughts. The supervisor is further instructed to be most attentive to the therapist's strengths, resourcefulness and creativity.

Once the role assignments have been completed, the instructor continues with instructions for the process of the TES.

Part One: The first part of each set of TES is non-verbal; that is, while the supervisor observes and records his/her own observations and reactions, all communications between therapist and patient are engaged in without use of words, be they spoken, written, or acted out by means of pantomime. However, both Therapist and Patient can express themselves, deliver their messages, responses and interventions by means of non-verbal sounds, facial expressions, movement, touch or smell.

The first part of each set may range in time between 8-10 minutes depending on the length of the full session. However, time devoted to this part of the experiment should not exceed ten minutes. The intensity of this non-verbal exercise generates such depth of experience and wealth of data that to spend more than ten minutes in the interaction creates in both Therapist and Patient an overload of feelings and information. Conditions of overloading tend to generate confusion, frustration or anger,

4. I prefer to instruct trainees at the end of the session preceding TES to remember behavior and attitude of an autistic patient they have been acquainted with in the past or imagine such a patient according to the literature they have studied. In either case to be aware of as many details as possible.

thus creating unnecessary barriers to learning. On the other hand, by removing the distancing effect of words, the intensity of the interactions are enriched and conducive to creativity. These conditions, at least partially, are due to the tendency for the quantity and quality of observable data, accessed during this non-verbal process, to be more honest, direct and less defensive than during verbal interactions. For example, within the context of the TES, the therapist cannot ask, "How are you feeling now?", "What does that make you feel like?" or say, "When I mention your mother, you avert your eyes." Meanwhile, the patient cannot respond by saying, "I don't know.", "I don't have any feelings." or "Why do you keep bringing up my mother?" Thus, as the therapist and patient engage in their communications, they have to draw upon their creativity and upon behaviors and attitudes stripped of the usual, familiar and stereotypical social or therapy interaction. Although these conditions initially arouse some anxiety, the trainees rapidly (usually within 3-5 minutes) settle into the newness and challenge of this part of the TES. Relaxing into their roles, the trainees tend to tap their spontaneity, authenticity and creativity. Later, they discover that in this context the "figures" or salient aspects of interaction are more clear and their observations match their partner's experience more accurately than they could ever have imagined to be the case.

Part Two: At the conclusion of the first part of the experiment, the second part ensues. During this 10-15 minute sequence, the Therapist and Supervisor are invited to interact verbally. The members of the triad arrange themselves with the Therapist and Supervisor facing each other in preparation for a supervisory interaction and the person who was the Patient sits to the side of the Therapist-Supervisor dyad. In this position the Patient is now an observer of the Therapist-Supervisor interaction. While observing, s/he is to take notes on the Therapist-Supervisor interactions as well as on the congruence between the Supervisor's and Therapist's observations and his/her, i.e., Patient's, experience during the non-verbal part of the experiment.

The Therapist is instructed to initiate the dialogue by sharing his/her impressions from the first segment of the experiment, what s/he experienced and observed, which interventions s/he made and believed to have been effective, which interventions seemed ineffective, what feelings s/he had about the Patient and about interaction with the Patient, what s/he wanted though did not dare to initiate, which responses from the Patient seemed important or determining of Therapist interventions, etc. The Therapist is also invited to ask questions of the Supervisor or to request feedback. The Supervisor then responds, sharing his/her observations, thoughts, feelings, feedback, evaluation and suggestions of alternative interventions. The focus of the feedback and evaluation is to be primarily on the Therapist's strengths, resourcefulness and creativity; suggestions and interventions are to be primarily responsive to the therapist's questions and concerns.

Part Three: After approximately ten minutes of part two have elapsed, the trainee who was Patient joins the Therapist-Supervisor dyad and shares his/her observations of the interaction between Therapist and Supervisor as well as his/her experience as a Patient. At least some of the Patient's feedback is to focus on the Supervisor's and Therapist's strengths, resourcefulness and creativity. For approximately ten minutes, all members of the triad interact. The triadic interaction concludes the first set of the experiment.

It is understood that within the time allotted, not all or even most of the impressions, feelings and observations will be communicated. The participants are instructed to be selective according to their judgment of what is most important to communicate now. The remaining data is to be recorded in the supervision learning journals.

Rest, digestion and integration of the experience

At the conclusion of the above process, all triads are instructed to disperse and for the following ten minutes participants are encouraged to engage in a solitary activity, e.g., a walk, getting a light refreshment, or sitting quietly in as comfortable place as can be found. It is strongly suggested that the participants do not interact with each other during this time and thereby clutter "the field" or vitiate the integrity of the experience they have just concluded.

Triad Experiment Sets 2 and 3: When the group reconvenes, if no urgent or very important clarifying questions are to be addressed, the second set of the experiment is initiated. The redistribution of roles follows the order presented in Figure 4.

The process of set 2, and later set 3, repeats the process of the first set. At the conclusion of set 2, the participants are once again invited to "stretch" and rest for ten minutes without interacting with others. The same instructions follow the third and final set of the experiment.

Processing of the experiment

Having completed the three sets of the experiment, the whole group of participants reconvenes. At this time the trainees are usually fatigued and saturated with the richness of the experience. Nevertheless, at least a short time needs to be devoted to "debriefing" in the context of the whole group. The instructor suggests that all judgments about design and efficacy of the experiment be put "on hold" until the following session. The members of triads are invited to share briefly their feelings, perceptions and learnings about themselves and others. For example, a participant might offer the following comment: "...after the first few minutes of being the Patient, I was quite into it – I was very cognizant of my Therapist's movements. The slightest suggestion of proximity would scare me and all the sounds extraneous to our dyad were annoying....I both wanted to be attended to and I was scared of it..." A participant having assumed the role of Therapist might say: "I felt quite foolish when we started – I think I felt more self conscious than the Patient....it was difficult to stay focused on the Patient, not to look over to the Supervisor for some moral support or to watch or listen to the sound of other triads' actions. I would have never been able to predict the extent of my elation when the Patient looked at me directly and made that first contact..." Supervisor comments might consist in part of the following message: "I couldn't stop from thinking how glad I was that I didn't have to be the Therapist in this set – then I got kind of panicked that I would have to do it eventually anyway. I was trying hard to follow the Therapist's interventions, she seemed so patient and calm to me. I think that calmness relieved me as well as influenced the Patient."

As noted above, the participants' reactions to, analysis of or judgments about the design of the experiment are to be "on hold" until they are recorded in the journal or shared during the following session. That is, questions raised at this time, e.g., "I still think using words would have made this whole experience more productive, why couldn't we do it half and half?", should be recorded and addressed during the following session(s). The debriefing session should take no longer than thirty minutes.

Experiment follow-up

Participants of the training are instructed to take time between the end of the TES and the next meeting to record additional observations, reactions and other experiences during the experiment in their supervision learning journal. Further, during that interval, each participant is to write out at least two facilitative behaviors, attitudes or qualities of the colleague who was their Supervisor. They are also asked to comment on the colleague who was Supervisor when the participant was in the role of Patient. Such observation might consist of: "When Sally played my Supervisor, her observation of my discouragement at one point and her telling me how to use this kind of feeling productively, sort of reframing it for me, was very useful." Another observation might consist of : "Stan was very still when I was in my Therapist role, but I still could feel his presence. That experience of him continued during our 'supervisory' interaction. He said very little, but his attitude, his non-verbals were powerfully supportive. He also was very skilled in building on my comments and turning them into insights." An example of Patient feedback to his/her Therapist's Supervisor might be as follows: "I could see how carefully Stan observed when he was a Supervisor for Sally. He seemed to have recorded my slightest moves and reactions when I was a Patient. He offered Sally some interpretations based on those observations and they were right on the mark; I mean they matched my experience and motivation in the process of being the patient." These written statements are to be submitted to the corresponding colleagues at the beginning of the following session. At the appropriate time the trainees are invited to share the descriptions of their facilitative qualities with the rest of the participants. Further, the instructor can use these descriptive statements of the trainee's strengths in advancing the discussion of how to build on these qualities in the process of developing the skills, talents and attitudes of a psychotherapy supervisor. This and other aspects of debriefing the experiences and related meanings aroused during the TES will need to be attended to and discussed/dialogued about for the duration of at least one full training session.

In summary, the TES is designed as a simulation experiment during which the trainees have an opportunity to experience their functioning in the role of a Therapist versus the role of a Supervisor, to be observers as well as participants, and receive feedback about their resourcefulness and creativity at being Therapists versus Supervisors.

Didactic Material Related to TES

During and at the conclusion of processing the TES, the instructor also facilitates discussion of related research and literature. I find at least three subjects of discussion that integrate well into the processing of the TES: 1. qualities of an effective supervisee; 2. qualities of an effective supervisor; and 3. models of supervision. Although data gained from the TES provide relatively limited information or direct experience with regard to what makes a supervisee an effective consumer of supervision, the immediacy of the experiential data is important. This information can be supplemented by the materials gathered during previous sessions, especially those devoted to the SLL.

Qualities of an effective supervisee

Exploration of qualities manifested by an effective supervisee is intended to provide the student of supervision with knowledge of those aspects of their supervisee's behaviors and attitudes that will be productive to facilitate and promote.

Beginning supervisors, as well as supervisors at other stages of development, do well to realize that perhaps the most significant and most necessary quality of a supervisee is his/her motivation to learn about the practice of psychotherapy and about his/her own dynamics relevant to the role of therapist and supervisee. In the process of this learning the supervisee also needs the courage to let go of some of those assumptions, attitudes and practices which have been useful in other contexts, e.g., being a student of a purely academic subject. The supervisee needs encouragement to test out and adopt new assumptions or premises, new attitudes and new practices which are useful in the role of being a supervisee.

Further, the supervisee needs to use the supervisor as a source of modeling, feedback, evaluation and as a guide who challenges the supervisee's own resources, experiences and creativity. "Learning requires some frank admission of dependence on a Teacher", says Kadushin (1976). Thus, the supervisee benefits by confronting his/her own vulnerabilities, fears, defenses, prejudices and, whenever possible, articulating awareness of them to the supervisor. It is well for the supervisor to remember that s/he can work productively with the supervisee's anxieties, and/or defenses against the anxieties, only when the supervisee invites that work to be done.

It is of utmost importance for the supervisee to keep the supervisory contract (see Chapter 7) in his/her awareness so as to deliver on those aspects of the contract which are his/her responsibilities. S/He also should be willing to initiate a renegotiation of those aspects of the contract that are not benefiting the process of professional development and the learning relationship.

In more concrete terms, the supervisee should come to the supervisory sessions with the questions s/he intends to have addressed or answered during the supervisory session, to articulate these questions, and to confront the supervisor when the answers or guidance offered do not seem to be adequate, understood, relevant or useful. Cohen (1980) points out, "Students, knowing that they will be evaluated, are often reluctant to say what they really think, in short, to 'push' supervisors" (p. 79). The issue of evaluation will be addressed elsewhere in this book. It is sufficient to note that the supervisee needs to exercise a heavy dose of professional and personal courage in confronting his/her supervisor. At times the risk of confrontation seems more dangerous than beneficial to one's professional development. Indeed, some supervisees, having made an accurate assessment of the defensiveness or fragility of their supervisors, make a wise choice to withhold a "push" at their supervisors. A capable supervisor, however, is sensitive to the supervisee's assessments, misassessments and/or fears and encourages appropriate confrontation. For it is precisely out of such encounters that valuable growth of both the supervisee and supervisor emerges. To quote Cohen

(1980) further, "A thorough airing of differences between supervisee and supervisor regarding dynamics and techniques of therapy is an underused resource in training therapists, especially at the doctoral level" (p. 79).

Once again I emphasize that in the context of the goals set for this training program, enumerating characteristics of an effective supervisee is only for the purpose of enhancing the supervisor's functioning. Having awareness and knowledge of what improves a supervisee's effectiveness in supervision, the supervisor can communicate this information to the supervisee directly or indirectly and thus not only improve the supervisee's quality of functioning and learning, but also promote his/her own effectiveness.

Indeed, the division between supervisor and supervisee effectiveness is somewhat arbitrary. For optimal results the supervisor and supervisee are interdependent and both are on a learning journey. To this point, I once again quote Krishnamurti (1976), "Now if you are learning all the time...there is no need to follow anyone. Therefore, the division ceases because both the teacher and the disciple are learning. Both are moving in the same direction at the same time" (p. 7).

Qualities of an effective supervisor

Although the TES provides the trainees with some direct experience regarding the effective qualities of a supervisor, the information gained from the SLL should be supplemental in enlivening examination of the literature related to this topic.

It is difficult to assess the effectiveness of the supervisor without considering the qualities and behaviors of his/her supervisee. However, for purposes of reviewing research and literature relevant to the beginning supervisor, I will suspend consideration of the influence that the supervisee's qualities, behaviors and attitudes have on the effectiveness of the supervisor.

According to Marshall and Confer (1980), supervisors productively effect the supervisory process in at least four ways. They, "1. afford an atmosphere that encourages trainees to grow as therapists by communicating and resolving insecurities in their role; 2. adopt a style of communicating suggestions and corrections that will enhance supervisee confidence, acceptance, and satisfaction; 3. devise methods to close the gap between student report and actual patient behavior; and 4. avoid debilitating attitudes that detract from her/his working relationship with a supervisee" (p. 96). All easier said than done. The supervisors need not only skills which can implement the conditions outlined by Marshall and Confer, but also positive reinforcement to continue developing such skills.

Thus, the skills enumerated above do not emerge spontaneously nor do they develop in a vacuum. Required and systematic training of psychotherapy supervisors is first and foremost a prerequisite for turning out effective supervisors. However, enough has been written about this matter in the introduction to this book. Of more immediate concern is the extent to which the training program presented here supports the supervisor's future effectiveness and ability to manifest what Marshall and Confer have specified as advantageous supervisory behaviors and attitudes. An invitation to assess the effectiveness of the program according to criteria Marshall and Confer consider as having merit can be extended to the trainees. In this manner they are alerted to engage in monitoring the value of their training as well as to be vigilant about fostering effective supervisor qualities in developing their own supervisory skills. The trainees can also be invited to identify criteria developed by other authors and to monitor their development as supervisors according to those frameworks.

Research conducted by Goin and Kline (1974) indicates that preferred supervisors tend to make more didactic comments about patients and recommend more facilitative techniques than do the less effective supervisors. Goin and Kline's data further indicates that the supervisors rated as more outstanding were neither passive nor authoritatively directive. Ability to modulate the authority, be appropriately active and have the skill of good timing in the use of both is not an easy goal to achieve. However, the effective timing of the supervisor's proactive versus reactive attitude is at least partially facilitated by the agreements made between supervisor and supervisee in negotiating the supervisory contract.

Many authors have emphasized the importance of establishing a set of specific, explicit and measurable goals of supervision (Archer & Peake, 1984; Fox, 1983; Rotholtz & Werk, 1984). Authors have also discussed the effects of such clarity of goals on diminishing the anxiety inherent in the evaluative aspect of a supervisory relationship (Cohen, 1980; Freeman, 1985). I suggest that the contract agreed upon between the psychotherapy supervisor and his/her student needs to go beyond establishing clear goals. The contract should be inclusive of such minor matters as where, when, for how long meetings will take place or how many absences of either party might be tolerable, as well as such major agreements as how to deal with emergencies, how telephone contacts will be handled and expectations of how theoretical or approach differences will be managed. Although both supervisor and supervisee must continue to be cognizant of the content and management of the supervisory contract, it is the supervisor's responsibility to model the productive use of this awareness.

In his review of related literature, Hess (1987b) considers the "ideal supervisor" as having versatility, i.e., ability and willingness to use a range of teaching techniques. Clearly, just as a clinician tends to adjust a technique to the patient need, so a psychotherapy supervisor must adjust his/her approach to the supervisee's learning needs, the patient's personal growth/health needs, and the development of a relationship between each of the pairs.

Brannon (1985) suggests the following approaches which have been useful in the process of supervision: brainstorming; role play; modeling behavior; guided reflection. Brannon's suggestions are especially and most explicitly congruent with the training program described in this book. The supervisor's versatility needs to be bridled. In at least one context, however, a supervisor's versatility in shuttling between being a supervisor and being a therapist does not promote good results. A number of authors, who have examined the supervisory process, have emphasized the importance of keeping the focus on supervisory tasks and not on psychotherapy. Carifio and Hess (1987) speak to this issue as they point out "...it appears that in most theory and research in the supervision field, the use of psychotherapy during therapy supervision is not recommended" (p. 247). This conclusion reflects the beliefs of Bruch (1974) and Archer andPeake (1984) that the parameters of material to be dealt with in supervision should be discussed and clearly maintained. A supervisee's personal difficulties which do not affect his/her clinical work directly are not proper topics of supervisory discussion (Cohen & DeBetz, 1977; Lambert, 1980; Weiner & Kaplan, 1980).

The inadvisability of engaging in psychotherapy during supervisory sessions is at least partially due to findings that skill building and direct instruction seem to be more beneficial for supervisee development than delving into the supervisee's personal background or experiences (Payne, Weiss & Kapp, 1972). Rosenblatt & Mayer (1975), through an examination of student accounts, found that a supervisor who used a certain therapeutic style, i.e., the style that focused on the supervisee as the patient and examined his/her personality structure, was the one most objectionable to the supervisee.

On occasion even a senior, though perhaps untrained, supervisor will succumb to doing psychotherapy rather than supervision. However the tendency is most prominent among beginning supervisors. Ekstein and Wallerstein (1978) attend to this phenomenon in the following manner: "Why is it that the one who becomes acquainted with a training method such as that described in these pages so frequently feels tempted to think of it first in terms of psychotherapy? We believe that this has to do with a special learning problem which is perhaps typical for most of us. The one confronted with something new will try at first to reduce the new to the familiar. The psychotherapist who becomes a teacher of psychotherapy will frequently be tempted to fall back on skills that represent prior acquisitions" (p. 255).

A supervisor, for example, who is overly passive and laissez-faire might be seduced by the supervisee, who in an effort to avoid dealing with confusing or challenging issues of doing psychotherapy and under the guise of examining countertransference, will delve into personal difficulties, genesis of low self-esteem, etc. A supervisor who fails to redirect the supervisee's material to the business of supervision enters by default into the role of a psychotherapist, abandoning the role contracted for by the supervisee. This behavior can also be caused by the supervisor's lack of professional self-esteem, fear of seeming insensitive, ignorance of proper boundary or lack of skill in management of the boundaries. Lack of professional self-esteem can also influence the supervisor to be overly critical, distant and humorless. In contrast, an effective supervisor feels free to interrupt the supervisee's personal ruminations, recognize without sounding critical the importance of the material in the supervisee's life, gently suggest it is an issue to be dealt with in the supervisee's private psychotherapy and return to the business of supervision. Under usual circumstances the supervisee should, even when interrupted and redirected, feel supported.

The supervisor's tendency to take on the role of therapist with the supervisees is outranked only by a tendency to take over the therapy of the supervisee's patient(s). In these instances the supervisors are barely, if at all, attentive to the supervisee. Instead, all of their focus is directed on the patient. The patient is hypothesized about, diagnosed and corresponding interventions are prescribed. The effect of such supervision often results in the supervisee becoming frustrated, disempowered and/or confused.

Being therapist to the supervisee or being surrogate therapist to the supervisee's patient are frequently manifested by fledgling supervisors during supervisory training. However, when these tendencies appear in the supervisor's later career, after s/he is expected to have achieved a certain level of expertise in psychotherapy supervision, it is most likely due to the supervisor's personal characteristics. Thus, for example, a supervisor who is overly controlling will tend to function during the supervision sessions as the therapist of the supervisee's patient.

Even though, theoretically, a supervisor might know that good supervisors should be supportive (Bruch, 1974), non-critical (Melchiode, 1977), confident, enthusiastic, open to supervisee's questions and input (Albott, 1984), ability to apply these attitudes and approaches calls for integrating them through practice and processing of that practice. This integration in turn calls for the supervisors to have received supervisory training and to have continued that training at appropriate intervals. Lacking training opportunities, the supervisor's attentiveness to other facilitative qualities, i.e., expertness, trust and attractiveness (Dorn, 1985), might be omitted or presented so self-consciously that the productive supervisory process is undermined by the corresponding tension.

Finally, trainees in the program are alerted to the quality and timing of supervisor feedback. Carifio and Hess (1987) provide a summary of the salient variables involved: "Some investigators have suggested that direct and immediate feedback that is closely tied to student's performance can be an invaluable part of clinical supervision (Barth & Gambrill, 1984; Freeman, 1985). Freeman (1985) comprehensively outlined a number of important considerations for the supervisor delivering feedback. It should be 1. *systematic* (objective, accurate, consistent, and reliable feedback that is less influenced by subjective variables); 2. *timely* (feedback is delivered soon after an important event); 3. *clearly understood* (both positive and negative feedback are based on explicit and specific performance criteria); and 4. *reciprocal* (feedback is provided in two-way interactions in which suggestions are made, not as the only way to approach a problem, but as only one of a number of potentially useful alternatives)" (p. 247).

Frequently, participants of the training program are gratified by their awareness that, in the segment of supervision they delivered during the TES, they practiced according to many of the criteria for delivering productive supervision. In this context, I alert the trainees to the differentiation between feedback and evaluation. Although all evaluation contains feedback, not all feedback must be of an evaluative nature. The matter of differentiation between evaluation and feedback will be addressed in a subsequent chapter. Here it is sufficient to say that the manner in which the supervisor evaluates and delivers that appraisal to the supervisee is part and parcel of the supervisory process, and that evaluation or feedback can be used as a constructive learning tool or as a weapon of intimidation and control.

Models of supervision

The experience of supervising during the TES provides the trainees with immediate, though limited, data regarding models of supervision. The data can be supplemented by information gained from the SLL and the contents of discussions during the training sessions. By this stage of training, trainees should have a sense of what models they have preferred to use in the past, what models they might choose in their practice of supervising and how their professional development influences the choice of model.

The supervisory models most commonly recognized are labeled "didactic" and "experiential". Carifio and Hess (1987) point out that, "most of the early studies on the differences between didactic and experiential methods focused on these processes as different and mutually exclusive (Payne, Weiss & Kapp, 1972; Uhlemann, Lea & Stone, 1976)" (p. 248). In contrast to treating these models as mutually exclusive, Hart (1982) organizes a significant part of his book, *The Process Of Clinical Supervision*, according to the sequential use of three methods or models: Skill Development Model (akin to the didactic model); Personal Growth Model (akin to the experiential model); and Integration Model.

The Skill Development Model is focused primarily on increasing supervisees' skills in dealing with patients. Supervisor and supervisee, explicitly or implicitly, abide by the supervisor's expert power. Implied in this model is a hierarchical structure in which the supervisor is the one who has the knowledge and skills which the supervisee does not have and needs to learn. In using the Skill Development model, the supervisor is in a "one-up" position and the supervisee in a "one-down" position. The hierarchical distance between supervisor and supervisee (French & Raven, 1960) is based on and supported by the supervisor's expert power, and these mutual positions influence all aspects of the supervisory relationship and the corresponding learning process.

The Personal Growth Model is focused on the development of the supervisee as a person. Emphasis is on enhancing the supervisee's personal and interpersonal behavior patterns and their effects. In contrast to the skill development model, the hierarchical distance in this model is decreased. Though more moderate, this model can range widely within the continuum of hierarchical structure as a function of the personalities, values and attitudes of both supervisor and supervisee.

The Integrative Model, according to Hart, is the most inclusive one in that it combines the didactic and experiential models. It is most appropriate for use with a mature supervisee who has had exposure to the Skill Developmental Model and the Personal Growth Model in that order. The goal of this approach is to help the supervisee integrate his/her acquired skills and personal awareness into effective client relationships. Here the supervisor promotes minimal hierarchical distance between him/herself and his/her supervisee. Instead, a consultative relationship is built and used in the service of collaborating primarily on examination of and learning about the supervisee-client unit, and secondarily on examination of and learning from the supervisor-supervisee unit and the corresponding parallel process.

The above discussion resolves the mutual exclusivity of the didactic and experiential methods. According to Hart, these methods instead of being mutually exclusive,should be applied in a sequence which corresponds to the developmental levels of professional growth. Thus, Hart points out, "The Skill Development, Personal Growth, and Integration models of supervision should not be conceived of as mutually exclusive or as implying the sole use of a particular model for a supervisee's entire supervision" (p. 161). The tendency to choose one or a combination of models according to personality and characteriological tendencies of supervisors and supervisees should not be underestimated. A student supervisor, following his/her understanding of the models, has an opportunity to adopt any one of them, combine them or use them in sequence.

Skill Development, Personal Growth and Integrative models correspond to the developmental models of supervision introduced by a number of other authors and investigators: Blocher (1983); Heppner & Roehlke (1984); Hill, Charles & Reed (1981); Hogan (1964); Litrell, Lee-Borden & Lorenz (1979); Loganbill, Hardy & Delworth (1982); McNeill, Stoltenberg & Pierce (1985); Miars et al. (1983); Ralph (1980); Reising & Daniels (1983); Stoltenberg (1981); Worthington (1987). Not surprisingly, the authors converge in citing both theoretical and empirical data which indicate a supervisee's tendency to change from a dependent posture to an increasingly independent one. Thus, the evolving therapist initially uses supervision to focus on didactic material; and in time and with experience s/he prefers to focus on personal and interpersonal awareness and later yet on development of increased versatility and integrity of therapeutic approaches. Further and more detailed exploration of the developmental models of supervision will be addressed subsequently in the context of matching the student supervisor with his/her supervisee [Chapter 6]. At this time, however, trainees can use the data gained from their SLL and subsequent training sequence to review their own development as supervisees and to select the model which will be most comfortable to use in supervising.

In summary, the TES experiment provides the trainees with a range of experiences, some of which can be related to the didactic material focused on the beneficial qualities of supervisees, supervisors and on the models of supervision.

5

Mapping the Scape Three Views

Since we have come to the understanding that science is not a description of "reality" but a metaphorical ordering of experience... It is not a question of which view is "true" in some ultimate sense. Rather, it is a matter of which picture is more useful in guiding human affairs.

Willis Harman

THE IMPORTANCE OF the Triad Experiment·Session in preparing the trainees for supervision resides not only in its inherent experiential value, but also in providing experience based data which can be used to flesh out and enliven the didactic, conceptual components of the program. Fundamental to preparing trainees for the practice of supervision is familiarizing them with concepts which will serve as organizing principles for selecting and assembling information gathered in the supervisory process.

A major aspect of the supervisory process is the manner in which the supervisor selects and organizes supervisory data for the benefit of the supervisee's learning. The organizing patterns that I expect the trainees to be conversant with are based on: 1. the phenomenon of parallel process; 2. the phenomena of the Gestalt Cycle of Experience and the Gestalt Interactive Cycle; 3. the phenomenon of bipersonal field. These three ways of viewing and organizing supervisory data are by no means exhaustive of the patterns that lend themselves as tools of organizing the supervisory process. However, I have found these three conceptualization options to be especially useful for deriving meaning from and planning interventions for supervisory encounters. The three options can be used independently of each other, in supplementing each other, in sequence or according to supervisor's and supervisee's current needs. Many of the trainees will tend to adopt and use only one of the patterns – the pattern most congruent with their theoretical preference. Others, appreciating the compatibility of the patterns, combine them and use them on different occasions and/or when working with more than one supervisee, e.g., applying patterns according to the supervisees' different needs or according to their different theoretical preferences.

Parallel Process

The concept of parallel process as a phenomenon of the supervisory relationship was addressed as early as 1955 by Searles (1955). Searles, who refers to this phenomenon as a "reflection process", notes that "processes at work currently in relationship between patient and therapist are often reflected in the relationship between therapist and supervisor" (p. 135). Hora (1957), Kubie (1958) and Arlow (1963) took further notice of this powerful way to understand supervisory interactions. Later, a number of researchers (Doehrman, 1976; Loganbill et al., 1982; Aldrich & Hess, 1983; McNeill & Worthen, 1989) focussed their explorations on the various and many features of parallel process. However, parallel process in the context of psychotherapy supervision is most clearly and most extensively identified, examined and applied by Ekstein & Wallerstein (1978) in their text, *The Teaching and Learning of Psychotherapy*.

Although, in concert with Doehrman (1976), Ekstein & Wallerstein (1978) observe that the phenomenon can be manifested on different occasions by both supervisee and supervisor, their focus is primarily on its manifestation by the supervisee: "...many a beginning therapist, selecting the patient's material, distilling it through the vehicle of the emphases dictated by his own needs, and presenting it thus to the supervisor...discovers that what he sees and presents often so closely parallels comparable problems he himself experiences in supervision. Whether it be of beginning, of termination, or of process in between, therapist and patient *seem* to be constantly working on the same problems. Only as the student is helped in the resolution of such difficulties in himself, will he be able to see objectively enlarging aspects of the patient's problems. It is as though we work with a constant 'metaphor' in which the patient's problem in psychotherapy may be used to express the therapist's problem in supervision – and vice-versa" (p. 179).

When the concept of parallel process is presented and discussed during the training session, the awareness of the phenomenon arouses a sense of recognition among the trainees. However, the recognition seldomly extends to memory of how this process was handled or resolved during their past experiences of being supervised.

Parallel process can also be identified in a supervision student's presentations during the training sessions, i.e., s/he has a tendency to focus on those aspects of the supervisee's difficulties which s/he experiences and manifests during the training sessions. Thus, communication patterns and problems between patient and therapist reverberate in the relationship between the therapist and student supervisor and further in the relationship of the student supervisor and his/her colleagues or instructor during the training sessions. Alerted to the potential for parallel process manifesting during training sessions, the trainees can use this tool for organizing the data presented by their colleagues and the data presented to them by their supervisees. The parallel process perspective can also be used by the trainees as a tool for guiding their supervisees to significant dynamics manifested by their patients.

The major considerations for addressing issues of parallel process in the context of the training program are: 1. whether the student is ready to be confronted with the recognition and management of parallel process during his/her training group presentations; and 2. on the basis of this knowledge how to guide interventions in his/her work with the supervisee.

The Triad Experiment Session (TES) provides the trainees with some rudimentary examples of parallel process. During the debriefing of his/her role as a Supervisor, a trainee might point out: "I wasn't really sure that I could contribute very much or be of much help. The Therapist, I think, did quite well – I couldn't think of anything else or anything better to do, so I was probably kind of useless..." In the context of the parallel process it is important to link the Supervisor's comment to an earlier statement by the Therapist: "At times, I felt quite helpless...my strongest move I think was my adapting to the patient's rhythm....Otherwise, I could not think of much to do..." Though the Therapist's ability to adapt to the rhythm of a primitive patient can be considered a powerful intervention, the Therapist's reality is that of feeling helpless. The Therapist continues: "She looked at me with that vacant 'what's the use' look. The Patient appears to have given up." Here we can witness the Supervisor picking up the Therapist's reverberation of the Patient's look of having given up and reporting his/her own feeling of helplessness, then repeating it in the presentation during the training session. Another participant may manifest the parallel process as s/he says: "You know the TES was very powerful, but now I am not sure we are getting anywhere with the processing of it, at least I don't have much to say about it anymore..." Once again giving up, helplessness is manifested.

The instructor, subject to his/her evaluation of the trainees' readiness to hear it, might point out the parallels noted above and thus introduce to the trainees an opportunity to choose between keeping the attitudes they have expressed or experimenting with different, perhaps more risky points of view. In weeks to come, when the trainees begin the actual supervising of junior colleagues, the phenomenon of parallel process is reviewed for those who choose it as their organizing principle and apply it to their work with supervisees. Thus, manifestations of parallel process often clarify and facilitate processing of the trainee's experience of supervising his/her supervisee as well as clarifying the content and manner of presenting that experience during the group sessions.

The Gestalt Cycle of Experience and Gestalt Interactive Cycle

The Gestalt Cycle of Experience, initially conceptualized by faculty members of The Gestalt Institute of Cleveland and elaborated upon by other gestalt therapy theoreticians, is well summarized by Nevis (1987) in *Organizational Consulting: A Gestalt Approach*. He describes the Cycle of Experience as, "...the process by which people – individually or collectively – become aware of what is going on at any moment, and how they mobilize energy to take some action that allows them to deal constructively with possibilities suggested by the new awareness" (p. 1). Nevis elaborates, "The Gestalt Cycle of Experience integrates the behavioral aspects of sensation, awareness, energy mobilization, contact, and resolution or closure into a complete unit of human experience. The ability of individuals and human systems to move smoothly through the phases of the Cycle is considered essential for healthy functioning and learning" (p. 4). In the application of the Cycle to the context of psychotherapy supervision, a supervisor will function optimally when s/he has sequential access to his/her sensation, awareness, energy mobilization, contact and resolution. That is, the supervisor needs to 1. experience hearing and seeing the supervisee; 2. integrate and relate sensation based information to personal awareness; 3. motivate/mobilize him/herself on the basis of this information to form an intervention; 4. deliver (verbally or non-verbally) the intervention message to the supervisee; and 5. listen/look/accept the forthcoming response.

Elaborating on the interactive aspect of the Gestalt Cycle of Experience, Nevis says, "To capture the situation...of two or more people,

Zinker and Nevis (1981) have conceptualized the 'Gestalt Interactive Cycle'. The phases of the Cycle of Experience remain the same as for individuals, but attention is now focused on the Cycle for each individual and the interactions among the members of the system" (p. 31). Since each individual functions according to his/her own rhythm, the cycles of two or more people may differ. The differences emanate from the length of time each person tends to devote to each phase of the cycle, the level of energy mobilized and exhibited by each person, and each person's potential to stop short of completing the cycle, thus getting stuck at this unfinished point of experience.

The supervisor, for example, following his/her own rhythm, might become frustrated with the supervisee's tendency to stay in the awareness/mobilization of energy part of the cycle longer than s/he usually does. The supervisor might consider the slowing down as unproductive, as a manifestation of resistance, or as acting out. For example, the supervisor asks the supervisee a question; the supervisee looks down and remains quiet for a number of seconds without an apparent or obvious attempt at answering the question. The supervisor considers this behavior as a resistance or another type of distancing. S/he then, without checking his/her interpretation (introducing another unfinished cycle), reiterates the question with a tone of annoyance or demand. The supervisee who might have just mobilized his/her energy to respond to the first question, but hearing the supervisors annoyance, becomes confused, self-protective, resistant or distant. Such an occurrence complicates and tends to preclude closure of the interactive cycle. In contrast, another supervisee in response to the supervisor's question might quickly move from the sensation (hearing the question), through the awareness and proceed without the slightest pause to mobilizing energy and to the action phase. This rapidity (impulsive manner) of response may elicit a disorganized, lengthy and redundant answer, i.e., the supervisee continues to elaborate on that answer, clarify it a number of times, repeat the information that had already been offered, etc. The supervisor becomes sufficiently impatient to say, "So, what is the point here – I don't believe you are addressing the question I have posed." At this juncture the supervisee, if in a previously established atmosphere of learning, alliance and trust, has the option to slow down and decrease the apparent anxiety raised by the question. S/he might rise to the occasion, allow the awareness to organize the direction of mobilized energy and produce a more adequate answer, thus completing the Gestalt Cycle.

On the other hand without a previously established trust, or due to a range of other circumstances, the interruption may not have a successful outcome, e.g., the supervisee withdraws from contact and thus precludes closure. In that case the cycle will tend to remain unfinished, creating a barrier to future ease of contact and resolution.[5]

From the context of the Triad Experiential Session a trainee describes his/her experience in the role of a Supervisor in the following manner: "It seemed like such a great opportunity to do something supervisory, to act as a supervisor, but I just didn't know what to say – except, 'Well, you seemed to do o.k.' So I felt kind of inadequate." Then she turns to the Therapist and says, "What do you think, what could have been a helpful observation or suggestion?" The Therapist, without a pause to allow adequate time for development of the Cycle of Experience, answers, "Well I think I behaved as if I was quite helpless myself. I found it very frustrating to have the Patient move from one physical position to another one, over and over again, it seemed impossible to make contact, I just felt useless. I mean it is impossible to have the patient be so resistant and to feel that something can be done that is helpful. Actually I remember once reading about a case like that, a really crazy kid, he would just hide under a desk..." The Supervisor, having assured him/herself that s/he had waited long enough, interrupts by saying, "A while ago, Sue, I was wondering and I asked you whether I could have been, in my role as supervisor, more useful to you than I seemed to have been, and I don't hear you responding to that question." Silence – now Sue, the Therapist, seems to move through the experience more slowly, allowing the energy to be organized, and says, "I just went on some tangent. I don't know why, but all of a sudden I got anxious... [silence]. I think I thought that you might have been implying that I wasn't very good as a Therapist, and then I couldn't even think in which way you could be helpful – I just lost it for a moment – now, let me think whether you could have been more useful to me. [silence] I don't think so, you were very supportive, and you pointed out some things I did well which I didn't even know about and that was useful to me." At this moment, from the perspective of the Interpersonal Experience Cycle, the trainees have proceeded to the point of contact and closure.

In time, when the trainees begin supervising, they will have an opportunity to use the Interactive Experience Cycle as one of the organizing principles. In a manner similar to the phenomenon of parallel process, the interruptions in the gestalt cycle can occur during the training session just as in the sessions between the student supervisor and therapist. With the instructor's reminder, the trainees can also be aware of the manifestation of parallel process and how it can supplement the use of the experience cycle. For example, the student supervisor might interrupt his/her cycle of experience, when s/he presents during the training session, at the very same point that his/her supervisee manifested his/her interruption, and further it reflects the precise point at which the supervisee's patient became stuck.

5. The volume of unfinished business, in my experience, is in direct proportion to the level(s) of resentment and defensiveness. The consequence of such a relationship produces an unproductive learning environment.

Bipersonal Field

The Bipersonal Field (Langs, 1976) is one of Robert Langs' numerous books dealing with issues concerning the interpersonal context of all psychotherapeutic interactions. Langs refers to having borrowed the term, "Bipersonal field", from Baranger and Baranger (1966). He describes this phenomenon in the following fashion: "In essence, this concept indicates that psychotherapy takes place within a clearly defined physical and psychological field or space... This field is defined by the framework which not only sets off the therapeutic situation from all other realities, but also gives it its specific characteristics, attributes, and powers. The two polarities of the field are, of course, the patient and the therapist, and the processes within the field relate to their interaction. Their interaction takes place along what I have called the interface of the bipersonal field, and the location of that interface depends on the moment-to-moment contributions to the field from both the patient and the therapist" (p. 48).

Langs (1976) focuses his attention primarily on the interactions between therapist and patient, although he does make many allusions to how supervisors should conduct the work of supervision. Langs, as a supervisor, derives his data from and focuses his commentary primarily on the therapist's verbatim reports of what transpired during the psychotherapy session. On the basis of these reports Langs enhances the therapist's awareness of how the patient is instructing the therapist about "breaking the frame", i.e., failing to uphold full and complete confidentiality, failure to maintain anonymity, neutrality and commitments to time and fee, or other ways s/he is mismanaging the therapeutic alliance, such as offering inappropriate interpretations. All communications, according to Langs, have meaning only in the context of the bipersonal field of patient and therapist. The patient also, according to Langs, unconsciously knows what is best, i.e., most healing, for him/her and s/he communicates this knowledge in a metaphorical way to the therapist. All of the patient's communications, on some level, allude to the therapeutic interaction, all of them arise from the bipersonal field, and all productive, therapeutic work emanates from awareness of that interaction. The supervisor, when s/he functions effectively, works with the patient as a team (via the supervisee's descriptions of therapeutic encounters), instructing the therapist about the therapist's proper work. The supervisor listens to the report of the patient's metaphoric feedback and decodes these messages. On that basis the supervisor determines when or what the therapist's mistakes in treatment were and how the patient will reiterate these mistakes to the therapist during the following psychotherapy sessions. Hence, this model at times is referred to as a predictive model. To test his/her own accuracy in supervising, the supervisor predicts the patient's attitudes and behaviors which, due to the therapist's mismanagement of the therapeutic encounter, will emerge as resistance, anger and confusion during the following sessions. When the therapist perceives the predictions to be validated by patient attitude and behavior, it is accepted that the supervisor was on "the right track".

Extrapolating from Langs' model, one can assume that the supervisor is also capable of mismanagement and misinterpretation which will effect the nature of the supervisee's response to him/her. The instructor, along with the other trainees, will then function as a team with the supervisee in setting the supervisor back on course. Once again the predictive aspect of the model will prove whether the consultant's decoding was correct or incorrect.

Not withstanding some of the obvious objections to Langs' model based on the phenomenon of "selective perception", or "self-fulfilling prophecies", his bipersonal model of supervision represents a powerful and an intriguing potential for enhancing the understanding of supervisory events. This enhancement is based on two premises: 1. all significant events of the supervisory session will emerge from the bipersonal field, i.e., the interactions between the supervisee and supervisor; 2. the supervisee, having absorbed the patient's unconscious message of feedback to him/her, will metaphorically instruct the supervisor about a correct process of supervision. At this juncture of ideas about supervision, one might see the striking similarity between the bipersonal field and parallel process. Just as in the parallel process, the supervisee selects to report those aspects of the patient's difficulties that converge with the supervisee's own area of conflict or blind spot, so in the bipersonal field the supervisee reports those aspects of patient behavior that correspond to the supervisee's lack of awareness. The process, once more established, will manifest similar repetitions or mirroring of conflict between the supervisor and the supervisee and, further down, between the supervisee and the patient.

Due to the significant portion of the TES being non-verbal, it is more difficult to apply Lang's model to the data gained from that experiment. Later, when students work with actual supervisees, the model becomes more obviously applicable and its implementation can lead to some powerful and impressive results. However, even in the context of a non-verbal experience, such as the TES, some patterns amenable to interpretation based on Langs' model are possible. For example, during the TES, a student in the role of Supervisor observes the Therapist who works with what appears to be an agitated, hyperactive, noncontactful Patient. The Supervisor also observes this same Patient hugging a piece of cloth and repeatedly shifting the focus of her gaze between floor and chair. The

Therapist later reports to the Supervisor that the Patient's incessant physical mobility not only was a barrier to contact, but made it impossible for the Therapist to focus and to get her bearings. This in turn causes the Therapist to feel helpless, "kind of useless", and lost. The Therapist appears agitated in reporting this experience about the Patient; the droop in her shoulders could be interpreted as a feeling of defeat. The Supervisor further notices that the Therapist does not mention the patient's other activity, i.e., hugging the cloth, moving a finger slowly over the back of her hand and shifting her gaze, which can be indicative that the Therapist's perceptions are selected according to her own tendency to unfocus and feel helpless when in an anxiety provoking situation(s). The Supervisor might also have a sense of his/her own energy being scattered or unfocused. The awareness of this state can later, during the supervisory encounter, be countered by a deliberate slowing down of his/her own movement, which will tend to be mirrored by the Therapist. The Supervisor then explores with the Therapist what other activities she, the Therapist, was aware of during her work with the patient. With some prodding and slowing down, the Therapist might recall the Patient's other activities. On the basis of the awareness of these other activities, it is interpreted that the Patient was instructing the Therapist to be more gentle (as the patient's finger on the back of her hand) and to slow down by standing still (standing, gazing at the floor) or sitting in the chair (gazing at the chair). The Patient needs the therapist to slow down. It can be predicted therefore, that the Therapist, having missed these instructions, will find the Patient continuing her hyperactivity; it could also be predicted that if the Supervisor had missed the Therapist's tendency to be unfocused herself, the Therapist would increase this behavior during future supervisory sessions.

The above example provides us with the phenomena which illustrate Langs' bipersonal interpretation and also illustrates the parallel process. Finally, from a gestalt therapy perspective, we might proceed by instructing the Therapist to enhance the patient's awareness, actively replicate the behavior and feelings by, e.g., mirroring the finger on the hand, thus potentially organizing energy, and in this case even making contact with a chair, i.e., the Therapist would model by means of sitting in the chair.

In summary, the understanding of supervisory data can be based on the use of the three discrete principles or patterns of data selection and organization, i.e., 1. parallel process, 2. Gestalt Cycle of Experience and Gestalt Interactive Cycle, and 3. bipersonal field. The organizing patterns can be combined and used according to what seems to be most appropriate at the time in the particular circumstance. Later, and with growth of their experience, the students of psychotherapy supervision will select from, modify and add to the conceptual models which they have studied. Thus, *new* and original models are created; models congruent with the supervisor's personality, type of practice and congruent with the zeitgeist.

Some of these patterns are articulated in the literature and/or passed down by word of mouth and practice to the students of supervision. However, and regrettably, it is my guess that many of the original organizing principles go unnoticed and are eventually lost.

Part III

Transition From Preparation To Practice

6

The Differences That Make the Difference Matching Supervisor in Training with Supervisee

But remember that becoming educated means being stretched. So be experimental. Try some things that are unfamiliar to you.

Paul Nash

...having the generosity to let a thing be what it is, the patience to come to know it, a sense of the mystery in all living things, and a joy in new experience.

M.C. Richards

THE TRANSITION STAGE of training, though in a sense still a stage of preparation for actual supervising, is nevertheless different from the preceding stage. The significant difference emanates from the added responsibility that the participants of the program face during this stage of training, i.e., the responsibility of making the initial contacts with the potential supervisee(s). Even as the Supervisor in Training (SIT)[6] continues to spend all of his/her training for supervising time in the training group with the other trainees, s/he is beginning to focus some attention on his/her supervisee(s).

In order to have at least one supervisee assigned to each SIT, the instructor of the training program needs to identify sources of potential supervisees. The search for the sources of potential supervisees is simplified when the instructor has the cooperation and support of the corresponding academic department's administration and of institutions used by the doctoral program for placement of its students. When the training is offered

6. In this chapter and chapters to follow, the students of supervision will be referred to in an abbreviated form as SIT, standing for Supervisor In Training. This nominology seems appropriate at this juncture of the student's development when s/he begins to supervise.

at a professional school, the majority of supervisees are 1st year students participating in their first clinical placement. An additional source of supervisees is supplied by volunteers from other local graduate programs in mental health services.

In preparing the SIT for making an informed choice of a supervisee(s), if choice is possible, the SITs are directed to review Stoltenberg and Delworth's (1987) work on developmental approaches to psychotherapy supervision and the literature on learning styles, e.g., Ekstein & Wallerstein (1978), Fox & Guild (1987). They are also invited to examine their own teaching style, skills and limits as indicated to them by the data gained during the Preparation for Supervision part of the training. It is suggested that the SIT record and revise his/her preferences in his/her supervisory learning journal. When the process of SIT-supervisee matching begins, s/he organizes the journal entries and submits them to the instructor in written form.

Variables in Matching

In part, matching and assignment of supervisees depends on the ratio of potential supervisees to each SIT and on logistics, e.g ., working hours, scheduling problems and in some instances the geographic distance that both SITs and supervisees would need to travel in order to meet. Additional considerations include a number of variables that can promote a productive supervisory relationship. The salient variables that support a satisfactory supervisory relationship can be divided into four categories.

1. Professional development:
   a. Supervisee's level of professional development.
   b. Supervisor's level of professional development.

2. Clinical experience:
   a. Supervisee's preference for supervisor's specific clinical experience, e.g., work with substance abusers or chronic inpatient population;
   b. Supervisor's preference for a supervisee working with a specific clinical population.

3. Theoretical orientation or school of thought:
   a. Supervisee's preference for a supervisor's familiarity with a specific theory or school of thought;
   b. Supervisor's preference for a supervisee's familiarity with a specific school of thought.

4. Gender, age:
    a. Supervisee's expressed preference for a supervisor of specific gender and age;
    b. Supervisor's expressed preference for a supervisee of specific gender and age.

Before I proceed to discuss the above categories in detail with the SITs, I like to underscore and warn them of the fact that even when the instructor matches SIT and supervisee based on all of their expressed preferences, there can be no assurance of a productive or high quality experience. Unforeseen and unattended to supervisee and/or SIT personality variables are of particular importance in this context. These personality variables interface with what Ekstein and Wallerstein (1978) have referred to as the supervisee's "learning problems" and "problems about learning", as well as the SIT's "teaching problems" and "problems about teaching". Although these paired problems present the supervisory dyad with significant barriers to a well functioning supervisory process, awareness and examination of these problems can provide the supervisee and SIT with rich opportunities for learning.

1. Professional development

Level of professional development is a function of academic achievement, longevity of practice in the appropriate field of endeavor and the ability to demonstrate the benefits of experience and competence. Among the major mental health disciplines (psychology, psychiatry, psychiatric social work and psychiatric nursing), professional development is measured by achievement of appropriate degrees, acceptance by pertinent accrediting bodies, and by seniority in the field of practice. Similarly, before terminal degrees are awarded, professional development in the field of psychotherapy is measured by advancement in an academic program and amount of supervised practical experience. It is not clear to what degree accuracy of professional development is rendered by these measurements. Study of the work of Stoltenberg and Delworth reduces the nebulous aspect of assessing professional development. The SITs, therefore, are directed to read and study Stoltenberg and Delworth's (1987) research and writings.

In the context of the matter at hand, I suggest that the SITs attend especially to Stoltenberg and Delworth's considerations regarding the levels achieved by supervisors and supervisees and implications of these levels on matching supervisors and supervisees. Thus, SITs familiarize themselves with the notion set forth by Stoltenberg and Delworth that the Level 1 supervisor should appropriately supervise only the Level 1 supervisee. "We have noticed in our own work not only that Level 1 supervisors who are themselves Level 2 counselors often provide adequate supervision to Level

1 trainees, but that the necessary task of aiding the trainee with cognitive formulations helps the supervisor to work through some of his or her own Level 2 confusion. In our experience, some Level 2 trainees are far better supervisors (provided they are matched with Level 1 supervisees) than they are counselors. The Level 2 counselor who is also a Level 1 supervisor often finds that the need to provide basic structure for the beginning supervisee helps to resolve some of his or her own confusion and ambivalence" (p. 155). It is advantageous, therefore, to match the SIT with Level 1 therapists. However, as I have noted, sometimes due to a limited number of available supervisees, the optimal matching of SIT with supervisee is not possible.

The mismatch can also occur when the instructor either ignores the importance of supervisor/supervisee developmental levels or when s/he makes a poor assessment of a supervisee's and/or SIT's level of development. Thus, despite best intentions, a developmentally important mismatch may occur, e.g., a SIT being matched with a Level 2 therapist.

The negative outcomes of the above match, according to Stoltenberg and Delworth, exceed those in the match between a Level 1 supervisor and a Level 3 supervisee. In the later case the tendency of the supervisee is merely to wait it out or regress temporarily to Level 2. It is disturbing to know how frequently, during my years of instructing, I encountered advanced graduate students who reported merely waiting out their engagement with supervisors that seemed inadequately trained to conduct productive supervision with Level 3 supervisees.

However, a mismatch between SIT and a supervisee has somewhat different consequences when this occurs in the context of the training program rather than at a place of work or supervisee's placement. Even a poor match can turn into a beneficial learning experience when the SIT is backed up by a good support and processing system consisting of colleagues and the instructor of the training program. Although the path of a poorly matched supervisory pair might be trying for both SIT and his/her supervisee, it can provide each of them with unexpected learning benefits.

As do Stoltenberg and Delworth, Alonso (1985) also focuses on the importance of supervisor development. Alonso's observation and thesis is that, "supervisors change over time [and that their development moves] along a fairly predictable continuum throughout their professional lives" (p. 53). Within the limits of this book, however, I focus only on the overlap between Alonso's description of a "novice supervisor" and my observations of the SIT. Alonso (1985) aptly points out that "it is not unusual for a novice supervisor to present a somewhat rigid stance with the trainee around the work, and feel threatened by the therapist's attempts at friendship; the supervisor may be feeling that he could work or play, be a supervisor or a friend, with little confidence about what constitutes a proper balance" (p. 56). In view of minimal, if any, training or current guidance, achieving a graceful, proper balance is as difficult as experimenting is risky. After all, inappropriate limit setting can be as professionally embarrassing to the supervisor as it might be harmful to the supervisee. Further elaboration of boundary and limit setting issues is presented in Chapter 12.

The affiliative needs during this early stage of supervisor development engage the supervisor's empathy and understanding of the trainee's struggles. "Thus, on the one hand, the new supervisor can empathize better with the student, but, on the other hand, he may need the student to comply in order to save them both from embarrassment" (Alonso, 1985, p. 61). In time, this dilemma might be resolved only to be superseded by new challenges. "As the new supervisor feels more secure in his capacity to survive in the role, i.e., to be a viable supervisory object for the trainee, he may become more vulnerable to strong competitive feelings toward the therapist who is, after all, a peer" (p. 62). Later, in addition to the competitive and controlling feelings experienced by the new supervisor in the process of adjusting to appropriate levels of intimacy with his/her supervisee, s/he may be confronted by intense and sexual fantasies of closeness. According to Alonso, "...in this pairing, fantasies of sexual intimacy may emerge, leading to feelings of guilt and secrecy" (p. 63). It is "the new supervisor's awareness of such affects [that] remains the best safeguard against regressive actingout of instinctual drives..." (p. 63).

Again, as in earlier discussions of Hess's Level A and Stoltenberg and Delworth's Level 1 supervisors, I point out to the trainees that, in contrast to Alonso's experience of a "novice supervisor", the SITs have the advantage of participating in a training program. During these sessions they discuss and experiment with the range of behaviors and interventions which, among other advantages, provide them with opportunities to test limit setting adjustments. Being supported by a group of peers who experience similar supervisory encounters, the mistakes in the adjustments of intimacy are neither as humiliating nor do they carry as heavy a penalty as they do in the lonely world of a novice supervisor at his/her place of work.

In the process of discussing and negotiating the supervisory matching, the SIT can be forewarned about the many balancing acts, described by Alonso (1985), which they may encounter and with which they need to deal. However, the full impact or meaning of these phenomena do not emerge until the SIT has engaged in the process of supervising.

2. *Gender or age*

Both SIT and supervisee should have an opportunity to express and, if possible, discuss their preference for specific gender or age of their learning/teaching partner.

Although most female SITs tend to request a female supervisee and male SITs request a male supervisee, it is well for them to know that there are advantages to same sex match as well as to a cross-sex match. For example, concluding their research on supervisory behavior and sex role stereotypes, Petty and Odewahn (1983) point out data which indicate "...that male social workers are not coping well with assertive behavior from female supervisors while female social workers expect female supervisors to be more assertive in an effort to overcome sex-role stereotypes may cause female supervisors to experience more resistance from male subordinates. If this scenario is real, female supervisors of mixed sex work groups may experience more role stress than their male peers" (p. 19). These findings suggest that stress may well be reduced by matching a female SIT with a female supervisee. However, distinct learning opportunities emanate from cross-sex matching. Indeed some authors (Alonso & Rutan, 1978; Brodsky, 1980) recommend that the cross-gender match in supervision is a necessary professional experience. Not withstanding the value of a male-female supervision pair, I have preferred to accede to the SIT's and to the potential supervisee's preference for specific gender match. At times, however, a choice will need to be made between the SIT's preferences and those of the potential supervisee. In that event, it is of greater importance to attend to the supervisee's rather than the SIT's wants. The supervisee might be in a less favorable position of power, while the SIT has the advantage of responding to the challenge of learning from a less favored match by employing the extensive support system of other trainees and the instructor.

The large majority of SITs, as expected, prefer supervisees who are close to their age or younger. When beginning to practice in a new role, it is understandable that one's confidence needs bolstering by whatever means from whatever source and therefore a supervisee's age seniority can be perceived as a threat. Thus, if at all possible, I do my best to match the SITs with supervisees who are chronologically younger. This type of match also seems favored by most supervisees. However, at times this arrangement is precluded by superceding considerations. It is reassuring then for SITs matched with older supervisees, as it is informative for the other SITs, to be aware that age according to many authors, including Stoltenberg and Delworth (1987), correlates minimally, if at all, with developmental level of the therapist.

While complications resulting from unfulfilled requests can be difficult, the potential for learning about new attitudes and mastering new personal and professional resources in such circumstances can be equally rich.

3. *Clinical experience*

The SIT's request for being matched with a supervisee who works with a specific clinical population, e.g., substance abusers, should be carefully discussed with the SIT. It is important to explore why the SIT prefers that specific category. If s/he feels that his or her expertise gained from having worked with that population might be helpful to the supervisee, s/he needs to be encouraged about his/her many other, more basic skills, e.g., active listening, mirroring, limit setting, that are applicable across clinical populations and would be of greater use to a novice therapist than specialized approaches. It is also important for the SIT to be reminded that the other participants in the training program and the instructor will provide a consultation resource. Thus, they will have access to at least some knowledge of how to handle issues of specific populations, e.g., chronically ill, agoraphobic patients, etc.

The supervisee's requests in this context must be attended to from another point of view. A potential supervisee is not expected to know what supervision can and cannot offer to them. A request for a supervisor with experience in treating a specific population or having a specific clinical expertise should be taken seriously and, if at all possible, acceded to and fulfilled. One must also keep in mind that a supervisee is very likely to have additional supervisors at the training institution and that one of those supervisors will have expertise in the requested specialty. This condition fosters the SIT's freedom to offer a more general supervision of psychotherapy, i.e., introducing to the supervisee skills in: forming and maintaining appropriate relationships; creative listening; observation; organizing psychotherapeutic data according to a theoretical stance; and a range of supportive interventions. Of course, in cases in which potential supervisees are matched with a SIT who has experience in treating a specific population, the SIT by default, if not by design, obtains his/her preferred match.

4. Theoretical orientation or school of thought

Though theoretical differences are frequently considered to be an important variable in supervision, Markowitz (1958), as other authors, e.g., Karr & Geist (1977), have pointed out that the facilitative conditions in the supervisory context are more crucial for success than the theoretical orientation(s) of the supervisory pair.

In contrast to the common assumption that a supervisor will work more productively with someone of the same theoretical orientation, it has been my experience that this similarity is often over emphasized. Differences in theoretical orientations tend to become problematic only when other aspects of the relationship do not work. The converse is also true. When the relationship is well tended, e.g., communications are clear, experiences of mutual trust and the learning alliance are strong, differences in theoretical orientations are enriching to both the supervisor and supervisee.

Further, the rigors of matching according to theoretical preferences will depend at least partially on one's belief about whether content and process of supervision should correspond to the model of psychotherapy that the supervisor identifies with and uses in his or her practice, or whether supervision can be generic and not associated with any one school of thought and practice.

In my opinion and congruent with this book's intent, a major aspect of psychotherapy supervision can and should be of a generic nature. This stance does not preclude the SIT's personal style which might be heavily influenced by a specific school of thought.

The SIT is expected to be aware of his/her tendency to think and conceptualize according to the preferred school of thought or theory and to discuss this preference with the supervisee. Being aware of these built-in differences, the supervisory pair can plan on how the differences will be managed and/or how they intend to learn from them. These conditions exist in contrast to the conditions in specialized training settings, e.g., strategic family therapy, behavioral therapy, cognitive therapy, gestalt therapy. In those situations, courses of training usually have a discrete content and predetermined length of training time. A professional psychotherapist should, and usually does, have supervised training and experience in psychotherapy before s/he engages in specialized training. His/Her professional development should continue after the specialized training and throughout the years of his/her practice.

Thus, it is my belief that the SIT can reach out to and, with the help of a support system, manage a supervisee with any theoretical perspective. Common to all schools of thought are skills: in forming and maintaining a productive relationship; listening and observing; using messages and observations to validate the other's existence, sense of worth and creativity; enhancing awareness of feelings and options. The particular foci, organizing principles, meanings and corresponding technology might differ, but the SIT should be able to adapt sufficiently to promote the supervisee's own process and discovery.

I suggest that a SIT's preference for a supervisee with a specific theoretical or therapeutic orientation be heard, discussed and, if at all possible, redirected to a new set of possibilities inherent in a flexible approach to psychotherapy supervision. Potential supervisees, however, usually do not have a clear preference for a specific theory or therapy orientation. When they do state a preference, it is well to accommodate them as much as possible. Thus, once again, if not by design then at times by default, the SIT ends up being matched with a supervisee of the same or similar theoretical orientation.

Logistic Limitations

As previously mentioned, the best laid plans for matching are at times impossible to actualize due to limits in availability of time and related issues of geographic proximity. The logistical complications are minimized when there is institutional and administrative support for the training of supervisors and when this support is carried out in concert with and the support of the placement sites. For example, a psychology graduate program may have special arrangements with a number of mental health centers and or hospitals where placements are available for advanced as well as beginning students of psychotherapy. In such circumstances the advanced students can be assigned the beginning or less advanced trainees for purposes of student supervising. This additional arrangement allows the administrators and instructors of both institutions, i.e., school and placement facility, to negotiate an appropriate contract regarding the inherent legal issues.

Although it might be difficult to identify enough potential supervisees for each SIT to have even one person to supervise, Hart (1982) makes a cogent argument that the beginning supervisor should have at least two supervisees. As he points out, "...each student should have a minimum of two supervisees for individual supervision. Having two supervisees allows the supervisor to examine the differences between supervision conducted with each supervisee and to consider different approaches that need to be used in either case" (p. 228). I am in complete agreement with Hart regarding the advantages of having two or more supervisees per each SIT. Although the process of matching might be more complicated, circumstances permitting, practice with multiple supervisees offers the SIT an opportunity to engage in an invaluable self evaluation and develop increasing versatility in the practice of supervision.

In summary, of the four major categories for matching of SIT with supervisee, the level of professional development is the most important. While other variables are important to consider, discuss and, whenever possible, take into account, the potential supervisee's preferences receive priority in all categories under consideration.

7

Road Maps and Bridges
Planning the Supervisory Contract

To live only for some future goal is shallow. It's the sides of the mountain which sustain life, not the top. Here's where things grow. But of course without the top you can't have any sides. It's the top that defines the sides.

Robert Pirsig

A CONTRACT IS a basic, though at times only implicit, ingredient of any relationship, e.g., marriage, employment. The more features of any relationship that are consciously and explicitly negotiated and agreed upon, the smoother or more meaningful the relationship's journey will tend to be. Likewise, in the context of the supervisory relationship, a conscious, explicitly articulated agreement will ease the navigation of the process and keep it focused upon a shared destination.

Supervisory Contract

Establishing a supervisory contract between supervisor and supervisee should be an obvious and essential component of the first, or at least very early, session(s) of supervision. It was with some astonishment that, based on trainees' reports, I repeatedly learned that the supervisors at some of the most distinguished training institutions did not suggest or negotiate a specific and detailed supervisory contract with their supervisees. There was of course no shortage of institutional contracts (considered frequently as "nuisance" paper work), prepared and requested by the corresponding administrations of each participating institution. A hands-on process of negotiating a contract between supervisor and supervisee falls far short of being a standard or common practice. In the few supervisory relationships where contracting does take place, it tends to be unsystematic, inadequate in detail and insufficiently concrete. During the later sessions of supervision and review, or when necessary, a renegotiation of such agreements tends to be equally unsystematic and thus inadequate as a tool for maintaining an optimal quality of the supervisory relationship.

The content of this contract serves to clarify goals and establish parameters for many aspects of the supervisory activity. However, of equal importance is the process of negotiating, reviewing and, when indicated, renegotiating of the contract. Initial negotiation of the supervisory contract effects mutual empowerment of both parties and therefore facilitates establishing a supervisory relationship. During later stages of supervision, in the event of difficulty or conflict, the contract should be used as a basis for reassessment and, if necessary, for renegotiation of unworkable or unproductive agreements. Finally, the supervisory contract serves periodically as the ground for supervisor and supervisee evaluations.

Introduction of the SIT to the supervisory contract

To begin planning the contract, the instructor requests the SITs to apply their knowledge about and experience of supervision gained thus far, including special attention to the SLL experience, the definition of supervision, the TES experience and the corresponding didactic material. On the basis of that knowledge, the SITs are invited to write out a list with a minimum of three and a maximum of six items that they would *want* in this contract; a minimum of three and a maximum of six conditions that they would *demand* from their supervisees; and a minimum of three and a maximum of six criteria that they would use to assess the response to the wants and demands. (It is important for the SIT to be clear about the difference between *want* as an expression of personal feeling or preference, not necessarily assuming an accommodation from the other, and *demand* which implies a rule according to which the conduct of the relationship is expected to conform.)

Upon completion of the lists, the participants share items on their lists with other SITs. In the process and/or as a result of this sharing, the items prepared to be considered for inclusion in the contract are refined, added to or omitted. Some of the basic components of the contract are thus defined. Although many items of the contract tend to be shared by all participants of the training program, some of the conditions are more idiosyncratic (e.g., one SIT will demand no smoking during the supervisory sessions) or fit the personal or teaching style of one or only a few of the SITs (e.g., that an articulated summary mark the end of each supervisory session). Each SIT also knows that most of the content of their version of the contract will be presented for consideration by, and negotiation with, their supervisee.

Some basic variables of the contract

The instructor of the training program facilitates the discussion of the supervisory contracts to include the following items:

1. Space Variables: Negotiation about place of meetings is at times more complicated than either SIT or supervisee expect it to be. Both SIT and supervisee usually have full schedules and at times their placements are at institutions geographically distant from each other. However, the willingness to or not to accommodate is indicative of either party's initial motivation or resistance to this supervisory engagement. In this context the SIT also needs to consider the significance of turf on which the meetings would take place and the corresponding power implications.

2. Time Variables: SITs will need to facilitate the negotiation of the following items: a. frequency of meetings (usually the preferred frequency is once/week); b. duration of each meeting (usually one hour is preferred); c. day of the week and time of the meeting; d. duration of the contract between the SIT and his/her supervisee (if in a predoctoral, professional school context, 12–16 weeks is usually recommended as the preferred duration, with ten weeks being the minimum); e. vacation times (vacation time[s], if at all possible, should be coordinated to coincide); f. time constraints regarding cancellations of established meetings (usually the supervisor would expect a 24-hour notice); g. makeup time (the expectations regarding making up the missed sessions by either party should be explicitly stated and corresponding arrangements agreed upon).

3. Goals of the particular supervision: In this segment of negotiations, the SIT articulates his or her goals for supervision and devotes at least equal time and energy to learning about the supervisee's expectations of and goals for supervision. Then, the SIT has an opportunity to talk to the supervisee about those expectations and goals which s/he, the SIT, feels competent and willing to deliver. On the basis of this dialogue, the SIT and supervisee can proceed to set their supervision goals. For example, the supervisee says: "It will be important for me to get at least some basics about how to begin doing therapy or counseling or whatever it is that I'll be doing with these chronic and terminal patients. I'm not sure I will know how to get it going – you know working with these kinds of patients and their families...is kind of scary. I think it might take a special skill and I just hope that I won't complicate their lives or deaths any more than necessary." SIT: "O.K., I hear you presenting few issues or goals. First of all we might need to examine what is the nature of the service that you will be delivering. I think I can help in differentiating the services and together I believe we will be able to identify the appropriate approaches, be they therapeutic or counseling in nature, supportive or another kind. I have experience in forming and maintaining relationships corresponding to those services and in empathic listening skills. On the other hand, I have never worked with cancer patients and therefore in that particular aspect of your work I am limited. Will you have another supervisor whom you could use as a resource for that particular need?"

Other expectations of the supervisee might consist of the SIT being supportive, being patient with a beginner's naivete, modeling appropriate professional behavior, etc. Goals can consist of acquiring creative listening skills, learning when to interrupt or ask a facilitating question, or how to set and maintain limits.

4. Choice of Focus: The supervisory pair needs to agree on what seems to be most profitable to the supervisee's development at that time. Accordingly, they will choose: a. intensive supervision, i.e., focusing on and following the treatment of one patient only; b. technical supervision, i.e., focusing on any one of the supervisee's patients (need determined by supervisee) or any related professional issues; c. combination of intensive and technical supervision, i.e., following the treatment of one patient for half of each session and spending the remainder of the session focused on other patients or other issues, e.g., ways of dealing with a patient's spouse who interferes with and refuses to come to therapy or how to handle greeting of the patient in the waiting room.

5. Supervisee's Method of Recording: The supervisory pair needs to agree on what appears to both of them the most productive method of recording the therapy experiences for the purpose of learning from them in supervisory sessions: a. process notes (preferred mode for intensive supervision); b. audiotapes; c. videotapes; d. structured or unstructured verbal presentation of therapy content and process by the supervisee.

6. Supervisee's Method of Presentation: Interfacing with the method of recording, is the supervisee's method of presentation during the supervisory sessions. The method of presentations can be negotiated according to what the supervisor considers to facilitate the process of supervision and what the supervisee believes will serve his/her learning style. Thus, if the process notes are used, the supervisor might demand that they be delivered a minimum of 24 hours in advance of the supervisory meeting time and the supervisee may feel the need to underline the segments of notes describing a difficult or unproductive interaction. If audiotapes are used, the supervisor might request that the supervisee mark off passages s/he found to be most or least productive, etc. When verbal presentation is used, it can proceed by means of vignettes or the sequential process of the session. The SIT or the supervisory pair will also need to decide whether this form of presentation will have a specific structure. For example, the SIT might suggest that his/her supervisee: a. present the context of the problem encountered; b. describe in detail the interaction at the point of encountering the problem; and c. frame, if possible, appropriate questions. If a question about a problematic encounter is not accessible to the supervisee, the supervisor might indicate that s/he is available to facilitate identifying that question.

7. Issues of Confidentiality: One of the most important aspects of negotiation between SIT and supervisee must be the extent of confidentiality that they can, and that they intend to, keep. The SIT has the luxury of not having legal responsibilities and no usual institutional training responsibilities. Therefore, the evaluations within the pair can be kept private and encapsulated. However, the SIT must also be aware to what extent the obligatory evaluations in other contexts of both the supervisor and supervisee can and do compromise the strict observance of confidentiality. The supervisee should be informed that this supervision will be processed with other SITs during training sessions. Though the SIT reassures the supervisee that his/her identity will be protected by use of a pseudonym, both SIT and supervisee understand that a pseudonym is not a foolproof measure of anonymity. The pair must also decide for what reasons the SIT or supervisee, preferably with each other's consent, may seek out additional consultation.

Other issues in this context might be considered and agreed upon: Will full confidentiality be kept about personal information which might emerge during the supervision sessions? If there is an obligation to the institutional process, how much process or content of the supervision will be included in the required evaluations of the supervisee or supervisor? How free is the supervisor or supervisee expected to be in discussing supervisory experiences and judgments of the supervisor, or other details of the supervisory encounter, with colleagues, with fellow students or faculty members who are not directly involved in the training program?

Issues of confidentiality are especially difficult to assess during the negotiation of the supervisory contract. Due to the supervisee's and SIT's inexperience, anxiety or other factors, at times it might seem that relatively easy and clear agreements about confidentiality have been made. However, at times only a few sessions into the supervisory process, agreements may turn out to be inappropriate and needing renegotiation, e.g., if the place of meeting is in the supervisor's home, this may compromise the supervisee's sense of privacy. In general, issues concerning confidentiality need to be addressed periodically and especially at those times when there is awareness of conflict within the supervisory pair.

Since, customarily, the SIT's supervisee will be receiving concurrent supervision from one or more other supervisors, it is important to clarify and, if necessary, negotiate the nature of the boundaries and how these boundaries are expected to be observed among all the parties involved. For example, it is well to anticipate whether the possibility that an overlap among the SIT and supervisors' input or responsibilities might be preferred and judged as productive. Some supervisees like to have the opportunity to present their work with the same patient/same session to different supervisors. The SIT has the opportunity to negotiate this condition with the supervisee's other supervisor(s). On the other hand, some supervisees might experience such multiple presentations and input as confusing or creating an unnecessary overload of information. Likewise, some supervisors will be more comfortable about allowing their supervisees to present similar material to another supervisor(s), or in this case, the SIT and some supervisors would be uncomfortable with such dual presentations. In the former case the instructor of the supervision seminar would of course need to be watchful of potential triangulation, competition among the SIT and other supervisors, and/or of the imparting of conflicting information.

Furthermore, the SIT might feel considerable insecurity and anxiety about having other, more senior, supervisors supervise the same case(s) s/he is supervising. If at all possible, the SIT should be assigned supervisee(s) who are not required to duplicate all of their supervisory needs with other supervisors. In these cases the instructor and the supervisors who assume legal responsibility over the cases supervised by the SIT must keep an especially clear and regular set of direct communications.

Since SITs can have no legal accountability over the supervisee's patients, logistically and technically this might present a complication. However, a variety of arrangements to resolve the complication(s) can take place. A staff person at the supervisee's placement site might be assigned to respond in the event of emergencies, or a staff person can be assigned to oversee case management but not be involved in an ongoing processing of the actual treatment. (The issues involved in the legal responsibilities of supervisors calls for further discussion and are addressed in Chapter 12.)

8. Issues of Feedback and Evaluation: The process of feedback and evaluation is at the core of the supervisory relationship and related conflicts. The supervisor, if not constrained by institutional demands, may have some preconception of how, when and to what end evaluation should take place. However, since this is one of the most sensitive components of supervision, it is also the one that requires the most negotiation. The SIT, having no formal responsibilities over the supervisee, is usually free of the institutionally required evaluations. Thus, this supervisee/supervisor pair can choose to whom, if anyone else, their mutual evaluation(s) will be communicated.

A. *Supervisee evaluations:* the supervisee and SIT may both assume that the SIT will engage in periodic evaluations of the supervisee. However, the manner of evaluation (systematic, structured, unstructured, written, spoken, open-ended, recorded in written or audiotape form) and the frequency (weekly, monthly, or middle and end of supervisory engagement) need to be negotiated.

B. *Supervisor evaluations:* the supervisee and SIT need to decide whether and how the supervisor will be evaluated. It can be the same or similar to the manner and frequency of the supervisee evaluations, or it can differ on any of the variables outlined above.

As with any of the other components of the negotiated contract, so with evaluations (but perhaps with a special attentiveness to this component), the circumstances and supervisory relationship might change and periodic renegotiations might be appropriate. For example, in the case of conflict between the supervisee and SIT, some change in manner and frequency of evaluations would be indicated.

It is important for both SIT and supervisee to be clear about differences between evaluation and personal or professional feedback. Whereas all evaluation is inherently based on judging and judgments, feedback does not have to include a judgmental attitude. A vignette that characterizes an evaluation interaction at the end of a session might proceed as follows. (Notice the italicized words implying judgement, thus setting the stage for increased distancing and or other defensive responses.)

Supervisee: *I don't think* interruption *is a good* approach in this case. When you interrupted my description of the patient's father, *you were cutting me off* and so missing what I believe to be some very important information...*so I think you have a wrong picture* of the patient and do not understand my being so cautious with him.

Supervisor: I understand your concern, but as I have pointed out, *in my judgment*, you were getting off the track and complicating the matter more than necessary. However, if the information about the patient's father still seems very important to you when we meet next time, I will be glad to have you finish that description.

Supervisee: O.K. I know *you are good at* remembering this sort of unfinished business; today when you remembered my concerns about greeting

the patient in the waiting room, *I thought that was really good.*
Supervisor: Yes, I know, it is difficult to keep many things in mind when one is just beginning a new skill. However, I think your presentations *have improved*, they are considerably more concise, clear and to the point than even a few weeks ago.

In contrast to the above interactions, similar content is described in the following vignette. (Notice the *italicized* words indicate the language of experience rather than judgment. When the implication of judgment is reduced, distancing and other defensive responses tend to decrease.)

Supervisee: *I feel taken aback* when you interrupt me as you did when I was describing the patient's father. And then I wonder whether you have sufficient information to understand my caution with the patient.
Supervisor: I understand your concern and I can see how *some things that seem important to you might seem less important to me*. However, if the matter about the patient's father still seems important to you when we meet next time, I will be glad to have you finish that description.
Supervisee: *I appreciate* your remembering this sort of unfinished business; today when you remembered my concerns about greeting the patient in the waiting room, I *felt good* – seen, heard by you.
Supervisor: It is difficult to keep all the things in mind when one is just beginning, but I experience greater ease in following the summaries you present to me. *I can follow you now much more easily* and so our work seems to have that same increased ease.

In summary, Supervisors In Training frequently are aware of many aspects relevant to the contract from their past supervisory experiences. Although the instructor of the program guides the general outline of the contract, each SIT has the freedom to add details that fit his/her own style. The final form of the contract, as pointed out above, is determined on the basis of negotiation between the SIT and his/her supervisee.

The supervision contract provides the SIT and supervisee with the basic ground upon which they sow the seeds of the supervisory process. The content of the contract consists of: an agreed-upon place and time of meeting; goals and choice of focus; method of recording and presentation; definition of and agreements about confidentiality; preferred modes of feedback and/or evaluation. The process of negotiating the contract further provides the SIT and supervisee with an opportunity to get to know each other, test out and/or establish a basic rhythm of the relationship, and for the SIT it provides an opportunity to gain some sense of the supervisee's needs and learning style.

Thus, the contract not only lays the ground for the activities of supervision, it also provides an important component of the "holding environment" (Winnicott, 1965). Further it creates a framework for monitoring the effectiveness of the supervisory relationship. The latter task is accomplished by means of initiation of a regular review and, if necessary, renegotiation of the original agreements.

8

Survey Of The Scape
Assessment Variables

Some find themselves ignited by glimpses of the whole; sight is what opens them to their energy. They strive on perception. And some find themselves unbound by their interaction with others. They are made more authentic by touch. Still others need vast open spaces in which all the thorny shrubs they've tucked around their passion are blown aside. And others need to drown in music before they stop fighting the deep.

Mark Nero

FINALLY, BEFORE THE actual supervising begins, I introduce the SITs to concepts used in assessing the supervisee's learning and defensive styles. In the process of examining these concepts, the SITs raise the awareness of their own defensive styles and the effect these styles might have on the supervisory relationship.

Supervisees' Learning Styles

Fox and Guild (1987) enumerate a range of learning styles studied and described by Witkin (1977), Myers (1976), Kolb (1974) and Gregoc (1979). In concert with the above authors I have observed that the learning styles of SITs and supervisees cluster around four dimensions:

1. Level of field-dependency vs. tendency for inner-directed style. One can expect the field-dependent supervisee to rely on supervisor evaluations, feedback and direction more than the inner-

directed supervisee. On the other hand, Bernstein and LeComte (1979) found that the field-dependent counselors were more positively disposed to feedback than were the field-dependent counselor/trainees.

2. Preference for presentation of information in a linear form (logical, orderly) vs. in a wholistic, metaphoric way. This dimension can be expected to influence the choice of interventions used by the SIT in his/her work with a supervisee.

3. Preference for an inductive, intuitive process of learning and tendency for risk in gathering knowledge vs. preference for a deductive process, needing access to concepts and understanding before acting. Stoltenberg and Delworth (1985) discuss the contrast in this dimension of learning style as learning by doing vs. learning vicariously. Some supervisors prefer the experience to precede consideration of the theoretical material relating to that experience. Other supervisors prefer to have access to reading material for the purpose of studying the theorectical underpinnings of an approach or intervention before they feel comfortable experimenting with it. The training program tends to structure the process of training with experience first, and examination and analyses to follow. However, the SITs are provided with opportunities to use the readings and didactic material offered in a sequence that they prefer. Further, they are cautioned to attend to the preferred style of their supervisees and to adjust their instructions according to the needs or preferences of the supervisee.

4. The supervisees will differ in their preference for emotionally intensive vs. distant, structured learning relationships. The SITs are reminded throughout their supervisory practice, by each other and the instructor, to be attentive to adjusting the emotional distance between themselves and their supervisees as a function of a range of events and processes encountered during the supervisory relationship. Interventions effecting these adjustments are modeled to the SITs by the instructor during the training sessions.

The SIT, having discussed and negotiated the content of the supervisory contract, will have at least minimal, if not a significant and adequate amount of information regarding the supervisee's level of field-dependency, preference for linear versus wholistic processing of supervisory material, preference for an inductive versus deductive approach in examining the supervisory material, and tendency for an intimate versus distance-based supervisory relationship. For example, a supervisee who requests the SIT to decide what would be the most useful way of recording the therapy sessions for presentation during supervision sessions is manifesting his/her field-dependency. On the other hand, the SIT must also consider to what extent the field-dependency is exaggerated by the supervisee's developmental level and how the tendency might change in the process of the supervisee developing his/her professional therapeutic skills. Indeed, many aspects of the learning style can reflect the supervisee's developmental level and thus potentially need adjusting to by the SIT as the supervisory relationship evolves.

Supervisee's Developmental Level

As indicated above, the supervisee's learning style reflects his/her level of development as a psychotherapist. Significant data useful in assessment of the supervisee's development can be derived from the process of negotiating the supervisory contract. For example, a supervisee who prefers and negotiates for structured, content-oriented supervision can be assessed as being in the early stages of development. Although SITs are directed to read Stoltenberg and Delworth's (1987) work in the previous stage of training, at this time they are invited to return to the material and be ready to apply it to the initial assessment of their supervisee.

Stoltenberg and Delworth (1987) describe in detail psychotherapy students at Level 1, at Level 2 and at Level 3 of their professional development; for each of the levels they also describe a corresponding behavior for optimizing learning.

Level 1 supervisees are described by Stoltenberg and Delworth as dependent and over-accommodating to their supervisor; their awareness of self and others tends to be low; they tend to over-identify with their client's lives; they manifest high motivation as well as high anxiety and low self-esteem; they prefer training of circumscribed skills and adherence to a preferred theoretical orientation. Thus the supervisor of a Level 1 supervisee will do well to provide a clear structure and offer specific techniques.

Level 2 supervisees, as they progress in their self-assertiveness, reduce the need to imitate their supervisor. As they enrich their own ideas about the productive process of psychotherapy, their theoretical versatility also tends to increase. However, the vacillation between dependence and independence, as a complication of increased personal and interpersonal awareness as well as fluctuations in motivation, results in tumultuous conflictual interactive processes with their supervisors.

The supervisor for Level 2 therapists will do well to minimize the imposition of structure, using less didactic focus while clarifying the inherent ambivalence and providing appropriate modeling. Prescriptive interventions are made only when it is necessary to protect the client's welfare.

Level 3 supervisees will have stabilized their motivation and firmed up their sense of autonomy, therefore they feel free to be dependent on the supervisor at appropriate times. They have increased their self-awareness to the point of productive empathy with their clients and a more complete ability in use of self. The supervisors of Level 3 therapists can be both flexible and person-oriented.

The above paragraph is included here for the purpose of closure and summary of Stoltenberg and Delworth's material. The SITs are well aware of the fact that it would be a most unusual and unwise decision to assign to them a Level 3 supervisee.

The outline of Stoltenberg and Delworth's descriptions is offered to the SIT as a potential, not an absolute, guideline. As with other conceptual material, the SIT is invited to use it in the form of a hypothesis more than a conclusion. Following the definition and description of the three developmental levels, Stoltenberg and Delworth (1987, p. 124) present a model of assessing the trainee, which the SIT can choose to use as presented or in a form modified to fit his/her needs. An additional resource for a systematic approach to assessment of the therapist's development is offered by Bradley (1989, p. 359-365).

During the transition sessions, the SIT's anxieties and related stress tend to rise and manifest in individual character defenses. To use the energy aroused by the many stress-related feelings in a constructive fashion and lighten the weight of new responsibility, I introduce the SITs to Satir's (1972) categories of defensive patterns and corresponding positions. The study of Satir's material allows the SITs to identify not only their own defensive tendencies, but provides them with a tool for assessing the supervisee's defensive styles and patterns that will tend to emerge in the relationship between SIT and supervisee. Some or many of the SITs are likely to be familiar with Satir's work; however, in the context of this training and with the instructor's encouragement to "ham it up", the SITs review their knowledge by acting it out and identifying with one or more of the positions defined by Satir. The process, usually accompanied by laughter, alleviates some anxiety and, as stated above, provides the SIT with an additional assessment tool.

Defensive Styles

Introducing the four defensive patterns, Satir (1972) points out, "whenever there was any stress, over and over again I observed four ways people had of handling it. These four patterns occurred only when one was reacting to stress *and at the same time* felt his self-esteem was involved..." (p. 59). These are the precise conditions that SITs frequently experience at the very beginning of supervising.

Satir's four identified patterns are placating, blaming, computer and distracting. Awareness of these patterns can facilitate understanding of an interaction, promote a serious as well as humorous interpretation of a behavior and open ways to alternate, at times, more productive behavioral options.

Placator

The first stance described by Satir is *placator*. In this case the person will tend to do just about anything to preclude the other's anger, rejection or judgment. The *placator* is a "yes person" trying to please at any cost.

Both supervisor or supervisee have been known to adopt the stance of *placator*, although it might be expected that supervisees, presumed to be in "one down" positions, would tend to adopt this stance more often than the supervisor. However the SIT, insecure in his/her own role and trying to satisfy the supervisee's expectations, can succumb to this pattern just as easily as the supervisee. The placating supervisee might say, "I feel so badly about being five minutes late, it is so foolish of me not to have allowed extra time for unforseen delays.... I hope it didn't inconvenience you; it won't happen again. If you'd like, I will stay five minutes longer." The placating supervisor responds, "Oh, that's O.K. You're not all that late, and you don't have to stay five minutes longer...unless, of course, you need to. By the way, I looked up the answer to the question you asked last time. I really am sorry that I didn't know the information last time.... I hope this will be helpful..." When supervisors adopt a placating stance and don't shift out of it during early stages of supervision (usually supervisor developmental Level 1 matched with therapist developmental Level 2 or 3), the supervision is doomed. The supervisor feels initially and progressively more useless and dependent on the supervisee for professional self-esteem. The supervisee might learn how to reassure and bolster the supervisor while abandoning his/her learning goals.

Blamer

A second stance described by Satir is *blamer*. "The *blamer*," says Satir, "is a fault-finder, a dictator, a boss. He acts superior, and seems to be saying, 'If it weren't for you, everything would be alright'" (p. 66). S/he communicates an attitude of blame and accusation. The supervisor in a blamer position might send the following message, "If only you would have followed my directions, the patient would not have terminated." or "If you hadn't gotten me off the track during our last session, I would have warned you to confront the patient's resistance."

The supervisee, having adopted a blamer pattern says, "Well, the patient walked out on me. I confronted her just as you told me to and she just got furious and walked out. I really should have listened to myself, but you were so insistent..."

Supervisor, as well as supervisee, tend to adopt the stance of *blamer* when they feel worthless and are desperately searching for some authority, some confirmation of their skills. When supervisees adopt this stance, the supervisor will do well to reassure the trainee, be maximally supportive and creative in focusing on those attitudes and behaviors that the supervisee can experience as productive. The supervisor, depending on personal proclivity, might also share his/her own experiences about being frustrated and discouraged doing psychotherapy and having had a supervisor who was not much help.

When a supervisor adopts the stance of *blamer* (most likely a supervisor at developmental Level 2, especially with a supervisee at therapist Level 2 or 3), the supervisee is likely to adopt either a fight or flight response. "Fight" might manifest as passive resistance to most or all of the supervisor's interventions, supplemented by vociferous complaints to persons in the supervisee's support system. It may surface as a counter-attack: "The way I read Freud, and I will bring that passage to you, intervening with the interpretation you suggest would completely destroy the therapeutic alliance."

A supervisee's "flight" can manifest as excessive fatigue or preoccupation during the supervisory session, being progressively more tardy, or missing an increasing number of the sessions.

Computer

Satir's third defensive stance is *computer*. "The *computer* is very correct, very reasonable with no semblance of any feeling showing. He is calm, cool, and collected. He could be compared to an actual computer or a dictionary" (p.68). Messages are communicated by the person assuming the computer stance by use of the longest possible words even when the speaker is not sure of their meanings.

The computer pattern is adopted when a supervisor's or supervisee's hidden feelings consist of loneliness and helplessness in making contact. The supervisor in a computer stance might send the following message: "It is manifestly evident that this particular circuitous intervention you have utilized to treat your patient's psychogenically induced symptoms produces results of a dysfunctional nature." The supervisee in that same stance might say, "It is reasonable to posit that this patient is craving the attentions of the opposite sex parent in service of addressing the decompensating pathogenic syndrome." When the supervisee adopts the attitude of a *computer*, the supervisor will need to exercise caution in fostering rapid or intense contact. On the other hand, responding with a similar posture, i.e., the posture of a *computer*, to the supervisee would also be unproductive. A delicate balance must be exercised between: fostering interpersonal contact and maintaining distance; being understanding yet contained and rational; being supportive and cautiously interpretive.

Distracter

The fourth stance that Satir describes is *distracter*. The *distracter* behaves and speaks with irrelevancies, does not answer questions and does not address the point of discussion or other interaction. The *distracter* simply does not make sense. The apparent discord with the environment and self leaves the person feeling alone and generates a further sense of loneliness and/or of being misunderstood.

The supervisor in the pattern of *distracter* might say, "I know that you were asking a question about transference, but it really might be considered to be an issue of a relationship or just being together...[The supervisor picks up a pencil and makes a note.] You know, it is not clear from what was happening in your interaction or what the literature related to this might really be indicating.... or maybe..."

The supervisee in the pattern of *distracter* might say, "I did ask the mother of the patient about his medication, or maybe it was the physician that I spoke to, or I meant to ask about the medication... In any case, it is too early to determine my effect on the whole thing. There are so many people involved with this patient I sometimes wonder..."

When the supervisor manifests the role of *distracter* (probably supervisor developmental Level 2 or possibly a severely anxious supervisor at a developmental Level 1), s/he precludes almost any potential for learning. The supervisee receives an overload of unrelated or inconsequential messages. Of the four stances above, this one is the most dysfunctional. A supervisee adopting the distracter stance might be doing so at least partially in response to the blamer stance of the supervisor. If the supervisor becomes aware of his/her contribution to the distracter pattern, s/he might be able to correct it or find alternative, more functional ways of behaving.

As with other defensive stances, it can be assumed that the person has a characteriological proclivity or a habit to adapt to their environment in a manner corresponding to that tendency. For example, the supervisor aware of his/her supervisee's tendency to be a *distracter*, will do well to model an alternative approach, consciously slow him/herself down in speech and mannerisms, present interventions in a calm, rhythmical way and intervene into the supervisee's distractor tendency by inviting him/her to take notes. This approach tends to organize at least some of the excess energy and to support the supervisee's need to avoid a face-to-face contact.

It is assumed that the four patterns described above would not be manifested in quite as extreme or explicit manner as described in the above examples. More commonly, the personal growth and awareness of the SIT and supervisee is at a developmental level which modulates or affects dysfunctional styles, thus the defensive patterns may appear in a covert manner. At times of anxiety, however, the tendency to regress may cause the patterns to become increasingly overt. The regression, however, should be short-lived. For the SIT the intervention into attenuating the regressive pattern should be facilitated by feedback from other SITs or, if necessary, from the instructor; for the supervisee the intervention should be facilitated by his/her supervisor.

The familiarity with and experience of one's self in one of the defensive postures facilitates the SIT's ability to be sensitive to and cognizant of their supervisee's defenses. The assessment of these defensive styles provides the SIT with a valuable tool for diffusing feelings of frustration or conflict.

In summary, the SITs proceed into the supervising phase of training with basic concepts about assessing their supervisees. Review of and/or familiarization with Satir's work enlivens this stage of training and provides it with a tool for assessing some of the supervisee's most salient defense patterns. During later sessions, even the slight suggestion of any of the four defensive styles can be role-played and used both as a humorous interlude and as a tool to enhance personal awareness, empathy with colleagues and empathy with supervisees.

Having released some of their anxiety by role play of Satir's stances, the SITs are invited to return to the business at hand. Those SITs who have not reached their potential supervisees are encouraged to proceed with scheduling their first supervisory sessions; those SITs who have made initial contact(s) with their supervisees are invited to share their progress and experiences of that contact.

PART IV

Practice Of Supervising

9

On The Road
Beginning Phase Of SIT's Supervising

> *There is a cycle, a return to one's own beginnings which occurs in the process of learning to supervise. It demands a mastery of self image, something rarely accomplished in two or three years of doing therapy. In the cycle, the supervisor is thrown back to his own first stage, is anxious, is inclined to overidentify with the beginning supervisee, or to become more circumstantial or controlling, or whatever one's customary coping patterns may be. Because he is still mastering his own insecurities, the beginning supervisor accepts the challenges of the beginning therapist more at face value and less as a part of the struggle of overcoming anxiety.*
>
> David Van Buskirk

THE BEGINNING PHASE of supervising is short in duration, i.e., approximately one-eighth of the total supervising time. There are three major tasks to be attended to during this phase: 1. initiation of the supervisory relationship; 2. negotiation of a supervisory contract; 3. on the basis of this negotiation process, assessment of the supervisee's learning style, professional experience; and 4. form a guesstimate of the defensive styles the SIT-supervisee pair will tend to stimulate in each other.

Following the assignment of supervisees, the SITs are instructed to make contact with their supervisee and to schedule the initial meeting. This step does not always proceed smoothly. Attitudes and behaviors manifested by the SIT during the early sessions of this phase are similar to those characteristic of the Level 1 Supervisor described by Stoltenberg and Delworth (1987). Anxiety accompanied by corresponding ambivalence about and reluctance to begin supervising might be high. Basic creativity and resourcefulness might appear to sag even as the SIT claims high motivation to begin the supervisory process. It is important for the instructor to exercise a heavy dose of empathy in addressing the initial barriers to forming a supervisory relationship and to provide encouragement and support of the SITs. The SIT, for example, reports during the training session: "I feel that I am failing at this. Just about all of you [addressing the other participants] seemed to have made contact and have sessions scheduled with your supervisee while I am still trying to ascertain whether I have the correct telephone number for the person assigned to me. I mean, I keep calling and it's either busy or no one answers." Instructor: "Yes, that can be very frustrating. How many times have you called?" SIT: "Oh, I don't know, three or four or maybe more, let me see...(SIT deflects question.) In any case, it is supposed to be a youth agency, so why would they not be answering during the day?" Though it might be easy to establish that the SIT has not exercised the simple solution of checking the accuracy of the telephone number or persevering with the calls more ambitiously, the ambivalence and other feelings related to the beginning of supervising are more difficult to identify or to discuss. The reluctant SIT needs a great deal of support and empathy to be able to conclude the above interaction with a statement, e.g., "I really have difficulty seeing myself in the role of supervisor and so my resistance is showing."

It is the instructor's responsibility to guide the SIT gently, though unrelentingly, to the above awareness and related feelings. Other early ambivalences need to be clarified, confronted and resolved as rapidly and as well as possible. The instructor's failure to facilitate resolution of this early resistance provides the SIT with a poor model and tends to solidify and/or increase a SIT's unproductive attitude. This in turn leads the SIT to model a similar attitude to his/her supervisee.

Furthermore, when the supervisor's tendency to procrastinate is left unconfronted, the initial contact with his/her supervisee can forestall the beginning of supervision for a prolonged period of time and thereby create the unnecessary complication of having one or more SITs being out of phase with the rest of his/her colleagues. Thus, for example, as a majority of these novice supervisors are initiating a mid-phase of supervision, one SIT may still be struggling to negotiate a contract and assess his/her supervisee's learning style or developmental level. This lag may create conflict within or scatter the focus of the training group.

Supervising Begins

The training sessions which follow the SIT's initial contact and/or first session(s) with the supervisee tend to be filled with a great deal of excitement. The individual agendas of the sessions range from final clarifications, e.g., "Should all the items of the contract be completed during the first session with the supervisee?" "This supervisee seems to fit into a Level 2 of counselor development, what should I do?" to requests for reassurances, e.g., "I requested a male supervisee, and I know there were not enough males in the pool, but I am not sure I can work with a female." or "I got so annoyed at this supervisee over her ambivalence about our meeting place, that I almost lost it and now I am afraid that I lost her. Do you think I should call her before the session we have set up?"

The trainees, especially now, tend to be mutually supportive, empathetic, glad to offer a range of suggestions and reassurances. The instructor needs to provide information or support only when these behaviors are not forthcoming from the participants of the training program. Some of the SITs, who were able to reach their supervisee rapidly and schedule a session within a day or two of that call, will have had one or more meetings with their supervisee. These SITs can address and respond to their colleagues' questions on the basis of the experience gained during the initial session. The SITs' sharing of impressions and observations of the initial contact with their supervisees tends to be received as encouragement by those SITs whose ambivalence about beginning the supervising has slowed them down.

During this phase of training, the SITs' and their supervisees' patterns of anxiety management are more clear than they will be in the future. Frequently, it becomes evident which of the patterns will present barriers to the productivity of the supervisory relationship and which ones might stimulate learning. Some behaviors during this earliest time clearly manifest as defense patterns described by Satir (1972). For example, an SIT reports, "My supervisee, Terry, looked so controlled. She was perfectly groomed and entered the office that we were meeting in as if she owned it... I think she fits into the computer defensive posture. Then she sat on the chair that I was going to sit in. You know, she did not hesitate, just walked in and it was as if she walked into her own office. 'Now,' I said to myself, 'this may be bad news – who's supervising whom anyway?' But aloud I said, 'Terry, I am pleased that you changed your schedule so that we could meet at this time...' Good *placator* aren't I?" In an apparently difficult introduction to her supervisee during the training session, this SIT demonstrates an excellent sense of personal awareness, skilled interpersonal observation and a sense of humor. Thus, her recovery from a difficult encounter appears rapid, the anxiety is contained, and the task of initiating the supervisory relationship promises to be well underway.

Another SIT reports, "Tina, my supervisee, came late to our first meeting. I thought that my being understanding about her excuse would be setting a bad precedent. After we introduced ourselves and sat down, I pointed out that we were starting ten minutes late and then I talked a bit about how lack of punctuality could interfere with the work of supervision.

It would have been very easy for me to get into a blamer posture. Then as soon as I stopped, I knew I jumped into the ring too fast and that I could just lose this supervisee right there and then. So I said, 'How easy it is to get lost the first time we try to get somewhere and...' so on. I think I covered my initial overbearing approach pretty well." This vignette portrays a style of anxiety management that could promote an escalation of the very same process that one hopes to diminish or contain, i.e., what is intended as empathy is poorly timed and might be perceived as an excuse and an indirect invitation to repeat the tardy behavior.

Whatever the defensive style of anxiety management used by the SIT, it is of paramount importance for the training program instructor to be alert to the trainee's need to be reassured, to facilitate mutual support among the participants of the training, and to invite continual review of the strengths demonstrated during the Triad Experiment Session (TES). The reassurances promote the SIT's ability to manage anxiety and thus enhance his/her willingness to confront fears, feelings of insecurity and confusion without losing face. In an atmosphere of trust and support, the SIT can feel free to confess to and and be humorous about his/her desire to be powerful, all knowing and an impeccably sensitive supervisor.

The instructor and/or training program participants are encouraged to follow the route of containing each other's anxiety by; recognizing and validating each other's feelings and concerns, using humor, using Satir's postures, sharing and exploring the meanings characteristic of assumed postures and suggesting a range of potentially productive options that can be exercised in promoting the early stages of the supervisory relationships.

In a supportive atmosphere the SIT is encouraged to articulate his/her vulnerability by sharing an experience common to many beginners: "I feel like a total impostor. Who am I to begin supervising when I'm not even certain about my skills as a therapist? Actually, before this I thought I knew much more or at least I began to have a sense of some competence, but now, I feel inadequate and scared."

The support and encouragement is especially important in view of the SIT's limited access to his/her real or attributed power. Even the very first contact by telephone or in person that the SIT makes with the supervisee reverses the usual power structure. It is common, for example, for supervisees, upon learning the name of the assigned supervisor, to initiate the contact with that supervisor and adjust to the supervisor's schedule. In the SIT's case it is, however, the supervisor, who upon receiving the name of the assigned supervisee, is expected to initiate the contact. After all, in this case we have a condition in which the supervisor needs the supervisee more than the supervisee may feel the need for this additional supervisor. The inverse power relationship is further complicated by some SITs feeling that by consenting to be supervised by an SIT, the supervisee is doing the SIT a favor, that they are indebted to this supervisee, or that the supervisee's expectations will far exceed the SIT's abilities to deliver on them. Indeed, for this supervisory pair to attain mutual benefit, the SIT must exercise the referant (relationship based) power more clearly and intentionally than supervisors usually do in many other contexts.

However, the SITs initially tend to underestimate their supervisee's appreciation of the opportunity to have a student supervisor do some of their guiding. The sense of appreciation is accented by the supervisee's awareness that this senior colleague will have no formal evaluation responsibilities and therefore provides them with an opportunity to be more open, more honest and less defensive than they tend to be with a supervisor who will make an evaluative mark on their professional future.

Finally, the instructor must remind the SIT that his/her introduction to and guidance of the process of negotiating the supervisory contract provides him/her with an excellent opportunity to exercise not onlyreferant but also expert power, i.e., power derived from demonstration of knowledge.

Negotiation of the Supervisory Contract

One or more of the initial supervisory sessions conducted by the SIT are devoted to negotiation of the supervisory contract. Agreement about place and time of meetings is sometimes established over the phone prior to the first meeting. Nevertheless, these logistics need to be reiterated and clearly established during the first session.

The process of sharing expectations for and negotiating of the supervisory goals and supervision focus (see Chapter 6) provides the SIT with valuable data regarding the supervisee's developmental level. This assessment, along with the assessment of the supervisee's learning style, is further fleshed out by observations made while discussing and negotiating the type of recording for and manner of presentation during the supervision sessions; discussing and negotiating the agreement about confidentiality; discussing and negotiating the process of feedback and evaluation. For example, an SIT with a supervisee who has neither experience in the conduct of an initial interview nor knowledge of available options in the recording of therapy sessions and presenting that material in supervision, has a different challenge than the SIT whose supervisee has extensive, unsupervised experience, feels comfortable in initiating the therapeutic contact, but has no experience with systematic recording and processing of therapy sessions.

Some SITs prefer to be systematic in conducting the contract process with the supervisee, e.g., "Tom, now that we have introduced ourselves, our task is to agree on ten items that will give a frame to our supervision process.

Let me enumerate them and then we can take them up one by one and, after some discussion, agree on how we will manage these particulars." Other SITs feel more comfortable in carrying on the discussion of the supervisory frame in a more informal manner, e.g., "Tania, our first session or two will need to be devoted to getting acquainted and in the process I will be pointing out some items which we will need to agree upon in order to give the supervisory process some shape."

When the SIT has covered all items on his/her list or in the process of covering the list, s/he can ask the supervisee to add whatever items the supervisee wants in the contract. The SIT also needs to state explicitly that, if need be, this initial contract will be open for renegotiation during the later sessions of supervision.

Some assessment of the supervisee's professional development is indicated by the information the SIT receives before selecting and/or during the matching with the supervisee, e.g., age, years of supervised training. Additional information is available from conversing with the supervisee and from observations made during the process of negotiating the contract, e.g., the supervisee points out: "I had a whole year of intensive supervision last year and it wasn't very useful. I think technical supervision as you described it will be much more useful to me..." This statement suggests need for further exploration which in the end might provide some detail not only about the supervisee's experiences and professional development, but also about his/her learning style, e.g., preference for inductive rather than deductive process.

The impressions and conclusions the SIT makes on the basis of the exploration and observations during the negotiation of the contract can be checked out with the supervisee: "I gather that having had the experience of the supervisor's focusing on your countertransference during the intensive supervision was not productive for you... You really wanted more general guidance about what to do and when to do it, and what results it might have. Is that so?" or "It seemed to me that you like to have an experience of something before you can think about it, rather than plan it out, conceptualize it and then initiate the actual experience of the process."

By the end of the beginning phase, the SITs will have shared and supported each other's feelings of excitement and sense of welcomed adventure leading them to a new level of professional self-worth and promise of new accomplishment. "I was surprised at how easy it was to agree on almost all of the items of our contract. We just seemed to have been on a similar track. It was so obvious that both of us want to make this thing work. It seemed like my supervisee really thinks that she can learn from me and I think it will be easier for her to be more vulnerable with me than with other, more senior supervisors," says one SIT. Another SIT points out: "It was such a relief, after the initial awkwardness, to find out that my supervisee and I have a lot of experience in common. We had the same undergraduate major and we both moved here to this city to go to graduate school. I know how it feels being in a strange city, starting school again... We both wanted to get through the contract rapidly and we both agreed that we might need to modify some of it as we go along. But now we just wanted to start the supervisory work..." A session or two later, "...so far I'm just amazed at how easy it is for me to hear just where my supervisee seems to be getting stuck, I remember that feeling myself and I am finally beginning to see how much I have learned in the past few years – it's all coming back. I never thought I could remember some of that stuff, or better yet, that I can really see, explain the application of some of the theoretical information I've been getting over the years."

Some SITs get into competition over whose supervisee seems to be better, smarter, more promising. By implication they are reassuring themselves and others of their own skill(s) and talent(s). Others feel more cautious, guessing with certain apprehension that the "honeymoon" stage might turn into a struggle. Still others are quiet because their colleagues' enthusiasm does not match their experience of doubts about their supervisee's motivation or about difficulties they might be experiencing in making contact. The instructor of the training program must welcome the reports of the SITs who are encouraged and excited and also be attentive to and invite special support and counsel for those trainees whose enthusiasm lags behind the others. If these early snags in motivation are addressed and handled productively and patiently, it might preclude the escalation of the SIT's negative response(s) and related complications during later stages of supervision. For example, the SIT, who earlier reported the experience of her supervisee's entrance to the first session as aggressive and intimidating, might continue experiencing the supervisee as distant and controlling. In exaggerated form the supervisor might experience the supervisee as being in what Satir (1972) describes as a computer (or perhaps as a blamer) stance. To intervene into what could develop into chronic or escalated discomfort, the SIT can be invited to role play the supervisee in two roles, first the computer role, i.e., maximally defended with rigid intellectualization, and secondly in the vulnerable role of a minimally defended person who feels helpless in making contact and who feels alone and lonely. The latter role needs to be acted out with words as well as posture, e.g., "I hope I didn't sound foolish or stupid when I asked that last question; I probably did. I should be more careful, let her talk. She doesn't have to know what I don't know. Oh...this is so difficult, so lonely..." Other participants of the training can also take a turn at role playing the supervisee, or exaggerating the role of *Computer* versus an insecure vulnerable person. The comical aspect of exaggerated "Computer stance" and the empathy with the supervisee's lonely inner part might tend to attenuate the SIT's own anxiety, defensiveness and helplessness. With a new attitude, a new view comes to awareness. From new views, new options emerge.

End of Beginning Phase

The first phase of supervising has been completed after most, and preferably all, of the SITs have: 1.completed the negotiation of the contract with their supervisee; 2. on the basis of the initial meetings and negotiations of the contract, ascertained their supervisee's approximate level of professional development, learning style and defensive style; 3. taken at least a brief time to process the earliest experiences with their supervisees during the training session(s); and 4. in service of confidentiality, assigned (or negotiated with the supervisee) a name by which the supervisee will be known during the training presentations.

The stage is now set for the second, middle phase of the supervising practice. At this juncture some SITs also begin shifting their development from the early experiences of anxiety, excitement and a sense of new pride in professional achievement into a sense of specific points of falability in the context of supervision. By this time the participants of the training, familiar with the rich resources that they have among themselves and with awareness that all are in the "same boat", can understand and empathize with each other, and assist each other in powerful and creative ways. Thus for most of the SITs, along with the new doubts, there is also a sense of ground from which they can grow, discover and be productive in the relationship with their supervisees.

In summary, the first phase of supervision consists of initiating the supervisory relationship; negotiating the supervisory contract; assessing the supervisee's learning style, defensive style and developmental level. The process of negotiating the contract serves not only to define the major parameters of the supervisory relationship, but to provide data useful in supervisee assessment.

10

Scapes Visited: The Voyage Of Discovery And Growth Middle Phase Of SIT's Supervising

> *I also recognize the value of relationship in struggling with problems, and in making decisions for action. Self-processes and self-other processes are at the heart of all resolutions and growth.*
>
> Clarke Moustakas

THE TASKS OF the middle phase of SIT supervising consist of exploring the role and relationship of supervision from as many points of view as possible. "...Look at one and the same event through two different frames of reference. These two frames mutually exclude each other but they also compliment each other and only the juxtaposition of these contradictory frames, provides an extensive view of the appearances of phenomena" (Heisenberg, 1974, p. 54). The multiple points of view allow the SIT to exercise his/her creativity and freedom of discovery. As Moustakas (1981) said, "...I recognize the multiplicity of choices, that there are many paths. ...I am almost never entrenched in one direction or in the notion that there is only one healthy way..."(p. 31).

The supervisor's task is the development of his/her relationship with, and instruction of, the supervisee. Tending to the tasks of development, nurturance and growth of the relationship is both difficult and rewarding. Some of these difficulties and rewards have been explored in the preparatory sessions of the training, some will be discovered as the process of supervising evolves.

The sessions of supervision training during this phase are focused on SIT presentations of the experiences they encounter with their supervisees and the corresponding discoveries, questions and/or difficulties. Presentations by the SITs and discussions of the supervisory issues provide the instructor with opportunities to model ways of confronting and resolving those issues. Participants of the training and the instructor, singularly or as a team, respond on a need basis as consultant(s) to the SIT who presents. Whenever possible or acceptable, the instructor and/or trainees suggest an appropriate role play activity to the presenter. This activity is designed to heighten the presenting SIT's awareness and empathy and to introduce the possibility of new options. In this and other more didactic ways the SIT begins his/her learning of how to handle the issues commonly encountered in the mid-phase of supervision.

Beginning the Middle Phase

At the beginning of the second or middle phase, the causes of the earlier anxieties usually have been ameliorated or significantly diminished. The repeated reminder that the new authority over the supervisees and their patients is mediated by limited responsibilities, i.e., that no institutional and/or legal responsibilities are expected of the SIT, continues to reassure the SITs that they are unlikely to do any irreparable harm. This awareness enables the SIT to feel comfort in experimenting with the new role and to take risks in working out the corresponding problems.

Ekstein and Wallerstein (1978) refer to some of the difficulties which a new supervisor experiences as "problems in teaching". In discussing these problems they point out that, "...we must give the supervisor time to detect and to work out his own problems in teaching" (p. 133). Fledgling supervisors participating in the training program have many opportunities to detect and work out their "problems in teaching". Although the detection and working out of the "problems in teaching" is not mutually exclusive with detection of the SITs' strengths and skills, most of the work at this time is focused on their vulnerabilities and those aspects of their attitude and behavior tendencies which will call for a measure of vigilance. In many cases the focus of the vigilance has been established during earlier preparatory sessions of the training. For example, if during the Triad Experiment Session the trainee in the role of Supervisor tended to disclaim the productive effects of his/her interventions, then the probability is that this deprecating attitude will manifest once again in the current supervisory contacts. To preclude poor modeling and a poor holding environment for the supervisee, the SIT's unproductive attitudes need to be monitored and intervened into by his/her colleagues and/or the instructor.

No matter how much preparation there has been, the SIT is bound to experience some surprises, some unexpected interactions, negative reactions to his/her interventions, occasional discouragement and regression to familiar, though in this context, unproductive attitudes and behaviors. Ekstein and Wallerstein (1978) point out that the supervisor, as well as supervisee, hope "to master the new situation in the same way that he has mastered previous ones, and at the same time is concerned lest this new situation turn out differently and that he may not be able to master the new with the methods of old.... The wish then to meet the new by making it into the familiar that one can master, and the concern that old methods will not apply might well occupy the minds of both participants. The beginning phase of supervision will be a reflection of this struggle, whose goal is to restore the new situation to an old... one..." (p. 83).

Thus, even with the benefit of the earlier preparation, the SIT may be tempted to act or, without awareness, slip into the role of the therapist. The way this might happen is not fully identifiable in advance of the actual supervision with the particular supervisee. However, the lack of certainty about exact pitfalls or unproductive attitudes serve the SIT well, for it is out of this unchartered territory that some of the most significant learning emerges.

For example, the SIT processing a very early encounter with a supervisee says, "Now I know that I can think fast on my feet but my anxiety gets the best of me sometimes. If I don't watch it I can easily become Satir's *pleaser*. Knowing that, and watching out for that, I can easily overcompensate and become aggressive. So I try not to get into either one of the polarities. But even though I know all that about myself, I almost blew it during the first session with my supervisee, Tanya. I just had to push at her indecision about the way to present at our sessions. Then the next 2-3 times that we met, things seemed to go O.K. I thought I was doing a pretty good job in navigating Tanya through a lot of angry feelings toward her resistant, hostile client. She said that she was feeling better or more secure when she left our supervision sessions. But when she got back with her client, she was just as stuck as ever and she was getting to feel more and more angry herself.

"During this last supervision session, Tanya said she just didn't want to end up feeling, after our sessions, as if she was doing 'O.K.', when she really was ineffectual. I got the message that I was failing in confronting her or in guiding her more aggressively. But I didn't say anything and I started wondering whether I had just been doing supportive therapy with her. Then she looked at me with a somewhat condescending look and said she hoped I would have the opportunity to present her dilemma with her patient and with me during my supervision training session. Suddenly I felt like a complete failure; I got ungrounded. She was clearly implying that I needed some help and I really wanted to say something nasty, but I smiled and said that I will make a special effort to present our process during the training seesion. I played the *pleaser*. Then I stopped and didn't know how to continue; I was tempted to interpret her behavior, to be in a kindly therapist role. But I didn't. I felt absolutely stuck. Tanya was not saying anything either, she appeared to be thinking and we didn't talk for a while. Then we spoke of some irrelevancies, just trying to diffuse some of the tension. The session ended shortly after that. I still felt terrible and, maybe I am projecting, but I think she smiled kind of an apologetic smile when she left, being a *pleaser* on the outside but feeling ineffectual/angry on the inside. I'm not sure why I had so much anger but I felt like punching her out." Silence.

One of the other SITs offers an observation, "Are you aware you're smiling when you tell us you wanted to punch her out?" The presenting supervisor nods, "Yes." Another SIT says, "I'd much rather focus on how tough that must have been for you, I mean finding out that you were out of sync with Tanya and then listening to her kind of nasty way of giving you that message. And you are so open here with us. I really admire that." Other SITs resonate with that message.

The instructor has an opportunity to point out that in supervising Tanya the presenter might have been caught in some behaviors that she has been familiar with as a therapist, e.g., waiting for confirmation of a theme before interpretation or confrontation. At this juncture the instructor can invite and structure an appropriate role play in service of diffusing some of the supervisor's feelings and finding new, more appropriate strategies for handling the supervisory role. For example, other participants might be invited to play out the conflict, i.e., the encounters between the SIT as *pleaser* and the SIT as sharp-tongued aggressor, perhaps *blamer*. Similar encounters can be played out between Tanya as the *pleaser* and Tanya as the aggressor. The parallel process should become rapidly obvious: empathy is likely to be raised, anger reduced; new, more productive attitudes and behaviors rehearsed by means of other role plays. The SIT might be prompted to say to Tanya: "It is so difficult to preserve one's sense of cool with angry patients. It is difficult to see them as sad, or scared at the moment of their saying something that 'pushes our buttons'. What do you think might make it easier for you to raise your level of empathy toward the patient?"

Styczynski (1980), one of the few authors who attends to the struggles of new supervisors, points out, "The supervisor's role is an unfamiliar one, combining various elements (i.e., responsibility, demands, intensity, and limitations) in ways that differ from previous relationships" (p. 36). Thus, what has worked well in other relationships and especially in a therapeutic relationship may prove to be ineffectual (or effectual for a much shorter duration) during supervision. Here, even the best intended, and I venture to say especially the sensitive and well informed, SIT might get him/herself into impasse and experience frustration. It is at this very juncture that the SIT encounters a learning opportunity.

Conflicts and dilemma during the middle phase of supervising

The deceptive similarity of the territory covered by psychotherapy and that which is more appropriately identified as supervision of psychotherapy is baffling. This baffling similarity is further compounded for the SIT when confronted by this dilemma: in forging ahead toward new destinations whether to rely on the tools and maps derived from other contexts or to travel using untested tools and rudimentary maps, thus risking a sense of helplessness and being lost. Frustrated, angered, disappointed, or even humiliated, the SIT wonders, "Why does this well tested intervention in psychotherapy, which seems so appropriate at this point of supervision, fall so flat?"

One of the SIT's strongest advantages at this time is having recent and/or current experience of being supervised. The SITs tend to empathize with the supervisee quite readily. The empathy-based interventions work well, relationships grow stronger, and the ground for exploration, confrontation and learning is thus solidified. On the other hand, when the supervisor overidentifies with the supervisee or becomes overly supportive and reluctant to confront anxiety-provoking issues, the above noted advantage turns against the learning opportunity. Further, emotional and experiential proximity with the supervisee complicates the role of the new supervisor by presenting him/her with the conflict of wanting to be the most liked, most available, most accepting, most competent and most rigorous (Styczynski, 1980).

During the middle phase of supervision, feeling, thinking and behavioral patterns which create difficulties, as well as those which benefit the learning process, surface and become available for examination. On the basis of this examination, no less than on the basis of the actual practice of supervising, the development of supervisory skills expands. This phase corresponds to and replicates the middle phase of any supervisory process. However, this middle phase should not be confused with Stoltenberg and Delworth's (1987) description of Level 2 (middle level) supervisors as it bears only a limited resemblance to that level of supervisor development.

Supervisor Development

Stoltenberg and Delworth (1987) describe the Level 2 supervisor as full of confusion and conflict. The supervisors at this level, according to Stoltenberg and Delworth, experience the process to be more complex and multi-dimensional than the process for which the novice supervisor had been ready. Motivation fluctuates, they may lose some necessary objectivity and manifest anger or withdrawal.

The lack of resemblance between the second phase of the SITs' attitudes and behaviors and Stoltenberg and Delworth's Level 2 supervisors is due to the fact that, even during the middle phase of training, the trainee is still likely to be, developmentally, a Level 1 supervisor. I say "is likely to be" because it is not clear to me the extent to which the supervisory levels of development and corresponding characteristics or patterns presented by Stoltenberg and Delworth (1987) would be modified had the supervisor participated in a systematic year-long training program prior to beginning further supervising.

Alonso (1985), who also has focused on the developmental stages of a supervisor, perceives the beginner as having certain advantages. In concert with Styczynski (1980) she describes the young supervisor as having the advantage of being facile in identifying and connecting with the supervisee. She relates this tendency to the supervisor's affiliative needs, "he also remembers clearly what it is like to be supervised, and to experience the distress of the learning regression in training" (p. 56). Alonso (1985) further points out the new supervisor's confusion about the frequently ill-defined role of supervisor and the conflict generated by redefining one's professional identity from being the person who is trained to being the person who is doing the training thus, "...joining one's mentors as a colleague" (p. 56). This condition is seldom manifested by the SIT undertaking systematic training. It is my guess that later, when the SIT enters the supervisory role in his/her postdoctoral years, this earlier training will have modulated and significantly diminished the confusion noted by Alonso. I invite the trainees of this program to monitor their development in view of the above information, taking into consideration my guess about their future experiences of supervising.

Another important factor influencing the content and process of the early supervisory experience is what Alonso refers to as memories of one's own training experience. These memories, when positive, provide the SIT with models of supervision; when negative they can interfere in the supervisor's development. Sometimes they can motivate the SIT to be different from his/her past supervisor without his/her having a repertoire of new, appropriate approaches, and not knowing what can be used in place of the disliked attitudes or behaviors. By default, lack of supervisory experience can result in a SIT's experiencing an absence of options, hence insisting on single or prescriptive interventions and, paradoxically, manifesting an attitude of rigidity similar to the one which the SIT might have tried to avoid.

The task orientation according to Alonso, though not congruent with my experience of SITs, may be weak and brittle. Nevertheless, even when task orientation is fragile, the basis for productive learning is inherent in the supervisory dyad linked by similarity and temporal proximity of experience.

Once again I underscore and remind SITs that some of the commonly reported experiences and perceived characteristics of new supervisors are modulated or absent among SITs who have been systematically prepared for the practice of supervising. SITs are also aware that the support and consultation system, consisting of the instructor and colleagues in the training program, is so strong and versatile in its range of perceptions, skills and feedback that they are fortified to proceed in exploring the new territory of supervision with a sense of potency and courage.

A Relational View of Supervision

At appropriate times, in the context of discussions relevant to the phenomenon of relationship, I return the SITs' awareness to the relational view of supervising. As healing in psychotherapy can be considered to be at least partially a function of a corrective relationship between the psychotherapist and the patient, in parallel form it can be said of psychotherapy supervision that learning is grounded in the potency of relationship between the supervisor and supervisee. Moskowitz and Rupert (1983) have pointed out that "Supervision....is a complex interpersonal interaction subject to the vicissitudes of all human relationships. The importance of these interpersonal or relationship aspects of supervision to the quality of the learning experience has repeatedly been emphasized throughout the supervision literature. For example, Cohen and DeBetz (1977) stated that success in supervision depends on the quality of the relationship between supervisor and trainee... Indeed one study found that trainee's perceptions of the quality of supervision were more strongly related to interpersonal aspects of the relationship than by the content emphasized by the supervisor" (p. 632).

Hess (1987a) also refers to the phenomenon of relationship as the core of supervisory functions. Following a brief review of work by Aldrich (1981), Aldrich & Hess (1983), Markowitz (1958), Netzky, Davidson & Crunkleton (1982), and Swain (1981), Hess concludes that, if there is a focal point in supervision, then the nature of the supervisory relationship is that point. On the basis of that conclusion, Hess introduces an organizing principle of supervision. The principle is based in part on Buber's (1970) concept of *I-Thou* in relationship. It is not within the scope of this work to review or elaborate on Hess's presentation of these unique and potent concepts; suffice it to state that in concert with Moskowitz and Rupert (1983) Hess attends to the unique and powerful effect of the relationship on the process of supervision.

The context of the above discussion also presents the instructor with an opportunity to review and facilitate discussion about relevant literature, i.e., literature which elucidates the distinction between functional and emotional relationships.

Functional versus emotional relationships

Hart (1982) describes a functional relationship as the relating in which "the supervisor and supervisee work to attain the goal of supervision as illustrated by what they communicate rather than how they feel about each other" (p. 33). In contrast, an emotional relationship is characterized by "facilitative conditions such as empathy, genuineness, and concreteness (Carkhuff, 1969)" (p. 33). Hart cites the research of Payne and Gralinski (1968), Payne, Winter and Ball (1972) and Goldfarb (1978), and on the basis of that literature concludes, "The level of facilitative conditions offered by supervisors is best conceptualized as a dimension on which all clinical supervision is based but one that is not sufficient for effective supervision" (p. 36). The conclusion is supported by Lambert (1974) and Leddick and Bernard (1980).

During the early phases of supervising, SITs tend to have difficulty in effectively combining the functional and emotional relationships. Communications tend to assume disproportionate dimensions of either functional or emotional components. Thus, the new supervisor might complain, with a sense of desperation, that for the third time the supervisee has looked surprised and acted confused about the supervisor's suggestion (eventually an instruction) to get more developmental/historical data from the patient. "It is as if Trisha [supervisee] lets my suggestions into one ear and out they go from the other," says Susan, the SIT. "She looks attentive, as if she understands, and she nods in response, but come the next session she acts surprised that I have a bit of annoyance in finding out that there are still gaps in her knowledge of a patient's development... Instead she just lets the patient take over and talk and talk." A colleague asks, "How do you express your annoyance?" Susan responds, "O.K., I think it's pretty obvious from the tone of my voice. You know, after I've let her describe an entire boring, unsuccessful session, I can't stand it anymore and I ask again, 'Do you know any more about the relationship between the patient's parents?' and she looks up at me like I said something completely new or outrageous..." Another trainee comments, "So you do not interrupt her much before close to the end of the session, tell her what might be more useful for the two of you to talk about or to tell her how you are experiencing the communication" (a bit of an overload and in parallel process a suggestion of functional rather than emotional relationship). Susan: "No, I am afraid it might get her to be even more resistant, I'm afraid I may end up feeling even more ineffective" (emphasis on the functional aspect of relationship continues even during the training group).

Another, perhaps more advanced, SIT points out process-oriented functioning corresponding to the emotional relationship: "I think that I know just about how you feel with Trisha because I think that I am feeling right now with you the way you feel when you supervise her... You seem to be so certain about what you're going for that I am afraid to point out a place you might be missing... I'm afraid you will turn away from me, and that would feel kind of difficult or distancing..." The predominantly functional focus of the relationship has been shifted to an emotional emphasis. (The latter interaction also corresponds to a feedback process in contrast to the former scene which suggests an evaluative process.) At this point a suggestion by other participants or the instructor to role play, combining the two ways of being, might prove productive.

During the mid-phase, or well into this phase, the interaction described above might have a new quality. In this case the SIT, Susan, says, "My supervisee, Trisha, and I have focused on her patient's need to use torrents of speech to distance. I reminded Trisha that she might be in a better position to discover the reason for or the foundation of that need by finding out more of the patient's history. Once again Trisha appeared confused by the remark. I asked her whether she indeed was confused and she said, 'Yes.' I was aware of some confusion myself, also of some annoyance, and I shared that with her. I continued by telling her that I remembered pointing out that particular exploration with the patient on a number of occasions, and though Trisha appeared to me to be attentive, the suggestion did not seem to have been followed through..." If, after some interaction based on this message, the supervisee fails to become aware of the "parallel process", or interruption of the "gestalt cycle", or failure to set limits within the "bipersonal field", the instructor can invite the SIT to build on the earlier message by saying to her supervisee, "And is that perhaps what happens to you when you work with your patient?" or "You and your supervisee seem to interrupt your energy at similar points of a gestalt cycle and if you are not liking your supervisee's guidance to set limits with her, the mis-alliance will continue."

During the mid-phase of the SIT's development, the didactic, instructional tasks are integrated with and are more gracefully generated by the relational or affective connection between the supervisor and supervisee. However, the major measure of time and energy during this phase is devoted to the SITs' presentations of the progress and/or the barriers to progress of the supervisory process, their own learning and the learning that their supervisee seems to demonstrate.

Each supervisor tends to encounter more pronounced difficulty with either functional or emotional aspects of relationships during one phase of supervising than during others. It may be in the initial phase (beginning a relationship, forming contracts) or the difficulty will appear during the middle phase (maintaining a relationship, confronting and resolving conflicts, identifying and productively using teaching and learning patterns). Some SITs do not encounter major problems until the end phase of supervising (letting go of the relationship, saying good-bye). During the phase which is most problematic for him or her, the SIT will request disproportionately more time to present and receive consultation (tendency to be dependent) or disproportionately less time to present and receive consultation (tendency to be counter-dependent) than is characteristic of him or her. Both tendencies need to be closely monitored and modulated by the instructor. The instructor's and the other SITs' feedback can serve to raise the SIT's awareness of quality of participation (and corresponding characterilogic tendency) as well as to facilitate the distribution of trainees' presentation time more evenly.

Supervisory Relationship: The Experience

"I also recognize the power of spontaneity and immediacy, the here-and-now experiencing.... Honesty and full human presence are essential ingredients of real growth." *Clarke Moustakas*

Especially during the middle phase of supervision, I encourage the SIT not only to present and receive consultation in a didactic form but also, as frequently as possible, to do so in an experiential form, i.e., here-and-now experiences. By here-and-now experiences I mean using the resources of the training group to engage the other SITs in explorations of a variety of role play or simulation exercises designed to address or illuminate a particular process or problem. The simulations and role plays enhance experiential learning and promote spontaneous insights; they augment empathy and enliven the more laborious process of analysis and interpretation.

Use of Satir's categories and other role play designs

Using role play, and Satir's (1972) categories of defensive stances, the SIT can be invited to explore the predominant stance that s/he adopted in the beginning of the supervisory relationship and any change in that stance that emerged during later stages of the relationship; they can role play the stance most characteristic of their supervisee vis-a-vis the SIT during early and most recent supervision sessions; or, using Satir stances, they can role play the manner which they imagine to be most characteristic of their supervisee(s) during therapy sessions with their patients.

Role play, using Satir's categories or other representations, can also be of a non-verbal nature, i.e., sculpting one's self or the other into a physical posture corresponding to the characteristic attitude, then attending to where physical tensions are created and what behaviors the assumed posture precludes, e.g., being unable to see the patient's full face. Non-verbal explorations are followed by verbal processing of the experience and discussion of the meanings that can be derived from it.

Processing of the role play with colleagues in the group can uncover a range of covert interactional material, expose the barriers to a productive learning process, as well as reveal the points of parallel process, the interruption of the Gestalt Experience Cycle, or breaks in the frame of the bipersonal field.

For example, as a SIT, Sandra, begins presenting the frustration she feels with her supervisee, Ted, she says, "He never accepts what I am saying without having to correct some of it or he adds some small irrelevant detail as if it was really important. So I think that he's always setting himself up to know more or he tries to show me that he knows it better... And he just gets me completely off the track. I end up being overwhelmed and of course end up acting unnecessarily dumb." Sandra's voice raises and she appears to be angry. A colleague asks, "Do you think Ted is aware of that behavior, that he uses it as a sort of strategy?" Sandra: "Well I certainly haven't been quiet about my experience and last time I said to him that, if he is serious about learning something in supervision, his continuous interjections of some details or some distractions will need to decrease or maybe I wasn't quite that blunt about it, but I know I raised my voice and I did sound quite stern... I suppose even angry." Sandra continued by noting that during the encounter Ted looked somewhat surprised and he said "in so many words" that he felt reassured that Sandra was serious about their supervision. Also Ted pointed out that lately he has had some health problems and that he was on an antibiotic and that it might have been interfering with his appearing interested or earnest. He continued to explain that the patient, Mrs. P, whom he was presenting in these supervision sessions, was such a scatter-brain that he himself had difficulty keeping all the data clear about her. Ted thought that Sandra might need to be reminded about some of Mrs. P's behavior and speculated that he might indeed, when he thinks of this patient, get into behaving sort of like she does and become this inept communicator. He continued, speaking of other circumstances in which he remembered having communicated badly. Sandra felt compelled to interrupt with a message implying her exasperation with Ted.

Sandra is invited to explore the relationship by means of Satir's modalities. Sandra assumes the stance characteristic of herself during the above interaction. She is surprised at how well she fits into the role of *blamer*. During the role play of Ted, Sandra becomes aware of his distracting or blaming position while he is with her in supervision and a blaming one while doing therapy with his patient. The role play of the patient, Mrs. P, reveals a stance of *distractor*. Colleagues in the training group play the other necessary roles and demonstrate to Sandra her contribution to miscommunication or misalliance. As an alternative, trainees can be assigned one simple message to be repeated until Sandra's awareness is heightened. For example, the message might be, "You're exasperating me with your interruptions." A colleague playing Ted might be assigned a message, "I have to interrupt because Mrs. P interrupts me." A colleague playing Mrs. P might be assigned the message, "You think you know me, but I know me better." The feelings created in repeating the messages without adding any other content are shared and processed. In a supportive, minimally judgmental atmosphere, the role plays are accompanied by a certain amount of humor and tension-relieving laughter. The SIT has an opportunity to play out a role that is more accepting and more productive than the behaviors s/he has repeated during supervision. The new behavior reduces the supervisee's anxiety and in turn influences the supervisee's relationship with the patient.

During or following the role play, interruptions in the "gestalt cycle", breaks in the frame of the bipersonal field or the "parallel process" come to the participants' awareness. From the point of view of Gestalt Therapy theory, the above vignette demonstrates how the interruption of a gestalt cycle at the point of arousal of energy (talk, information) needs to be corrected. Practice in making contact, followed by completion of the cycle, will tend to improve the relationship. From the bipersonal point of view, one might focus the role play on inadequate limit setting which creates misalliance in supervision as well as in psychotherapy. Parallel process is implied in both of the preceding interpretations.

On occasion the stance is not obvious. In such instances, the SIT can be directed to experiment with a series of the stances to test out which one has the best fit. On other occasions, the SIT may not be ready to reveal his/her defensive postures. In that event the instructor, sensitive to the SIT's lack of readiness, lets go the option of using Satir's categories and introduces an alternative approach, e.g., dialogue between the SIT and an SIT chosen for this consultation, or review of pertinent literature.

During the middle phase of the SIT's work with a supervisee, the SIT continues to increase his/her awareness of his/her characteristic defense tendencies and, as Ekstein and Wallerstein (1978) put it, of his/her problems about teaching. However, with guidance and experience, management of these defenses becomes increasingly varied and productive. Having freedom to experiment with the effects of the defensive postures and with alternative attitudes or behaviors, the SITs feel reassured that their habitual defenses will not have a lasting, damaging effect. They also become aware that observing these tendencies in a supportive environment and with a gentle manner will diminish them and their effects spontaneously. Claiming or owning the habitual postures of defense, with a dose of humor, turns them into a manageable vulnerability; confronting and sharing these vulnerabilities promotes the SITs' mutual understanding and empathy which in turn enpowers them to use a dose of humility in the process of supervising their supervisees. The supervisees in turn model this attitude to their patients.

The possibilities of role play designs are so profuse that enumeration of these interventions and discussion of their implications and effects would warrant an entire book. The history of its use and advantages of this intervention as a training technique are summarized by Akamatsu (1980). A few of these techniques are briefly described below.

1. SIT assumes role of self while the consultant(s) (other SITs) assume role(s) of the supervisee (whose behavior/attitude has previously been described).

   General instruction to everyone in each of the roles is: "Be in touch with your feelings and observations." Specific instruction to the presenting SIT: "At the point of described impasse, do something, anything that is *different* from what you did in the session with your supervisee, or do what you consider to be *opposite* of what you did during the session with the supervisee. Say out loud what you were secretly thinking/feeling during that interaction with the supervisee."

2. SIT plays self; two or three training group participants play roles of judges based on hypothesized or demonstrated "should" [archaic superego] which interferes with the SIT's integrity of action.

   Specific instruction to SIT: "Respond to those judges first from a position of disempowerment, then from a position of power. Attend to: difference in feelings; experience of options; barriers to your actualizing these options."

3. SIT plays supervisee as s/he knows him/her; another participant of training plays the SIT. Specific instruction to the participant who plays SIT: "Be in touch with your feelings, observations, act from the ground of your feeling." then, "Be in touch with your thoughts, act from the ground of your thoughts." then, "Combine the two if possible, if not, be in touch with what gets in the way of this integration."

4. SIT plays the supervisee. Two or more other training participants take turns in responding with one sentence or one phrase only.
   Specific instruction to SIT: "Play supervisee in his/her most resistant mode; repeat above 2- 4 times (or as many times as there are consultants who volunteer to play the respondents)."

In all variations of role play, repetitions of the role structures and variability of the role players facilitate awareness of obstructive behaviors and provide clues to the type of alternative behaviors that can be more productive.

Each SIT in a role can be assigned an alter-ego, i.e., a participant, standing in proximity to the SIT who is in role, speaks and behaves according to what s/he imagines the SIT feels or thinks but leaves unspoken or unexpressed. For example, the SIT in the role of supervisee says, "Oh, you sound as if you know, or as if you have met my patient." The SIT in the alter-ego role says, "You sure know how to take over. Now you've even taken over treating my patient."

The role plays can be designed in the form of human sculpture and without words or using one word or one phrase only. For example, the SIT assumes the role of self (on the basis of previous self-description) and sits on the edge of the chair leaning into the supervisee's space; the SIT who assumes the role of supervisee might be asked to react with one word to the other's posture. The range of role play possibilities is limited only by the creativity of the instructor, the creativity of the trainees, and by the willingness of the SITs to experiment, to explore their vulnerability and to be touched by the poetry of human experience.

My favorite experiment involves a somewhat lengthier role play than those described above and is not designed for a specific occasion, circumstance or impasse. This role play is introduced after the middle phase of supervising is well under way.

The worst supervisor. To engage the SIT's sense of humor and to emphasize in an unthreatening manner the dysfunctional aspect of some behaviors commonly manifested by "bad" supervisors, I suggest that during the mid or latter part of the middle phase of the SIT's work with their supervisees, a session be devoted to a parody of the supervision process. For this purpose the SITs are asked to role play the "worst supervisors".

Most SITs have at least some idea about what not to do in supervision. However, the specifics of these behaviors are not always clear. To lay ground for the experiment which opens up the opportunity to specify the dysfunctional behaviors of a supervisor, the SITs are reminded of a study by Rosenblatt and Mayer (1975). These writers looked at behaviors which social work students considered to be objectionable supervisory practices and concluded that the following styles were cited most frequently as negative: overbearing, amorphous, unsupportive and therapeutic. They further noted that students of supervisors manifesting these behaviors would often engage in "spurious compliance", i.e., appearing to agree with their supervisors in order to avoid appearing uncooperative and thus run the risk of receiving potentially harmful evaluations of their work.

However, on the basis of a research study evaluating doctoral students' supervision experiences, Allen, Szollos and Williams (1986) concluded that the "worst supervision experiences apparently were harder for our respondents to define by citing the presence of specific characteristics. Rather, they seemed better identifiable through the absence of effective teaching strategies and role-modeling. A majority of poor supervisors were characterizable as disinterested or inept, and a minority as authoritarian or exploitative" (p. 98).

The SITs are further oriented by being told that the session is based on Haley's (1986) paper, *The Art of Being a Failure as a Therapist.* Haley points out that, "What has been lacking in the field of therapy is a theory of failure. Many clinicians have merely assumed that any psychotherapist could fail if he wished" (p. 83). But the task is not as simple as it is assumed to be. Thus, for the purpose of instructing the therapist to have a competent, systematic approach to failure, Haley presents a "program of twelve steps to failure sometimes called the daily dozen of the clinical field" (p. 88). It is not within the scope of this book to present and examine Haley's carefully developed program. Any supervisor should have his or her own approach to failure and at least some clear images which demonstrate bad supervision.

Those participants who wish to engage in competing for demonstrating the worst supervisor are requested to pair off. In this exercise the SITs have an opportunity to discharge, relax, play and laugh. They also develop and express clear images of the bad, very bad and worst supervisory processes and of behaviors or attitudes which bring about the deplorable results of such supervision.

It is not as easy to create a suspicion-full, tense interaction or to be clearly nonsupportive, critical, provocative and domineering as it may seem. Nor is it easy to slip smoothly into a confused, self-effacing, low self-esteem posture or act the part of someone who is preoccupied, bored, unfocused, evasive or unresponsive. All the previous training mitigates against assuming such attitudes and behaviors. It is easier to talk about the supervisors who demonstrated nonfacilitating qualities or to be critical of such approaches. When it comes to actually impersonating such behaviors, messages and attitudes in a concrete form, the SITs need to put their training (and related pretensions), their professional maturity (and pretensions), and their altruism (and pretensions) aside. Setting the pretensions aside results in self-consciousness which gives way to spontaneity and laughter. The spontaneous responses of the persons playing supervisee are no less humorous and valuable in their impact. The interactions that result from such brave and ambitious demonstrations can provide the SIT with a long lasting series of useful images about how not to supervise.

The "Worst Supervisor" exercise provides the trainees with comic relief, while building further awareness of behaviors and attitudes which present a barrier to proper contact and learning. In exaggerating some of the qualities of supervisors who were difficult, the SIT experiences a catharsis and at the same time can laugh at his/her own mistakes or manifested defenses. The images, messages and interactions viewed during this session tend to be imprinted into the SIT's awareness and provide an invaluable overview of the pitfalls of supervising. (It is optional, but at times highly informative and "merry-making", to videotape these role plays and to view them at a later date.)

On the basis of this experience, just as Haley (1986) presents twelve steps to failure in psychotherapy, each SIT is invited to enumerate 12 steps to failure in supervision.

Supervisory Relationship: Conceptual Models

The three organizing conceptual models introduced to the SITs earlier (Chapter 5) are reviewed and examined at various points of the training. During the middle phase of the trainees' development, these models are used to organize the supervisory material, select relevant data for planning appropriate interventions, and adopt productive attitudes.

The choice of conceptual model, or combination of models, used by the SIT will also influence the manner by which s/he will handle supervisory issues which emerge at this time. For example, limit setting is of paramount importance in an orientation based on bipersonal field. In order to use this orientation well, the SIT needs to be intensely focused on maintenance of the frame and being vigilent about recognition of any incursions upon it. Adopting this stance, the SIT implicitely models it to his/her supervisee. Explicitly, the SIT points out to the supervisee any break in the psychotherapeutic frame between supervisee and patient. Learning misalliances need to be attended to with no less vigor than the psychotherapeutic misalliances. Although, as with any of the other conceptual models, the supervisor's personality will tend to color and modify the model to a certain extent, the Langs' orientation (bipersonal field) still leans to being more authoritarian than either the parallel process orientation or the orientation developed from the Gestalt Experience Cycle. That is, Langs' approach is grounded in absolute right (keeping the frame intact and delivering correct interpretation) and absolute wrong (failures in maintenance of the frame or missed and incorrect interpretations). In contrast the parallel process, as an orienting concept, provides the SIT with greater latitude of choice. Practioners viewing interactions from a parallel process perspective define the corresponding interactions as neither right nor wrong, but simply mirroring repetitions of a certain pattern. There is less certainty about whether the parallel behaviors or attitudes of a patient in therapy or a supervisee in supervision are absolutely right or wrong. Although the attention is frequently focused on parallel patterns of an unproductive nature, or parallel attitudes and behaviors which create a barrier, the effective or beneficial attitudes and behaviors can also become evident by means of focussing on the parallel process. Thus, the supervisor can manifest an attitude of perseverance in facilitating the supervisee's awareness of his/her anxiety that creates a timing error. This perseverance will then manifest in the therapist's perseverance in facilitating the patient's awareness of poor timing in confronting her spouse. Or in a similar circumstance, after a prolonged perseveration, the patient makes a decision. The decision appears to be well thought out and the patient feels good about himself and the therapy. The therapist experiences relief. In supervision this supervisee tells the SIT that he is now aware of the positive effects of supervision on his ability to choose appropriate therapeutic interventions and that this awareness makes the him feel good about the supervision.

The practitioners who adopt the Gestalt Experience Cycle tend to practice the least authoritarian attitude. The SIT who chooses this orienting set of principles attends primarily to the flow of energy, rhythm and adequate closures. The foci of the SIT are on the point in time and the manner by which interruptions in the flow of energy occur and what behaviors engaged in by either or both persons involved in the supervisory system produce the interruption. The SIT is to be sensitive to the rhythms of all persons involved, pointing out any complication, difficulty or interruption in completion of a process. In this approach, there is no implication of right or wrong. The judgment about what is productive or unproductive is limited by two considerations; what each participant in the relationship needs to modify in order to stay in contact with the other person, and what each participant in the relationship needs to modify in order to achieve completion of an interaction.

Issues of Mid-phase Supervising

The activity of the training group during the middle phase of training is organized around the sequential presentations by the SITs. The order of the presentations is determined at least partially by each SIT's need and readiness for consultation from his/her colleagues and/or the instructor. A number of recurring issues and corresponding themes are brought forth by the content of the presentations, the responses from other SITs to the presentations, the questions raised and the interactions created during the ensuing discussions. Some of the issues raised are idiosyncratic to the particular supervisor, his/her supervisee or their relationship; other issues can be expected to be of a generalizable nature. Dealing with and resolving the issues presented by any one SIT in the group context benefits the learning process of the other trainees. Thus, all participants in the training have an opportunity to be reminded of: their own "teaching problems" or "problems about teaching"; habituated patterns by which they interrupt their Gestalt Energy Cycle; component(s) of the supervisory frame about which they tend to be lax or unobservant.

The general issues emerging from the middle phase of SIT supervising experience tend to fall into eight categories: 1. limit setting and related ethical issues; 2. use of confrontation; 3. coping with conflict; 4. coping with resistance; 5. coping with power issues; 6. coping with gender, race and cultural differences; 7. differentiating between psychotherapy supervision and psychotherapy; 8. cognizance of professional and ethical standards.

Encountering the above issues generates a range of defensive patterns and other teaching/learning difficulties. However, in the context of the training group and with support of colleagues and guidance of the instructor, the SITs can reframe, modify or let go of the dysfunctional attitudes and behaviors in favor of more productive ones.

1. Limit setting and related ethical issues

The supervisory contract provides the SIT and his/her supervisee with the basic guidelines for defining the parameters of the particular supervisory relationship and the corresponding tasks, or what Langs (1976) refers to as the "frame".

The SIT, when properly directed by the instructor, readings and his/her colleagues, will have an opportunity to identify the supervisee's initial testing of limits. The testing can manifest simply as the supervisee's coming to the supervision session late, forgetting the process notes, audio-recording, or other agreed-upon record of the psychotherapy session, requesting change of time, expanding the length of sessions, etc. The supervisory contract, among many other of its functions, serves well in this context. The SITs are invited by the instructor to be vigilant and vocal with their supervisee about the testing or breaking of limits, and to use the contract as a tool for facilitating confrontation. Thus, for example, the supervisee's coming to the supervision session(s) late is addressed in the following manner: "Last time, you were five minutes late, today I believe you came even later. Nevertheless, we have made a contract for a 50-minute session to begin at 7:00 p.m. and now I wonder whether you are indirectly suggesting a need to renegotiate either the length of the sessions or the established time of our meetings." If renegotiation of this component of the contract seems indicated, it should take place early in the supervisory relationship. Should the supervisee continue to test the limit, problems about learning need to be addressed. Except in unusual cases, it is not advisable to invite repeated renegotiation of the contract after the middle phase of supervision is well underway, although reviewing segments of the contract can be productive at any time during any phase of supervision.

In time, and when the relationship between the SIT and supervisee is well established, the supervisee's intra and interpersonal dynamics become more apparent to the SIT and the motivation to test limits can be addressed directly, e.g., "You have been late five out of the eight sessions we've had. Now this indicates to me that you and I need to speak about the meaning of this tardiness more honestly than we have done so, thus far." Or the matter of attempts at extending the supervisory sessions might be addressed in the following way: "I know from what you are telling me that you are overwhelmed at times and that there are so many issues to present here that there is just never enough time to accomplish everything you had planned to. So it might seem at times that you don't get enough guidance from these sessions. And you tell me that the patient you present here complains about inattentiveness from her husband and her children and her co-workers, and when it comes time to finish her session with you she just continues talking or asking questions and you can't get her out of the door." A supervisee, who has attended to and absorbed well the material of previous sessions and the related readings, has adequate information to be aware of the saliency of this material. Working from a parallel process orientation, an intervention based on empathy and appropriate interpretation should be easy to design. For a less attuned supervisee, a more detailed exploration of the parallel process or other orientation and related issues might be necessary.

Many of the limit-testing behaviors are focused on what the SIT or supervisee continue to expect from each other in spite of what had been negotiated and contracted. Boundaries regarding outside socializing and/or relating to each other in a psychotherapeutic rather than supervisory role are the most frequent foci of testing. Both SIT and supervisee at times discover that it is easier to agree on a set of limits than to actualize or function according to them. On many occasions the limits can be reinstated simply by providing the supervisee with feedback, appropriate information, e.g., professional standards, or reminding him/her of the contract, e.g., "I would like to have dinner with you, but it would invade the parameters of our contract and undermine our work." or, "When you ask me what you should do about your mother's demands on you, I feel uncomfortable. I would like to be helpful but I know it is outside of our agreed-upon task of doing supervision." or, "I can hear how difficult it is for you handling your mother's demands. In which way do you think it might relate to your work with your patient?"

The SIT will also use the instructor's manner of setting and observing limits during the training session as a model for their setting and observing the limits during the supervision sessions. The instructor models the observation and maintenance of limits, models the manner of confronting failures of maintenance and, when appropriate, relates these failures to the standards and ethical principles of his/her profession.

2. Use of confrontation

Confrontations can take place between SITs and their supervisees, or among the SITs, or between the SIT(s) and the instructor. In all of the above cases these confrontations should be motivated by a desire to promote learning or the learning alliance, and they should have a corrective effect. That is, when the supervisee, SIT or instructor perceives a behavior which is outside of established limits, or when verbal components of behavior do not match the nonverbal ones, it is well to speak up and describe the behavior in question to the person who originated it. Predictably, most SITs find it easier to be supportive of their supervisees rather than to be confrontive. However, failing to confront can create a teaching-learning mis-alliance, a stalemate in the learning process, and thus deprive the supervisee of the necessary modeling of appropriate times and techniques for the psychotherapeutic use of confrontation. Generally, in the context of the relationship that is well tended, in an atmosphere of mutual respect and trust, the confrontations are well received and have an effect of increased understanding and awareness. On the other hand, when the relationship and learning alliance are fragile, the confrontation can be experienced with suspicion, defensiveness and hostility. Poorly timed or poorly managed confrontation can lead to conflict. Confrontations among SITs during group sessions usually have a positive, productive effect. However, when they arouse defensiveness, it is important to suspend the process of confrontation and attend to the underlying feelings.

Confrontation(s) of the SIT by the instructor during the training session is important not only as a tool used for maintenance of the learning atmosphere, but also as a model of the use and at times abuse of the tool. An example of the latter case can proceed as follows, "Susan, I am aware that for five minutes or longer, while I was speaking to Seth, you left the room two times. Is there anything wrong?" A "Yes" reply will necessitate recognition of and attention to the problem. If on the other hand the response is, "No, I just needed to stretch a bit." the instructor might continue, "As you might imagine, your behavior is quite distracting to me and perhaps to the others. I don't want to ignore you or the disruptions, so can you tell us a bit more about your need to stretch?" "Well, I had a hard day and have some difficulty in following what's happening here." Having been attended to may be quite sufficient for the SIT to terminate the disruptive behavior. If the same or similar behavior is repeated, a brief exploration of the dynamics and motivation for such behavior might be appropriate. For example, the instructor might explore in which way she has interrupted an earlier interaction with Susan: in terms of the Gestalt Interactive Cycle, Susan might still be experiencing the stage of energy arousal; or from the bipersonal perspective, Susan is giving the instructor a message that, unconsciously, the instructor has broken the "frame". Time permitting, the instructor should initiate corresponding inquiries. The instructor has the opportunity to model to the SIT an application of one of the three organizing patterns. The confrontation should not proceed beyond a description of the objectionable attitude or behavior, its impact and, if necessary, a brief exploration of its genesis. Additional interpretations or in-depth explorations tend to damage the learning alliance. In those instances when confrontations are rebuffed and result in unproductive or hostile interactions, they bring about conflict.

3. *Coping with conflict*

The potential conflicts in any relationship are inversely correlated with the clarity of the negotiated contractual agreements. Once again, I underscore the need for a detailed, clear supervisory contract for the purpose of diminishing anxiety, frustration, disappointment, anger and conflicts emanating from those feelings. Nevertheless, not all exigencies can be anticipated, not all circumstances predicted. Thus, even in the context of well-executed contracts, there is possibility of conflict. In supervision many conflicts arise from the clash of personalities, from an unacceptable breach of boundaries, from dependency needs or counter-dependency moves. Hart (1982) summarizes the range of issues that tend to create conflict in supervision: lack of clear, detailed communication about expectations; supervisor's use of a "technique that seems to be inconsistent with the agreed upon model for supervision..." (p. 216); too wide or too close hierarchical distance between supervisor and supervisee; supervisee's readiness to move to another goal while the supervisor is not ready for such a move; "resistance of supervisees to perceiving that their personal attitudes and feelings affect their clinical behavior" (p. 218); supervisor's disappointment in supervisee's slow progress; supervisor's competency in a specific area is not used; and finally, when "...the supervisee exceeds or is perceived to exceed the supervisor in level of either skills, personal growth, or integration" (p. 221).

The above enumeration is representative of the origins and content of conflicts encountered among the SITs, and between them and their supervisees. However, once again the SIT has the advantage of processing his/her experiences and conflicts in the context of a group of predominantly, if not fully, supportive colleagues. Within the medium of the group, SITs can explore and experiment with options to behaviors or attitudes which create conflict.

In dealing with resolution of conflicts, Hart points out that "resolution of an issue in supervision must be conceptualized as a temporary phenomenon that lasts until the occurrence of a new anxiety that reopens the issue" (p. 216). Thus, "a major concept is that the developmental stage of supervision affects the types of conflicts that occur. In the beginning of supervision both supervisor and supervisee are likely to have conflict over such issues as roles each one is to take, evaluation, goals, and the control each person is to have over the direction taken and content discussed. Later in the process, the conflicts typically arise over feedback given (or not given) to the supervisee, whether goals and subgoals have been achieved, the degree of hierarchy, or new techniques that are anxiety-producing. Much later in supervision when termination is near, conflicts may be present because of reluctance to terminate by the supervisor or supervisee or because of unfulfilled agreements regarding areas to be covered" (p. 219).

Due to having worked through a painstakingly detailed supervision contract, SITs and their supervisees do not tend to encounter conflict over the nature of roles they are to assume and evaluate, goals or control of supervisory direction. The conflicts most frequently reported by SITs during the early stages of their supervising relate to issues of confronting and maintaining limits. The content of these conflicts can range from such minor issues as being repeatedly late to forgetfulness and other "problems about learning".

It is imperative to confront and resolve the conflicts aroused during the early stages of the supervisory relationship. Neglecting to do so lays the ground for a learning misalliance and promotes the probability of more and/or increased intensity of conflicts during later stages of supervision. Research data on this subject are sparse. However, extrapolating from my observations of the complicating effect of unresolved conflicts in the early stages of any relationship leads me to conclude that this phenomenon is also characteristic of a supervisory relationship. This corresponds to my experience when instructing the training program and Moskowitz and Ruppert's (1983) observation that "...unresolved conflicts do indeed have a negative impact on the overall learning experience" (p. 633).

The training program presented here does not include a discrete component which addresses the teaching of conflict resolution. However, to accomodate those SITs who have or are developing a special interest in the subject of conflict resolution as it relates to supervision, pertinent references, e.g., Fisher & Ury, 1985; Moskowitz & Rupert, 1983, are included in the training program's syllabus/bibliography. Furthermore, throughout the duration of the seminar, the SITs are introduced to a range of options conducive to conflict resolution. Many of the options are created by the SITs during the discussions and role play generated by their supervising experiences. Other options are modeled by the instructor.

The approaches range from structures such as allowing, for the purpose of catharsis, the parties in conflict to speak for an established period of time without interruption, to having these parties role play each other's identities and thereby increase empathy for each other. On occasion it is useful to have other trainees role play the SIT, who experiences conflict, and the other person involved in the conflict. Such role play should include both the oppositional stances and the stances which culminate in productive communication. In other circumstances it is enough to check back to the details of the original contract and assert the agreements made at that time.

The following vignette demonstrates some of the interventions discussed above. The SIT, Seth, presenting the relationship with his supervisee, Tara, portrays her as talking uncontrollably. Tara appears to Seth as scattered and unfocused, persistently avoiding the issues which Seth perceives to be of paramount importance. Further, says Seth, "She's into art therapy and that's far from my training. So I let her talk and show off and I didn't even remind her once again that she failed to bring in written notes as we have agreed in the contract. I kind of withdrew and sat there being judgmental and feeling incompetent." Seth addresses the instructor, "I really don't think you did too well by matching her up with me." Here Seth is articulating his frustration and fear of his own inadequacies, his characteristic defense of distancing, and then assuming the stance of *blamer*. The instructor can initially handle the confrontation by accepting Seth's perceptions, then validating Seth's frustration and disappointment. The other SITs are then invited by the instructor to join in the validation process with expressions of empathy and understanding. As a consequence of this type of support, Seth will have an opportunity to reframe his feelings of threat into opportunities for growth and development. Since Seth has chosen to work with the conceptual model of parallel process, further exploration will focus on whether Seth is aware of his supervisee having experienced feelings and thoughts similar to his in her work with the patient. This component of the relationship can be explored through a short role play: Seth is assigned the role of his supervisee, Tara, while 2 or 3 colleagues assume the role of Seth. Insights generated by this role play are processed and the roles can be switched (Seth plays self, others play Tara). This role play is repeated 2-3 times to assess accuracy, increase empathy and generate intervention options. In this case, on the basis of the role play process, Seth becomes aware of Tara's torrents of speech as a defense against a sense of inadequacy in working with her patient, who she reports is refusing to pick up the art materials and "produce" anything and ends up behaving withdrawn and "sulking." Seth can now be in touch with, understand and empathize with the supervisee. Just as the patient affects the supervisee, the supervisee affects the SIT.

Following a period of further processing, e.g., "How did you feel in the role of Tara?", Seth experiences renewed motivation and potential for his work with the supervisee. From a position of empathy and renewed sense of self-esteem, Seth can envision and plan to set the necessary limits without the fear of risking intensification of a misalliance.

A particular conflict pattern with its underlying resistance is at times repeated. However, at the same time, the SIT's management of conflict usually improves and these encounters pose less and less threat to him/her. The content of the supervision session, e.g., specific listening skills or type of intervention used, are temporarilly placed into the background. The relationship issues come to the foreground, feelings are explored and validated, and then used to build a stronger learning alliance. As the SIT increases self-esteem in his/her new role, as s/he feels more secure and trusting in his/her relationship with the supervisee, the frequency and intensity of conflicts decrease.

On occasion, during this middle phase, the SIT encounters a seemingly unresolvable conflict between him/herself and his/her supervisee which is reflected in parallel form between the SIT and the instructor. The instructor needs to use a combination of clinical, teaching and personal skills to reach out, to empathize with the SIT and suggest new options or new points of view. The other trainees can be of special help to each other and to the instructor. Particularly at mid-phase of the training and mid-phase of SIT development, the understanding, support, empathy and suggested options coming from a colleague have a greater impact than similar interventions delivered by the instructor. During this mid-phase, as the SITs are adjusting the sense of their supervisory power, the instructor needs to tolerate, mirror and gently interpret temporary SIT alliances and/or distancing, even blame messages, directed at him/her. However, an ongoing closed system alliance among the trainees, fueling alienation of the instructor, indicates a training dysfunction which calls for careful attention and intervention. For example, two or more SITs are engaged in an exchange of ideas. In the service of equal time allocation to other issues or SIT presentations, a time limit is indicated by the instructor. The SITs are perturbed by the interruptions and by the suggested time limits to be observed. Additional SITs support the dyad's right to continue without the imposed limit. Other SITs indicate their impatience with the process and speak up for their time to present. The instructor may intervene by suggesting a time limited "fish bowl"[7] experiment. If this or other group interventions are not effective, the instructor can schedule a private conference between the troubled SIT(s) and him/herself. In cases of seemingly intractable conflicts, the instructor models to the SIT the use of an outside consultant. This device is useful, though at times difficult to initiate or manage. In a close knit group, even though temporarily torn by conflict with the instructor, the outside consultant becomes an intruder; to an alienated instructor s/he might seem to be a competitor. On the other hand, the SIT's repertoire can be enhanced by an example of how to expand and build upon a consultant's observations and interventions.

Not all difficulties encountered during these early wondrous and challenging times of supervising are resolved or used productively. An unresolvable conflict can occur, for example, when a relatively fragile SIT is narcissistically injured beyond his/her tolerance and his/her defenses preclude receiving understanding, supportive messages, interpretation or suggestion of interventions. The tension(s) created by such unresolved conflicts tends to drain the energy from a supervisor-supervisee relationship just as it deenergizes relationships in a training group.

When unresolvable or repeatedly inflamed conflict occurs between an SIT and instructor during the training group sessions, it is well to insulate such conflict in the best possible way and to continue the process of the training session without the expectation of achieving the usual levels of energy or trust. It is also the instructor's responsibility to consult with his/her colleagues about the trainee's intransigency and, if the out-

7. One of the opposing subgroups discusses their "gripe" in a small circle surrounded by a circle of those who are without access to discuss the matter with the inner group, only to observe and listen. Then the "outer" group exchanges places with the "inner" group

side consultations indicate a consistency in the pattern of the trainee's negative attitude and behavior, to initiate appropriate, remedial procedures according to standards of professional conduct (see Chapter 12).

In contrast to the occurance of difficult, intractable conflict between supervisors and their supervisees, or among SITs, or between SITs and their instructor, some SITs, due to their vigilance in preventing it, do not indicate, experience or report any conflict. During the training sessions, when conflicts are being processed, these SITs are supportive, accomodating and/or withdrawn. In their presentations they avoid reporting any conflict between them and their supervisee. Such SITs respond to their supervisee's strategies of control and domination on the one hand, or to manipulation for affection and support on the other hand with a laissez-faire attitude and/or by indirect expression of hostility. These SITs manifest difficulty in modulating and modeling vertical and/or horizontal distance, i.e., s/he, even though supported and guided by colleagues and an instructor, can become (just as his/her supervisee) too accommodating or too domineering, too close or too distant for the proper development of a supervisory relationship. Unproductive circumstances are more likely to persist when the SIT is reluctant to present material during the training sessions or presents selectively, focusing only on supervisory interactions which have been resolved, worked out well, or continue to be unencumbered by any difficulties.

The SIT's reluctance to present during training sessions can also be motivated by a desire to protect self from repeating unproductive or painful experiences of earlier presentations. The detrimental experiences can result from encounters such as receiving negative feedback or negative evaluations without being balanced by supportive comments or from having been overloaded by interpretations and suggestions without time and energy devoted to their digestion. Failing to confront these occurences, thus precluding resolution of a dormant conflict, distances the SIT from his/her colleagues, from the instructor and in parallel form from their supervisee.

Although the SIT's insecurities can contribute to conflictual and unsuccessful group encounters, unsuccessful or discouraging presentations can also originate from the behavior of an instructor who does not set limits on the quantity of feedback, evaluations and suggestions, or fails to structure adequately the SIT's interactions during the processing of presentations and role plays. It is the instructor's responsibility to intervene into and preclude an overload of information and/or overly negative feedback and evaluations from the other SITs.

Preventing an information overload is difficult in the midst of enthusiastic and creative trainees. Many of the SITs have creative, potentially productive observations to offer, a unique view to present and/or an

and the process is replicated. At the conclusion of this second set, the whole group processes the information generated during the two sets of the structure.

especially fitting interpretation and intervention to recommend. The fervor of the trainees tends to be high; their mutual competition, as well as their creative contributions, need the instructor's careful calibration. During the presentation process, it is the instructor's responsibility to be attentive to the SIT who is receiving feedback or suggestions. S/He needs to monitor SIT reactions, picking up verbal as well as nonverbal messages of saturation. At the same time, the instructor must be sensitive to those contributors who are absolutely "burning" with their observations, ideas or recommendations. The SIT presenting may also feel cheated by not having received all that was available. All of the above conditions can lead to conflict which in parallel form may create conflict in the SIT's supervising sessions and, subsequently, therapist's conflicts with patients. The balance between facilitating maximal participation and minimal overload during the training sessions is a delicate and at times difficult condition to achieve.

4. Coping with resistance

Closely related to issues of conflict is the range of attitudes and behaviors commonly labeled as resistance.

The SIT can encounter resistances in at least four contexts:

1. his/her own resistance to the supervisee's requests, feedback and evaluation;
2. his/her own resistance to the feedback and evaluation received during the training sessions;
3. resistances manifested by his/her supervisee to the views, suggestions or interpretations offered by the SIT;
4. patient's resistances reported by the supervisee.

The phenomena of resistance can be viewed and examined from the perspective of the conceptual models discussed in Chapter 4. In Langs' bipersonal system any resistance is interpreted as the patient's instruction to the therapist about mismanagement of frame or about a faulty interpretation. By derivation, the supervisee's resistance is an instruction to the supervisor about mismanagement of the learning frame and learning alliance, or having made faulty observations or interventions. For example, a powerful determinant of the supervisee's resistance might be the supervisor's failure to deliver on one or more of the agreements. Lack of punctuality, unexpected shifts in goals or infractions of confidentiality can be viewed as prompting the supervisee's resistance. From the same perspective, an SIT's resistance during training sessions can be viewed as an instruction to the trainees (consultants) and to the instructor about mismanagement of the learning frame and of faulty or poorly timed observations and suggestions. For example, an instructor's insensitivity to and/or failure to intervene when an SIT experiences overloading of suggestions and observations can result in the SIT developing a resistant attitude.

From the viewpoint of the parallel process system (Ekstein and Wallerstein, 1978), a range of personal tendencies and interpersonal events can be regarded as resistance. These authors, in their effort to differentiate psychotherapy supervision from psychotherapy proper, have wisely renamed many behaviors, which can be considered manifestations of supervisees' resistances, "learning problems", i.e., ways of acting and responding that have been determined by the needs of the therapist and not by the needs of the patient, and "problems about learning", i.e., characterilogically limited ways of reacting and learning.[8]

Just as the therapist-supervisee develops by overcoming "problems about learning" and "learning problems", so the SIT develops by overcoming "problems about teaching" and "teaching problems". The beginning supervisor may have some difficulty in hearing critical observations of his/her "teaching problems" and "problems about teaching". Just as the therapist hopes to master new situations in old and familiar ways, so the supervisor, especially the beginning supervisor, hopes to protect professional self-esteem while attempting to face and handle new situations and new types of relationships by means of old, now inappropriate approaches. The fear of being found inadequate or feeling shame over what appears to be failure can become a powerful barrier to development and learning. The SIT, for example, may respond to feedback experienced as threatening his/her self-esteem by interpreting, or deflecting, or otherwise questioning the motives of the colleague in a way which places the onus on the colleague who offered that feedback. Further, the resistance that the SIT manifests during his/her presentations and processing in the training sessions can reflect a similar resistance that s/he encountered with his/her supervisee.

Resistance from the perspective of the Gestalt Experience and Interaction Cycle can be viewed as an attempt to maintain a self-regulatory strategy. The influence of another person's rhythm, especially if that other person has assigned authority (therapist, supervisor, consultant, instructor), might be experienced as invasive, intrusive or aggressive, thus a threat to self-regulation. A SIT, for example, can in the process of presenting his/her work experience the other participants of the training, or the instructor, as organizing the presented material too rapidly (energy) and proceeding to the intervention (action) at a pace that does not match the SIT's rhythm. Thus, while this SIT is in the phase of awareness and the other SITs consulting to him/her are speeding ahead to the action phase, the SIT may protect him/herself by assuming a

8. Although I strongly support Ekstein and Wallerstein's effort to differentiate between psychotherapy supervision and psychotherapy by means of using different terminology,

resistant attitude; being confused, distracted, withdrawn – all maneuvers effecting a slow down of the process.

The instructor has a responsibility not only to monitor a trainee's resistance, but to model a productive response to it and to invite the other trainees to empathize with the SIT who is manifesting a resistant behavior. Any existing infractions on the frame can be examined, any suggestions of feeling inadequate, or ashamed, or humiliated must be carefully attended to and handled with respect and support. The instructor needs to maximize balancing the negative feedback and evaluation with positive and supportive messages. At this juncture s/he can also choose to share appropriate personal anecdotes or humorous and instructive stories from the literature.

At appropriate intervals the instructor needs to initiate examination of invasive, aggressive or discordant rhythms among the SITs. On other occasions s/he can initiate a slowing down or speeding up of the interactive process. For example, slowing down of a process can proceed in the following way: "I would like to suggest that we go back to Sally's description of her supervisee's blame-like reaction to her. Are you willing to engage in a short role play, Sally? Would a few of you volunteer to be Sally while she role plays her supervisee in the blaming posture?" If and when Sally and others agree, Sally and 2-3 volunteers proceed with a brief series (1-2 minutes per person) of role plays. The role play slows down the process of feedback, suggestions, confrontations and provides the consultants with an opportunity to raise the level of empathy toward Sally. Further, the process tends to increase Sally's connectedness to her supervisee. In the event that Sally refuses to engage in a role play, and/or other participants do not offer supportive comments, the instructor can initiate a message of support and communicate his/her own experience of empathy. The instructor models ways of coping with resistance to the SIT who will then model the same to the super-visee. The supervisee in turn can be expected to handle a patient's resistance in a similar way.

While the instructor needs to stay alert to the manifestations of resistance and to the foundations of such responses, once the atmosphere of support and trust has been established, the instructor intervenes infrequently. Having had the proper interventions modeled to them, the trainees intervene on each other's behalf. Most importantly, the practice of attentiveness to and productive defusion of the resistance during the training sessions fosters the SIT's productive management of resistance with their supervisees.

5. *Coping with power issues*

In his review of dimensions of power, Hart (1982) articulates his

their terms have not been widely adopted and thus use of them without linking the phenomena to the more commonly used terms of defense or resistance tends to be confusing.

premise that every supervisor is invested in influencing his/her supervisee, and that the influencing process is contingent on the type and amount of interpersonal power used by the supervisor. A SIT is also motivated by the hope of influencing his/her supervisee. This hope and investment in the process is tempered by the SIT's uncertainty about his/her own position and by an investment in learning about being a supervisor. Furthermore, the SITs know that their influence will be modulated as a consequence of having limited access to the powers usually exercised by supervisors.

French and Raven (1960) identify five categories of power: 1. reward power; 2. coercive power; 3. positional power; 4. expert power; 5. referent power. In most institutional settings supervisors are administratively superior to the supervisees and thus possess; positional power (their opinions and decisions carry more weight than the supervisee's opinions or decisions), reward power (supervisors have the responsibilities of evaluation and the privilege of granting special dispensations), and coercive power (determining demotions and reprimands).

Clearly, for the SIT access to positional, reward and coercive power is limited to a much greater degree than it is for full fledged supervisors. Although the SIT is generally considered professionally senior to his/her supervisee and capable of having informed opinions or making informed decisions, both the SIT and his/her supervisee know that the effect of these opinions is curtailed by the definition of the SIT's role. The reward power is limited by the confidential nature of evaluations and feedback; the coercive power is essentially non-existent. The lack of access to these sources of power and the corresponding reduction in responsibilities is experienced by the SIT as a great source of relief as well as a source of some consternation. Only in extreme situations, such as lack of response by a supervisee to confrontations about grossly unethical behavior, would the SIT be expected to report the supervisee to appropriate authorities or otherwise initiate censoring sanctions. Thus, having no access to positional, reward or coercive power reduces the SIT's options. The SIT's most effective substitute for these sources of power is his/her access to the counsel and support of other SITs and the training instructor. Strategizing about the difficulties they might encounter with their supervisees during the training session frequently empowers the SIT to continue productive and influential functioning with the supervisee(s). In contrast to other supervisory situations in which the supervisees are expected to implement the suggestions and guidance of the supervisor, the SIT can facilitate a learning environment in which the supervisees choose to proceed according to the SIT's guidance.

Expert power (derived from relevant respected knowledge, experience and/or professional advancement) and referent power (derived from a rapport, learning alliance and personal respect) are much more accessible to the SIT than the other categories of power. Although many researchers and authors have found that in supervision expert power is the most important source of influence (Olmstead & Christensen, 1973; Kadushin, 1974; Hester, Weitz, Anchor & Robach, 1976; Gale, 1976), referent power has a very special place in a supervisory relationship. It may even be argued that referent power, being akin to mentoring, has a life-long effect on the supervisee's professional career. In any event the SIT derives most influence from referent power. Both the young or new supervisor and the supervisee find it easy to identify with each other, and at times the supervisee's feelings reach a level of idealizing the SIT. It is also worth noting that referent power tends to support and enhance the SIT's expert power. The positive relational climate and the corresponding empathic bond between the SIT and his/her supervisee increases the SIT's referent power and the supervisee's perception and acceptance of the SIT's width and depth of expert power. It is not unusual to have a SIT report a supervisee's deep appreciation of material shared with and taught to him/her by the SIT. This material is frequently experienced as more valuable or unique than information received in other learning contexts. It would appear that inasmuch as positional, coercive and reward power are at a level significantly lower than in other supervisory relationships, the anxiety quotient is lower and the concepts or practices presented are more easily understood and accepted.

In the context of the training, the participants among themselves also exercise primarily expert and referent power. The instructor, on the other hand, has access to positional, reward and coercive power. However the instructor's exercise of positional power without careful modulation and restraint can destroy the learning and teaching alliance as well as model an attitude which, in the long term, is unproductive.

Just as in the supervisory relationship between the SIT and his/her supervisee, so among the SITs' and between them and the instructor, power struggles are bound to emerge. The type and intensity of power manifestations, as well as power struggles, depends not only on characterilogical tendencies of the SITs but also on the atmosphere introduced and maintained by the instructor of the training.

The supervisor's and supervisee's expectations for the supervisor's manifestations of "expert" power can stimulate a range of related responses which could seem linked to competition for other kinds of power. An insecure SIT can provoke an attitude of, "It should be done in this way because I know so and I said so!" or "I have experienced that many times and I know exactly how it is to be handled!" Although some supervisees may take kindly to such attitudes, perhaps even feel secure in the context of such messages, others might balk at them, find them invasive, resist them, and end up in an impasse with the supervisor. In the form of parallel process, the SITs then displace their frustrations upon the instructor. The instructor, thus challenged by an SIT, might succumb to using coercive power instead of using expertise, teaching and relationship skills. The participants of the training are usually quick to notice and to voice the instructor's failure to promote a productive learning environment. If the instructor is open to this feedback, s/he may help discover the root(s) of the projected power play and attributions or inappropriate uses of power. The process of this examination tends to sooth the learning alliance(s) and serve as a model for the SIT who can also be confronted with a supervisee's projections of a power play or who might need to curb his/her unproductive use of power.

To sensitize the SIT to coercive or positional power, role play during the training can be enhanced by a "one up"/ "one down" structure. That is, the SIT taking the role of supervisor might engage in interaction with another SIT who role plays the supervisee. The SIT who represents the supervisor stands up or stands on an elevated platform while his/her "supervisee" remains seated. The addition of a verbal component from that position in the form of a simple message, e.g., "I need to stop our session early...", is optional. The feelings of being in and interacting from these positions are examined and recorded for future use in similar, though not quite so obviously structured, encounters. The level of intimacy, at times influenced by coercive power, can also be examined by means of sculpting the supervisor and supervisee in a range of standing or sitting positions or by changing the seating arrangement of persons playing supervisor and supervisee so that they are closer or further apart. Finally, the power categories can be examined from the perspective revealed by the use of the three organizing principles discussed earlier.

The experiential, process-oriented character of the Gestalt Experience Cycle lends itself to the use of referent power more than expert power. In the context of the parallel process orientation, both referent and expert power are exercised more than in either the Gestalt Experience Cycle or the bipersonal field orientation. Bipersonal field organizing principles are the most congruent with the use of expert power and employ minimal access to referent power.

6. *Coping with gender, race and cultural differences*

The SIT is usually pleased to have been matched with the same sex supervisee and s/he tends to express some doubt or anxiety when matched with an opposite sex supervisee. Alonso and Rutan (1978) wrote a pioneering paper on cross-sex supervision for cross-sex therapy. In the paper reference is made to a general reluctance to discuss sex bias in supervision, "although other cultural differences, e.g., age status, nationality, and ethnicity, are attended to regularly" (p. 928). They continue, "Our experience indicates that there are serious gaps in the material being given by young male therapists in supervision as they present their female patients. The omissions occur especially in areas concerned with inhibition of healthy aggression in the female patient" (p. 928). This condition they attribute to the "long standing cultural bias combined with limited capacity for empathy that is normal for beginning therapists" (p. 928). It might be expected that a cross-sex supervisory dyad can offer important opportunities and learning benefits for all parties involved. If the situation is handled well, i.e., with encouragement to process, resolve and learn from the experiences of conflict or other difficulties, the expectations are fulfilled. However, the anxieties of the inexperienced supervisor, which are inherent in the process of using and modulating appropriate levels of assertiveness, aggression and intimacy, can outweigh the potential benefits of learning. Thus, in the case of a SIT for whom referent power is most available and most effective a same sex supervisee is preferable.

One of the most common supervisory tasks, which taxes the new supervisor, is recognizing and coping with inappropriate levels of intimacy. Thus, the SIT may be confronted by issues of seduction and related issues of boundary and limit setting. For example, a female SIT with a male supervisee might present her concerns as follows, "He seems to me to be doing a bit of a seductive scene and so far on the outside I have been able to keep cool about it, but on the inside I get annoyed, I get very angry.... and certainly I don't want to confront it head on. It would seem kind of presumptuous of me to say, 'Listen Tim, when you do such and such or say this or that it sounds like you are flirting with me.' Then if he says, 'There's nothing further from my mind.', I would just die..." When addressing this or similar issues, it is valuable to have both male and female participants of the program offer their reactions, observations and suggestions for interventions. Similarly, the input from both genders is valuable when the perception of a phenomenon has been influenced by the cross-sex composition of the supervisory pair as in the following example of a female SIT reporting, "I get angry when my supervisee, Terrance, demonstrates his ignorance about what abortion means to a woman; he speaks kind of flippantly about his patient who has had two or three or perhaps more abortions. To him it seems as if it is her habit or something like that–not a crisis or a loss.... and I'm even turned off about educating him about this matter..."

On the other hand, though many SITs prefer not to complicate the supervisory situation by having an opposite sex supervisee, they frequently discover that such matching can be beneficial. "I have maintained," said Brodsky (1980), "that one of the experiences necessary for training students to recognize their sex role biases is that they receive at least one segment of the total training experience in which the supervisor is the opposite sex of the trainee" (p. 513). The same notion can apply to the training of a supervisor. Brodsky emphasizes this as she continues, "...it is often very fruitful for cross-sex dyads to explore their perspectives about the client's problems from their own sex role vantage point" (p. 514) and "for both sexes, learning to treat male and female trainees equally is something that does not come naturally" (p. 515).

The SIT who ends up in a cross-sex match has the opportunity to examine his/her own preconceptions, to process positive or negative reactions that s/he has to a supervisee's work with the same or different gender patients. In doing so s/he not only enhances his/her own awareness of the inherent issues, but by presenting his/her supervisory experience during the training session, s/he also stimulates the thinking, feeling and learning about the issues among the other trainees. In the safe and supportive atmosphere of the training session, the SIT may explore his/her personal biases and inquire about subjects that in other contexts are more difficult to confront and examine. Using an earlier example of different reactions to percptions of abortion, a female SIT asks a male colleague what thoughts, reactions and associations he, as a male, has to the abortion procedure or how similar/different his reactions are from those she has reported held by her male supervisee. She might also request suggestions from him and other male SITs about confronting the supervisee's inappropriate attitude, and about interventions that from a male point of view would be non-threatening. The instructor can invite the trainees to engage in a role play in which they assume the opposite sex role, thus potentially becoming aware of some of their own prejudice and misconceptions. The female SIT could also benefit from having other women take turns in playing her alter ego. The instructions to those engaging in the role of alter ego are to guess at and articulate feelings that might be difficult for the SIT to say out loud or feelings that are outside of her awareness. The male SITs in the role play also benefit from having an alter ego assigned to play out feelings that are seemingly unacceptable or outside of their awareness. In contrast to the frequently polarizing effects of discussing issues involving male vs. female perceptions, outcomes of the above role plays tend to build empathy and enhance a sense of togetherness. Further, the presenting SITs can become aware of their own contributions to the unproductive aspects of contact complicated by their own misconceptions. On the basis of this awareness, the SITs can design and practice a series of new behaviors and supervisory interventions.

It is with a considerable sense of self-consciousness that I admit that, during the years of instructing the training program, I have not encountered any conflicts or issues generated by ethnic or racial differences. Nevertheless, the SITs are invited to familiarize themselves with the writings of Gardner (1980) and to be alert to the effects of cross-race or cross-ethnic supervisory encounters. Just as therapists working with patients of different race or ethnicity can become distant, rejecting, paternalistic, condescending or insensitive, so the supervisor can manifest similar attitudes and behaviors when supervising a therapist of a different race or ethnic group. As with other subjects of discussion, the processing of gender, ethnic and racial issues during training sessions not only enriches the awareness of these issues and generates new behavior options for the presentor, it also benefits the learning of the other trainees.

7. *Differentiating between psychotherapy supervision and psychotherapy*

Although this topic was dealt with in earlier sessions of the training (see Chapter 4), it tends to reemerge during the middle phase of SIT development. The instructor and other participants of the training can offer a review of the earlier didactic and experiential material relevant to this differentiation. However, the new experience of functioning in a supervisory role raises many new questions about the subtleties of this difference. In some cases the supervisor's concerns are stimulated by supervisees who seem to manipulate the supervisor so as to turn the supervision into psychotherapy. Equally significant is the SIT's tendency to function in a role that is more familiar to him/her, i.e., psychotherapist, than is the new, challenging role of psychotherapy supervisor. I, as others (e.g., Hess, 1980b; Ekstein & Wallerstein, 1978), have been pointing out that the psychotherapist who becomes a teacher of psychotherapy will frequently be tempted to fall back on previously acquired skills and will try to convert the teaching relationship into a therapeutic relationship.

Using any of the three organizing models, i.e., bipersonal field, parallel process or Gestalt Experience-Interaction Cycle, one might tap into the supervisee's dynamics and the potentially dysfunctional influence of those dynamics on the process of therapy. The SIT is then presented with the challenge of dealing with these psychodynamics without engaging in psychotherapy. Hess (1980b) points out, "Certainly the supervisor may be attracted to the psychotherapy model when the supervisee replicates a focal interaction that is occurring in the psychotherapy" (p. 24).

Thus, the SIT, Sara, wonders, "How should I have handled Tina's [the supervisee's] speaking so 'matter of factly', sort of like Satir's '*computer*', about the patient's mastectomy? She spoke of it as if it was a routine car wash or something...and I know that she was colluding with her patient, denying the feelings, ignoring the need for grieving the loss. Tina was complaining about how difficult it was to establish some contact with the patient, but I also felt somewhat protective of Tina because I know that just a month ago she had a cancer scare and that she tried to put it out of her mind and just went on as if it never happened..." An SIT asks, "So what did you do?" Sara responds, "I simply pointed out that the patient seemed to be avoiding dealing with the feelings of grief and loss and did she [Tina] consider that the patient's avoidance of making contact was really reflecting the avoidance of getting in touch with the painful feelings. Tina looked at me with a sarcastic smile and said that for someone like her patient who has to worry about where her next meal comes from, "the feelings and grief are a bunch of malarky." The parallel process and the interruption of experience at the sensation and awareness levels are obvious. Sara reports making another attempt at reaching the supervisee, "Does your patient's mastectomy bring up any of your own fears?" Tina looks away, then she covers her eyes, and Sara says, "I know she is crying, quietly crying and then sobbing and really I don't think she wants me to be watching that...so I was quiet. I hoped some marvelous insight would come to me or some voice from above would just give me a clue about an intervention...but I just sat quietly. I knew that I just opened a topic that could seduce us from supervision into psychotherapy and I had to handle it somehow. I thought, what will happen to our contract, to 'the frame', to my role as a supervisor? I said some dumb things like, 'I am sorry' or 'I see that you still have memories about your loss' or something like that, and I also pointed out that Tina's personal unfinished business might be influencing her work with her patient." The interaction seems to have been on an appropriate track. But Sara, still unsure of the limits imposed on her by the supervisory role, yet unsatisfied by her therapeutic intervention, is critical of her interactions.

To heighten Sara's awareness of an approach that can be taken by a psychotherapist in contrast to a supervisor, the instructor invites a role play in which Sara simply observes the interactions of SITs taking the roles of: 1. The supervisee, Tina, with an instruction to function according to the description of Tina's behavior; 2. The ideal supervisor responding to Tina's frustration; 3. The ideal psychotherapist responding to Tina's fears.

The role play can be repeated with different SITs taking on the roles. Sara is instructed to observe the role play and offer constructive criticism. The role play interactions should provide data which clarify the basic differences between psychotherapy and supervision of psychotherapy. The interactions which bring the supervisee's psychodynamics into the foreground should be linked to inquiry about how those interactions or awareness of particular dynamics can promote the work of supervision.

The conclusion of role play provides an opportunity to recapitulate that the intent of the psychotherapeutic relationship and interventions is resolution of the patient's inner conflict, increased self-regulation and other aspects of personal growth. Whereas the intent of psychotherapy supervision is to increase the supervisee's knowledge about and skill in providing the service of psychotherapy.

In a recently published paper, *Therapy in Supervision: An Unresolved Issue*, Burns and Holloway (1989) provide a careful examination of the multifaceted and difficult subject of how the process of psychotherapy fits into and/or contaminates the process of psychotherapy supervision. They conclude by stating that "the distinction between the process of supervision and content of supervision seems critical. We are suggesting that it might be entirely appropriate to use counseling skills (such as facilitative conditions) when the intent is to enhance trainee's understanding of their own reactions, behaviors and attitudes toward the client. However, it may not be appropriate to use such techniques with the intent to solely affect counselor change outside of the counseling role" (p. 56). Among those emphatically opposed to psychotherapy in the context of supervision are Altucher (1969), Banikiotis (1975) and Blocker (1983). Blocker, for example, points out that the supervisor who assumes a "self-appointed, unrequested therapist role is the epitome of egocentric insensitivity, and verges closely upon the unethical and unprofessional" (p. 29).

8. *Cognizance of professional standards and ethics*

The categorization of issues presented in the preceding sections 1 -7, is for the purpose or exposition somewhat arbitrary and not considered mutually exclusive. Issues of gender, race or culture can affect issues of power, conflict and confrontation; inadequate differentiation of psychotherapeutic process from process of supervision can also stimulate power struggle, resistance, conflict, confrontation or call for limit setting. Nor are any of these effects mutually exclusive. Further, the meanings that one makes of any of the above phenomena and corresponding issues influence the choice of interventions and these interventions in turn can engender power struggle, resistance, conflict, confrontation and need for limit setting. Of greatest importance, however, is the interface between all the issues manifested during the middle phase of supervising and the impact of professional standards and ethics on their management.

During the middle phase, as it is throughout the training, the SITs are reminded that although they have no formal responsibilities to monitor their supervisee's professional standards, they need to attend to and integrate these standards of practice into the supervisory process.

By the time the trainee has reached the level of a SIT, the instructor of the training program can rightfully assume that the SIT's professional education and training has included exposure to and study of professional standards. However, the application of these standards does not become quite as salient or as confusing as it does when the student engages in the role of supervisor. Hart (1982) points out, "...supervisors carry out responsibilities and activities unique to their job roles and encounter situations which present challenges for implementing ethical standards" (p. 243). What are the limits of dual relationships? To what extent does one limit socializing with one's patients, supervisees or supervisors? What does one do when confronted with a case that raises themes reminiscent of *Tarasoff v Regents of University of California* (1974)?

Although the SIT has no formal responsibilities beyond the clinical supervising of their supervisees, it is important for them to be aware of, to monitor and when necessary to confront a range of infringements that their supervisee might make upon the patient or that the SIT might make upon their supervisee, e.g., failures in confidentiality or other indications of poor boundary management. The SIT is directed by the instructor to review the *APA Ethical Principles* (APA, 1981), *General Guidelines for Providers of Psychological Services* (APA, 1987) and related literature, e.g., Hess (1980). During the training sessions, the SIT, at times, needs only to report his/her observations and corresponding management of the supervisee's ethically poor or questionable conduct. At other times, the SIT needs to clarify the standards for him or herself and/or request that training time be devoted to the particular issues of professional standards and ethics.

The most challenging ethical issues raised by the SITs concern a supervisee's conduct which seems destructive to the task of psychotherapy. A supervisee, for example, might lack even a minimum tolerance for ambiguity, s/he might demonstrate a lack of ability to listen to and work with a patients' affect, or s/he might report and demonstrate behaviors so bridled by personal difficulties, e.g., depression/hypermania, that functioning in the role of therapist appears inappropriate or dangerous for the patient.

Hart (1982) states that "supervisors, through continual trainee evaluation and appraisal, should be aware of the personal and professional limitations of the trainee which could impede future professional performance" (p. 245). How is one to be sure of the appraisal's accuracy or of the correspondingly appropriate nature of interventions? The SIT, having limited supervisory experience, might doubt his/her objectivity or the validity of his/her perception, wondering to what extent s/he might be misapprehending the supervisee's dysfunctional behavior. On other occasions, the SITs identify with the rough beginnings of a fledgling therapist and may not be certain to what extent the dysfunctional behavior is due to commonly experienced anxieties of a beginner. The instructor and the trainees also need to be attentive to the manifestations of parallel process, the SIT's projections and/or projective identifications. Implicitly or explicitly, the trainees expect the instructor to model the management of an overly fragile or seemingly inept SIT and thus be instructed in management of the inept supervisee.

Other frequently encountered questions about ethical conduct address a range of boundary issues: "What should my supervisee do to warn her patient's wife about his violent ideation?" "Should my supervisee tell the patient's mother about her son's treatment?" "Should I discourage my supervisee's bringing in a lunch for me?" "Can I, after our session, go out for a coffee with my supervisee without damaging our rapport?" "How can I refuse my supervisee's countless offers to help me in closing up the office for the night?"

The complicated nature of the above issues and the importance of understanding and managing them warrants a discussion beyond the scope of this chapter. Thus, Chapter 12 of this book is devoted to presenting and discussing the standards and ethics related to psychotherapy supervision and the implications for the training of supervisors.

Finishing the Mid-phase of SIT Supervision

As time draws close to the end of the middle phase, the SITs feel increasingly reassured about the nature of their supervising; they feel good about the bonding between themselves and their supervisees; they experience closeness to their SIT colleagues and the instructor. They also are aware of their growing edge, accepting gaps in skills and knowledge inherent at this level of professional development, and anticipating opportunities for further growth. All of these conditions mitigate against an enthusiasm about termination. Nevertheless, at this time the SIT needs to review and confront his/her past experiences and difficulties in facing terminations. The instructor needs to review and present issues relevant to the processes of termination and evaluation.

Although awareness of the new professional identity is mobilizing, the full experience of this newness comes after the next stage of SIT development, i.e., termination of supervising.

The pre-termination phase of the supervisory training ushers in a multiplicity of feelings; pride, affection, sense of imminent loss, confusion, relief, resignation. The SIT who experienced him or herself as a "*blamer*" in an earlier role play, now begins once again to manifest some of the blaming behaviors, e.g., "I simply can't reach my supervisee about termination since he's always in some sort of crisis; whether it's with a patient or with his own life. He's just so narcissistically preoccupied that I don't have a chance with him!" In the following chapter I will address in greater detail themes and processes characteristic of this ending phase of training and supervising.

In summary, the middle phase of SIT supervision is a multifaceted experience rich in learning potential. Experiential and didactic material is used to confront, process and resolve an interdigitated set of issues ranging from limit setting and use of power to ethics and professional standards. By the end of this phase, reluctant as they might be, SITs are gearing up for the final stage of supervising which consists of termination, evaluation and celebration.

11

View From the Summit End Phase of Supervising

Events grow to cataclysmic size and intensity in proportion to their not being noticed.
J. Hillman

Trials never end, or course. Unhappiness and misfortune are bound to occur as long as people live, but there is a feeling now, that was not here before, and is not just on the surface of things, but penetrates all the way through.
Robert Pirsig

THE OBJECTIVES OF the third phase of SIT's supervising are: engaging in the process of termination; completing the final supervisor-supervisee evaluations; partaking in a celebration.

Termination

Saying "good-bye" in the context of supervision, as in many significant relationships, can arouse feelings of fear, anger, sadness, hope or tendencies to deny, avoid and otherwise resist facing the inevitability of ending. Some of the most subtle characterilogically determined resistances may emerge at this time. A number of authors (e.g., Bruner, 1957; Ekstein, 1965; Loewald, 1960; Stewart, 1963) have compared termination to the process of mourning.

Psychotherapy supervision is usually a significant professional relationship which has evolved over time and which is based on a series of significant encounters. When this relationship has produced a sense of accomplishment, learning and growth, it is difficult to let go of its continued potency and promise. When this relationship has produced a sense of disappointment, lack of learning or growth, it is difficult to let go of the original hopes and expectations of what could have been. Each person, supervisor or supervisee experiences and manages the process of saying "good-bye" in a unique manner and each relationship affects the individual's patterns of saying "good-bye" differently. Thus, it is with caution that I offer generalizations regarding the phenomena manifested during the process of termination.

Reluctance to engage in termination

Among the most salient and common issues of termination are denial of ending or other manifestations of resistance to engaging in the process of ending. Since the SITs are alerted to the task and issues of termination by the corresponding entry in the syllabus and by the instructor's reminders of the corresponding changes in focus, it would seem difficult to escape cognizance of the pre-termination and termination processes. Nevertheless, the avoidance can be strong enough to create "blind spots" regarding the imminent new phase.

The instructor of the training program facilitates the ending by reminding the SITs of the date of the last session and by drawing attention to the themes suggestive of termination. Still, just as the supervisee, alert at some level of consciousness to the approaching termination of the supervision, may collude with his/her patient in raising and nurturing a range of critical issues seemingly unrelated to the termination, in parallel form the supervisor may be seduced to postpone and ignore addressing termination issues. For example, as termination is about to begin, the supervisee reports that the patient's son had just run away from home. Even though the son had returned, the supervisee is insistent that the supervision session needs to be focused on the logistics of dealing with that event. The SIT might be able to interpret the metaphoric nature of the event (leaving, separating, not saying "good-bye"), but the emotional upheaval experienced by the patient may capture the supervisee's full attention and may preclude focusing on termination issues.

As Stoltenberg and Delworth (1987) point out, this form of resistance to termination tends to characterize female dyads in supervision and therapy more than cross-sex dyads or those dyads consisting of male members. On the other hand, a male SIT might be very convincing in his description of a disciplined and systematic handling of the termination, yet concludes his presentation during a training session by revealing that his supervisee cancelled the last session. Here, in line with the observations of Stoltenberg and Delworth, I suspect that although the

SIT appears to proceed with termination in a technically correct manner, his attitude and nonverbal communication sabotages the termination process.

It is not unusual for a SIT to report themes of loss, death or destructiveness in his/her work with the supervisee and fail to recognize these themes as the supervisee's messages, at his/her unconscious level, which indicate preparation for termination. The supervisee-therapist deals with the same phenomena in his/her work with his/her patients. For example, a SIT, Sandy, presents a vignette from the supervision session in which her supervisee, Tracy, seemed to be despondent about work with a patient and yet unwilling to hear Sandy's guidance. Tracy's patient is dealing with a life threatening disease and during the particular therapy session the patient speaks of the senselessness of life and deprecates further efforts to survive. Tracy asks the patient why she is focusing on death now when symptoms related to the disease have subsided and the most recent reports from the physician are encouraging. The patient offers a token response, "Well, one never knows," then begins enumerating her friends who died over the years and the circumstances of their deaths. Tracy is baffled and points out to the patient that she does not seem to have heard Tracy's previous remark. Inwardly, Tracy is conscious of some anger and some sadness related to the recent loss of her own father. The patient claims to have heard the therapist's earlier remark and not to have known what to say about it, except that it seemed to her that Tracy just did not understand—really didn't know how it feels to have to live with a serious disease and the related thoughts of loss. The therapy session proceeds to the end without significant contact.

During the supervision session, Sandy suggests to Tracy that the patient seemed to have been hinting about her need for more empathy, and inquires how Tracy felt when the patient spoke of her losses and implications for her own death. Tracy responds by saying that she might have been a bit angry because the patient seemed to have been wallowing in her pessimism, feeling unnecessarily sorry for herself. Sandy then wonders whether it was the anger that influenced Tracy to proceed to an implied interpretation rather than to authentic recognition of the patient's fears and sadness. Tracy reacts somewhat defensively, explaining that it would have been unproductive to continue empathizing with and thus infantalizing this particular patient. Sandy feels lectured to by Tracy and becomes a bit angry. The remaining part of the session is tense. After mutually agreeing to finish five minutes early, Tracy and Sandy leave in a somber mood, sympathizing with each other about all the work that needs to be done at the end of an academic year. Sandy parts with the remark, "April is the cruelest month except when there are still some 'incompletes' to finish in May or June..."

Sandy presents the above interchanges during a training session with considerable confusion and self-reproach. It seemed to her that, having established a good relationship with her supervisee, Tracy, the session was some sort of an aberration. She was also aware of the parallel process in having missed the appropriate opportunities for making contact, but she was puzzled about why now, at this particular point in time, the mistakes occurred.

Another SIT asks Sandy whether she was aware of an overall theme. Sandy looks even more confused and embarrassed. Observing this, others in the training group point out the need to recognize Sandy's frustration and they give her a bit of support, thus precluding continuation of an unproductive parallel process.

At this juncture, as the other trainees point to Sandy's blind spot (fear of good-byes or of finishing on a bad note), the instructor needs to be wary of the delicate balance between using an intervention which increases the SIT's embarrassment about her confusion and using an intervention which produces and colludes with Sandy's denial. The embarrassment and related defensiveness or anger, emerging as the program is coming to a close, can complicate the training group's termination process as well as model to the SITs an unproductive procedure. Avoiding a confrontation regarding the issue at hand also models an unproductive procedure to the SITs. In the service of minimizing Sandy's embarrassment and facilitating her getting out of the impasse, the instructor suggests a role play structure designed to support Sandy and provide the means for further exploration of the impasse.

With Sandy's agreement to proceed, the rȯle play is designed as follows: one at a time, up to four of the seminar participants are invited to adopt the role of Sandy. Each in turn speaks as Sandy from three orientations: 1. expressing the censored, unexpressed feelings she experienced during the supervision session; 2. expressing what she might be experiencing and not saying now during the training session; 3. expressing a fear of something which is out of Sandy's awareness. For example, the first volunteer to play Sandy articulates Sandy's unexpressed message to her supervisee: "Where do you get off lecturing me? You are the one in trouble. If you'd just keep quiet and listen you might find out that I'm trying to help you!" At this juncture Sandy has an opportunity either to affirm or correct the representation. If no correction is necessary, the person in the role of Sandy continues with expressing Sandy's currently unrecognized or unexpressed feelings: "Now, I probably look like a Bozo myself, no wonder I couldn't help my supervisee...I certainly would like to be finishing the year in a better way, but for the life of me I can't think of what themes I missed or what I'm missing now." Once again, Sandy is invited to correct this version of her feelings. Finally the third phase of the structure, i.e., expressing Sandy's unconscious or defended against fear, consists of the following message: "If there's one thing I hate, it's looking dumb at the end of things and now, just as we're coming to the end of the year, I feel more of a beginner than ever before." Sandy corrects the above message: "Actually I hate looking dumb at the beginning, middle or end, and the rest fits but it is a bit more dramatic than what I really feel. Also, I'm happy to report that I just got it! My dumbness has lifted, even though I still hate saying good-byes!"

If the presenter's awareness of the theme indicating ending and termination is sufficiently enhanced after the first enactment, she can stop the continuation of the role play. If she wants more information, the dramatization can continue with other volunteers playing the role of Sandy. At whatever point the presenter chooses to stop the intervention, the likelihood is that even though a blatantly blind spot is dramatized, the SIT feels supported and safe. In this manner, not only is a necessary insight achieved, it occurs in an atmosphere of comradeship and humor.

Termination process: Three perspectives

Termination, as other processes of supervision, can be viewed from the perspective of the three organizing concepts discussed previously: parallel process, bipersonal field, Gestalt Experience-Interactive Cycle, or any two or all three of the conceptual models.

Sandy's presentation provides a clear example of parallel process. The interaction between patient and therapist is not unlike the interaction between the supervisee and supervisor. It is also apparent from the dyad's intimations of death and loss, with corresponding ambivalence and unwillingness to stay focused on the subject of impending termination, that it is a diversion which results in frustration and dissatisfaction. The therapeutic misalliance is repeated in a learning misalliance and could well be repeated in a second learning environment, i.e., during the training session. However, once consciousness of impending termination is raised, the learning problem (difficulty in facing loss, saying good-bye) and problems about learning (difficulty in hearing the supervisor's feedback suggesting the lack of empathy with the patient's fear of loss) become obvious. The avoidance or denial of dealing with good-byes becomes untenable or at least very difficult to maintain.

From the view of the bipersonal field, data presented in the above vignette can be understood as indicating that the patient unconsciously directed the therapist to attend to the upcoming issues of termination. Just as the therapist's "blind spot" precludes the delivery of an appropriate interpretation to the patient, so is the avoidance repeated in supervision. The supervisee from his/her unconscious delivers to the supervisor an instruction to be alert to the feelings inherent in termination,e.g., confusion, anger. The SIT on the other hand only alludes to dealing with loss (by means of empathy), but does not interpret the major issue at hand, preparation for termination. For example, Sandy could have asked Tracy how the patient might react to the message: "You speak of all the losses you have experienced in the past and I imagine you feel that now, as our therapy is coming to an end, you don't want to think about an additional loss in your life."

In the context of bipersonal field theory, recognition of a supervisee's failure to interpret patient messages correctly can provide a basis for predicting future events indicative of resistive interactions. That is, during the session(s) following the one described, the patient in one case and the supervisee in the other, would deliver in metaphoric form the message about the missed interpretation. For example, the therapist may become aware that the patient is perseverating on the ugliness of her half dead plant and failing to respond to the therapist's interventions. Or the supervisee may mention the dingy appearance of the meeting room with the hope that it will be spruced up before next year.

Sandy's vignette, examined from the view of the Gestalt Experience-Interaction Cycle, would indicate a condition in which sensations were aroused and awareness was not engaged adequately, thus the corresponding energy had no clear or conscious focus. The behavior, unless based on the awareness corresponding to the specific sense arousal, will then be scattered, unproductive and lacking completion. Sensations experienced by the patient, therapist and supervisor all seem to indicate that energy is focused on the feeling of loss or fears of loss. However, there is no clear indication that patient, therapist or supervisor have this awareness. Once insight is reached, energy can be focused on articulating the fear, making contact and preparing for closure. The SIT can point out to the supervisee, "I also became aware of an image of loss. It seems that we are gearing up to face the issues of ending and of the loss that it implies. You and your patient ending the therapy; you and I getting ready to finish the supervision. In four weeks we will have our last session..." The supervisee will have an opportunity to express her other feelings and acknowledge the beginning of termination. This of course is assuming that the rhythm of communications is harmonious and thus no complications in the Interaction Cycle are introduced.

During the training sessions, only one SIT needs to articulate the significance of death or loss themes at the time close to the termination of supervising in order to stimulate the awareness of other SITs. Once this consciousness is sufficiently raised, the trainees become vigilant about recognizing themes indicative of ending. Simultaneously, they become alert to identifying interventions which can facilitate a productive process of ending. Nevertheless, every so often the collusion among the SITs to deny the ending might be strong enough to impel the instructor to remind them, explicitly and repeatedly, that the end of the training, as well as the end of their supervisory contract with the supervisee, is at hand, that termination themes will need to be attended to and any impediments to the process of ending intervened into promptly.

Common Themes in SIT's Terminating the Supervision

Gender issues

As mentioned above, Stoltenberg and Delworth (1987) point to the influence of gender variables on the process of termination. In their experience, congruent with Gilligan's (1982) observations, "females often experience difficulty 'saying good-bye' and males may have problems 'saying hello'. Supervisors...must be sensitive to the reality that, for at least some proportion of our female supervisees, this is a very difficult issue. For female supervisors with female supervisees, the danger is that the crucial 'good-bye' may not be said, leaving both participants in sort of limbo regarding their relationship and the work they did together. For male trainees, the 'good-bye' may come too easily, thus creating a pseudo termination in which affect is suppressed rather than acknowledged" (p. 177).

I am reluctant to generalize about males being less sensitive or less attentive to the range of feelings accompanying the process of "good-byes". On many occasions the male SITs are so conscious of the literature portraying the tendencies of their gender and so sensitized to consequences of interpersonally unproductive attitudes, that they develop a special vigilance about attentiveness to feelings. It would be easy to dismiss that sort of vigilance as overcompensation, or counter-phobic behavior. However, it has been my observation that many advanced male students of psychology and psychotherapy not only constitute a select sample, but over the years of study and training (often accompanied by personal therapy), they develop attitudes, sensitivities, skills and motivations more frequently associated with female developmental paths. Nevertheless, at appropriate times I do direct my students to keep Stoltenberg and Delworth's observation in mind.

Experience of doubt

One of the common themes that emerges during the termination phase is embedded in the experience of doubt. The SIT might begin to wonder, "Did I do enough? Did we accomplish anything? Was it productive?" Heeding Schafer's (1973) warning, I admonish the SITs that their narcissistic investment in supervisory results must not go beyond certain points of intensity. "Above all," says Schafer, "he [the supervisor] must realize that his ideal should be to do the best he can and not necessarily to get 'results' "(p. 140). That is, the supervisor, having been observant, available, willing to listen to supervisee feedback and use consultation, does not need to expect that the supervisee's patient has resolved his/her presenting symptoms, or that the supervisee is now fully versed in establishing appropriate therapy relationships, assessment of a specific personality disorder or a series of corresponding interventions. The instructor needs to facilitate the SITs' mutual support of the achievements accomplished during their supervision.

Some doubts about the value of the learning and the training that the SIT has offered are also voiced. This concern usually subsides when the SITs review (especially for the purposes of evaluation) the contents and process of that supervision and their experiences, encounters and growth during the process of training.

Passage of time

Another theme emerging during ending is surprise at the "rapid passage of time". That, which in the beginning of supervising, appeared to be a long, and perhaps too long, period for initiating one's skills as a supervisor turns out to be an experience characterized by such questions as: "Where did time go? Couldn't we re-contract for a few more weeks?", etc. Frequently, it seems to the SIT that there is so much more to be learned and taught at this time when the relationship has stabilized and is functioning well. The old saying, "Just as I have learned all the lines, they have changed the play.", reflects the sense of frustration about having to end at what appears to be an especially potent time. Sharing and mutual recognition of this theme facilitates the process of appropriate closure.

Relief

The themes of reluctance to end, doubt, frustration, anger or sadness about limited time left are balanced by themes of relief about the impending end of the academic year or of the training session and a sense of satiation, celebration and excitement about future professional responsibilities. The SITs and their supervisees frequently make a special bond. Their "good-byes" are characterized by warmth and feelings of sadness and respect. The supervisees often claim that the SITs who supervised them had been the most significant persons during that year or during all the past years of their training. The SIT is viewed as someone who could understand them, accept them and still offer many learning opportunities. The SITs on the other hand frequently sense that this was an entirely new kind of opportunity to test what they have been learning over the years and they appreciate the supervisee's willingness to accept their guidance and to promote mutual learning.

Disappointments as hopes

Amidst strong positive feelings, it is difficult for a SIT and his/her supervisee to focus on what might have been missing in this particular supervisory relationship, what either member of the pair might have failed to learn or to teach. It is difficult to identify specific disappointments or unfulfilled expectations. Difficult as it might be to focus, at the time of mutual respect and emotional closeness, on what might have been and wasn't, it is nevertheless an important ingredient of saying good-bye. It provides the SIT and the supervisee with the awareness of their growing edge. No matter how much each member of this dyad has gained from the other in the service of their professional growth, they need to identify the foci of additional learning and development.

One way of facilitating that task is for the SIT to initiate and conduct a review of the original (or revised) contract. How did it hold up, were all the agreements honored? If not, why? How were the failures in agreements handled? What articulated or implied expectations were not realized? What opportunities seem to have been missed? The items identified in this manner become the ground for future learning and thus the disappointments are reframed into new expectations, hope and excitement about the future.

Not only is the attention and time during the latter sessions of the training focused on how the SITs are proceeding in terminating with their supervisees, the SITs are simultaneously engaged in terminating their supervision training and this first experience of supervising.

It is the instructor's responsibility to weave in the termination issues at times when corresponding materials are presented by the SITs in their termination with supervisees during training sessions. Among the more important issues to address, during these final sessions of the training, are the SITs' unfulfilled expectations of the training and how these expectations can be translated into future plans and hopes.

Awareness of newly enriched professional identity

The review of the SIT's journey over the time of the supervision training reveals a newly enriched professional identity. As they finish this component of learning and training, SITs take a step into a level of professional functioning qualitatively different from the previous ones. The newly experienced identity prompts the SIT to be more curious about a range of new phenomena in the field of psychotherapy supervision. These attitudes of inquiry frequently result in plans to do related research. The area of psychotherapy supervision, still young and relatively unexamined, provides trainees with a range of new and challenging opportunities for further exploration and use of their creativity and research. The new supervisor, having been trained systematically in the rudiments of psychotherapy supervision, is in an especially opportune position to be a contributor to this practice and a researcher in the field of supervision.

Final Evaluation and Feedback

The process of termination forms the ground for the final evaluation. This component of the end phase of supervision should take place at least two weeks prior to the final session of the training. Observing this parameter provides the SIT with an opportunity to examine and discuss the content and process of the supervisor-supervisee evaluation during a training session and to use that as one more learning opportunity. Although the manner, frequency and other variables involved in evaluation have been previously agreed upon in forming the contract, at this time the SIT, as well as the supervisee, may need to reexamine the earlier agreements. They may choose to reiterate which components of the contract regarding evaluation continue to be satisfactory and which ones might need modification, elaboration or greater specification.

It is especially important for the SIT to be clear whether s/he prefers to conduct the supervisee's evaluation and to receive an evaluation from the supervisee in written form or by means of dialogue. In either case the SIT should have the issues to be addressed in this final evaluation prepared well in advance and carry out the evaluative process in a systematic manner. If the choice is to use a written form, the SIT must decide whether to construct an instrument for this purpose by her or himself, or with cooperation of other trainees, or in collaboration with the supervisee. Some SITs may prefer to use a well established and previously validated instrument.

The participants of the training are reminded of Stoltenberg and Delworth's (1987) compilation of *Instruments for Assessing Supervisors and Trainees* (p. 183) and are invited to review that material. The instructor may also distribute sample instruments constructed by SITs who participated in previous training programs.

Further discussion of written evaluation needs to focus on advantages and disadvantages of completing the questionnaire privately then discussing the content of the evaluation with the supervisee versus completing it in the presence of and in consultation with the supervisee. This decision might be based on or related to the developmental stages of supervisor and supervisee. A supervisor well matched with his/her supervisee, according to developmental levels, usually feels secure in completing the evaluation instrument in consultation with the supervisee. On the other hand, an insecure Level 1 supervisor matched with a Level 2 counselor might need more distance in the process of evaluation.

For those SITs who choose to proceed with evaluation by means of dialogue rather than use of a written questionnaire, the time of preparation for the evaluation is diminished, although their learning gains might also be diminished. To mitigate against the ambiguities in the spoken evaluation, the instructor recommends the use of audio and video tape recording with copies available to both the SIT and the supervisee. A further benefit of this intervention is that it provides a record to be reviewed or studied at a later time.

The instructor's non-authoritarian attitude during this last phase of the training provides the SITs with a model to be applied in their own termination with supervisees. Although an excessively resistant attitude may flare up in the early stages of termination, it tends to subside by the time of evaluation. If the resistant attitude persists into the evaluation stage, an authoritarian approach will merely solidify and complicate it. On the other hand, maximizing the student's options at the conclusion of the training tends to be received as a message of respect and collegiality, promoting the experience of "passage".

The information produced by the evaluations does not have to be communicated beyond the SIT and supervisee dyad. However, both SIT and supervisee know that within the constraints of anonymity some of the process and content of the evaluation will be discussed and/or consulted about during the training sessions.

Concomitant with the planning and completion of a final evaluation between the supervisory pair, the instructor also evaluates the SITs and the SITs evaluate the instructor. These evaluation questionnaires are usually provided by the academic or sponsoring institution and the completion of this questionnaire is mandatory. The completed evaluations are filed in the trainees' academic or continuing education records and in the instructor's faculty folder, respectively. The manner of humanizing or bureaucratizing this process is up to the instructor and students.

Celebration

Completion of the final evaluation, feedback and corresponding processing brings the contract between the supervisor and supervisee to its close. Termination is almost completed. At this point of ending, I recommend an additional step before the SIT and his/her supervisee complete the process. This final step is a functional punctuation of the end phase; it consists of a celebration. The form of the celebration, to be agreed upon by SIT and supervisee, can consist of having an informal dialogue about a topic of their choice over a cup of tea or the sharing of a full meal. This celebratory meeting can take place at the location of the other supervisory meetings or a new location, e.g., a coffee shop or restaurant. It can be scheduled at a regular meeting time or at a different time.

A celebration for the end of the training process is also planned; the time and place is mutually chosen by the SITs and the instructor. This event, which I refer to as a "punctuation" to the supervisory engagement, often has an atmosphere of merriment which alternates with serious, intellectually stimulating discussions. Professional hopes and research ideas related to the process of supervision are compared, discussed and mutually built upon.

The conclusion of the celebration meeting marks the completion of a very important passage in the SIT's professional life. Some SITs began the training with strong notions about what psychotherapy supervision is and how to function in the supervisor role. Others began the year with vague notions and a certain sense of amusement that it was not long before that they were similarly uncertain about their role as a therapist. The strong notions are usually modified; the vague ones are clarified, built upon and developed. The potency of the supervisory process is experienced and bestowed with a heavy dose of new respect.

From the very early sessions and explorations of their SLL, through the struggle of defining supervision, through the TES and through the time of studying the didactic material related to all of the above, the trainees are gearing up to the high point of beginning to supervise. With a certain sense of impatience, the SITs study the supervisory contract, issues of matching with and assessing of a supervisee. With some anxiety they embark on the process of supervising. The early sessions of supervision are promising, some of the later ones problematic, the final ones triumphant and satisfying. As participants in the training, the SITs have developed a close bond and frequently continue to use each other as a support system. Their basic preparation for and practice of supervising is completed.

Many will choose to continue the study and practice of supervision. Some will tackle the many unanswered questions about psychotherapy supervision in their dissertation research or during their post doctoral years of practice.

Evaluating the Program

The training program presented in this book does not have the benefit of having been researched or studied by independent observers.

The only data I have are the anecdotal data provided by the SITs who have completed the program and by their supervisees. Upon completion of the program and for a number of years later, a predominant majority of the trainees remember the training as beneficial and fulfilling. Their supervisees, as pointed out earlier, find the SIT to have been an especially useful guide. I concur with Taub, Porter and Frisch's (1988) point of view that having neither literature providing us with "adequate guidelines for training supervisors..." (p. 77), nor a way to approach this training from a non-specific, non-technical point of view, the only assessment data available are the trainees' feedback and evaluations. "Hopefully," point out Taub et al., "as the need to train supervisors becomes widely recognized, and well designed research studies on the supervisory process begin to appear in the literature" (p. 83), it will be possible to use more established guidelines in the development of the training programs for the supervisors of psychotherapy. For now, the program I describe in this book is offered as a training sequence to be experimented with as a whole or in parts; to be adapted to the specific needs of the populations trained; to be modified by a trainer's own ideas and creativity. Then the view of the new roads through the old scapes will once again challenge us to chart new maps.

Part V

Ethics And Supervision

Chapter 12, Ethical and Legal Considerations for the Supervisor, is a radical departure from the flow of the preceding text. The author of this chapter seems not to concern himself primarily with the training of psychotherapy supervisors as he does with the practice of the psychotherapy supervisor. This is accurate. Nevertheless, this chapter serves a very important function in the context of *Old Scapes, New Maps: A Training Program for Psychotherapy Supervisors*. It not only provides material which is relevant to any supervisor, it puts forward an ethical argument for the essential nature of psychotherapy supervision being regarded as an important area of specialization in psychology. This argument would be difficult to make in the absence of a detailed presentation of a training program for supervisors of psychotherapy. The preceding text presents such a program.

Herbert J. Hoffman, Ph.D.

12

Signposts and Signals
Ethical and Legal Considerations

> *Moral capacity may be thought of as the ability to be to be guided in one's behavior by the standards of quality to which one gives inner allegiance.*
>
> M. C. Richards

> *Our actions speak no matter what our lips do or do not say. Responses are values, and the responses we foster are values we teach.*
>
> M. C. Richards

IN THE PROCESS of supervising, the SIT will encounter many of the ethical issues with which supervisors are faced throughout their professional careers. Included among these issues are: limits of confidentiality; duty to warn; boundary maintenance, including social and/or sexual intimacies with a patient; dual relationships; supervisee misrepresentation or significant omissions of clinical material during supervision; supervisee's incompetence or impairment which is harmful to the patient(s). Consistent with the parallel process, each of these issues can emanate from the SIT or supervisee. In order to recognize and address these problem areas, it is necessary to have knowledge of the profession's ethical code, standards of practice for providers of service and a working acquaintance with pertinent laws and regulations. Even with such knowledge, ambiguity can arise.

At a time when psychologists and other mental health professionals are under close public, legal and regulatory scrutiny, it is in the providers' and the consumers' interest to bolster the qualifications of those who are vested with the responsibility of preparing competent practitioners.

This volume has presented a model for the training of psychotherapy supervisors which is designed to assist in filling a glaring gap in the profession. This gap has nurtured the unexamined assumption that to be a supervisor of psychotherapists, a psychologist needs no specific or systematic training in the skills of supervision. Despite this belief and the corresponding gap in preparation of supervisors, the profession has bestowed upon the "supervisor" an authority which serves as the linchpin for virtually all credentialing. In application to a licensing board, a specialty board or many professional organizations, the documentation of relevant experience gained under the direction of a *qualified supervisor* is essential.[9]

Health and mental health organizations are the major providers of supervised clinical and health services experience to psychotherapists in training. This supervised, documented experience becomes a critical element for establishing acceptable credentials when the aspiring psychologist seeks eligibility for licensure or certification. In spite of occasionally poor supervisory practices in institutional settings, the trainee's patients have the protection of access to a network of affiliated senior professionals and an array of facilities. However, once the poorly supervised psychologist is licensed, s/he is able to engage in the *independent* practice of psychotherapy without the requirement of access to resources for patient protection similar to those available at the training sites.

How then does a psychologist qualify as a supervisor? This question has been addressed in the *Introduction*. Basically, psychologists qualify to become supervisors as a mere matter of seniority, i.e., as psychotherapists gain more experience, they are considered eligible to become supervisors. The next levels of concern are: How does a governmental body, i.e., a licensing or certification board define the qualifications of a supervisor? How do voluntary credentialing organizations, e.g., American Board of Examiners in Psychology (ABEP) and The National Register of Health Service Providers in Psychology, define the qualifications of a supervisor? To answer these questions a review of the respective criteria is in order.

Consideration given by the ultimate gatekeepers to independent practice, i.e., the governmental regulatory authorities, to the qualifications of those members of the profession (the supervisors) who are most directly responsible for the training in clinical work performed by aspiring psychologists (psychotherapists), is minimal. A review of a sample of state rules and regulations will help to illustrate this point.

9. This book is concerned with the supervisor of psychotherapists, independent of the supervisor's specific discipline. For exposition purposes, the discipline of psychology and

State Rules and Regulations: A Sample

Massachusetts, the state with which I am most familiar, has incorporated into the Rules and Regulations of the Board of Registration of Psychologists minimal qualifications for supervisors. These qualifications specify that "supervision...shall be obtained from a licensed psychologist.... A psychiatrist who is certified or eligible for certification by the American Board of Psychiatry and Neurology, or a certified member of another bona fide psychological specialty..." (Mass., 1988, 3.06 [4]). Connecticut (1986), Florida (1982), Idaho (1985), Maine (1986), New Hampshire (1984), Ohio (1981), Rhode Island (1981) and Texas (1987) also specify possession of a license as adequate credentialing for qualifying psychologists as supervisors. However, Connecticut, Idaho, Maine, New Hampshire, Rhode Island, Texas and Vermont (1987) specify that, for licensing purposes, *only psychologists* are qualified to be supervisors of psychologists. Ohio, like Massachusetts, considers certain other licensed professionals as qualified supervisors. In contrast to the states requiring minimal qualifications, Idaho, Ohio, Texas and Vermont call for specific competence in the areas being supervised as a prerequisite for qualification:

> Idaho: "The licensed supervising psychologist's proficiencies will be commensurate with the services provided by the [supervisee]" (sec.K,1.l vii).
>
> Ohio: "The supervisor shall be competent in the area(s) of functioning of the supervisee. Competence can be demonstrated with appropriate academic training as well as experience in the area(s) to be supervised" (chapter 4732-13-02 [10]).
>
> Texas: "A supervising psychologist shall have adequate training, knowledge, and skill to render competently any psychological service which a supervisee undertakes. The psychologist shall not permit a supervisee to engage in any psychological practice which the psychologist cannot perform competently" (465.18, a.3).
>
> Vermont: "...receive credit...only if supervisor is qualified in that area [of practice supervised]" (Part 2.1 [2]).

The Rules Governing Psychologists in Ohio, as cited above, also provide a basis, i.e., academic training and experience, for testing the

psychologists who function as psychotherapy supervisors will be the focus of the material to follow.

competence of a supervisor in the areas in which s/he is supervising. Paradoxically, it contains no such test for assessing the supervisor's competence *as a* supervisor, e.g., course work in the theory and practice of supervision, or even specification of the number of years of experience as a supervisor.

The Delaware Psychology Rules and Regulations (1982) places more emphasis on supervisor qualification than most, if not all, psychology regulatory authorities. In the Delaware regulations it is noted that, "supervision of candidates for licensing requires that the supervisor has experience beyond journeyman practice levels. Supervising psychologists shall have at least two years of experience beyond the granting of their license and shall have training in the specific area of practice in which they are offering supervision" (3.D II.A). New Jersey (1978) also requires a supervisor to be two years beyond the granting of the license. Like Massachusetts and Ohio, Delaware accepts supervision by other credentialed professions acceptable to the board, though it places a restriction on the maximum hours of such supervision that is acceptable, i.e., no more than one-quarter of the supervised experience. Delaware also addresses the issue of competence in the areas of being supervised and does take the next step by directly speaking to competency as a supervisor, i.e., "It is the supervisor's obligation to limit supervision to those areas in which he/she has professional expertise, *as well as to develop the specialized skills necessary to render competent supervision* [italics added]" (3.D).

Voluntary Credentialing Bodies

The American Board of Examiners in Psychology (ABEP) and The National Register of Health Service Providers in Psychology, two voluntary credentialing bodies in psychological specialties, including psychotherapy, do not address the issue of academic qualifications of a supervisor. These credentialing bodies accept documentation of a formal internship as indicative of acceptable supervision. That is, the training and qualifications of supervisors, who are in a pivotal training role, are not specified.

National Standards

The American Association of State Psychology Boards, a member organization composed of Psychology Boards from fifty-two United States jurisdictions and eight Canadian Provinces, recently adopted *The Guidelines for Defining Supervised Experience in an Organized Psychological Internship Training Program* (AASPB, 1986). These guidelines were "based on or derived from several sources, including the *Directory of the Association of Psychology Internship Centers Criteria for Accreditation of Internship Programs* (APA), and the *Guidelines for Defining Supervised Experience in an Organized Health Service Training Program* (National Register)" (p. 2). This document contains a single criterion which refers to the qualifications for a supervisor. These guidelines specify that the agency providing the formal internship needs only employ two psychologists, "at least one of whom was actively licensed..." (p. 1), to function in the role of supervisors. Prior to this time, AASPB (1980) had promulgated the following qualifications: "Supervising psychologists shall be licensed or certified for the practice of psychology and have adequate training, knowledge, and skill to render competently any psychological service which their supervisee undertakes. They shall not supervise nor permit their supervisee to engage in any psychological practice which they cannot perform competently themselves" (p. 1).

It appears that at virtually all levels of training and accreditation, sparse attention has been devoted to identifying minimal course work and practice training in psychotherapy supervision to qualify psychotherapy supervisors. An exception to the above, though not widely adopted, is contained in two sections of the American Psychological Association, Division of Psychotherapy (1971) standards for doctoral education. Principle 9 of these standards holds that faculty themselves are to have received coursework and supervised practice training in psychotherapy supervision. The document further states that students are to receive training in psychotherapy supervision. While the professional schools in psychology have included the latter point in their curricula (Bourg, 1988), the former point, regarding the qualifications for faculty, has not been addressed.

The Ethics of Supervision

The role and function of a psychologist supervisor is referred to in the American Psychological Association's Ethical Principles of Psychologists (1981) and Standards for Providers of Psychological Services (1977). Familiarity with these documents is essential for SITs, not only because the conduct proscribed and the guidance contained must become an integral part of their professional identity, but also because of the influence a code of ethics has on the teaching/training function. The SIT is a role model for the aspiring psychotherapist and as such the SIT sets a standard for the supervisee's ethical behavior.

Stoltenberg and Delworth (1987) devote a chapter to Ethical and Other Issues in which they note Newman's (1981) "three major reasons for an examination of ethical issues in clinical supervision. 1. supervision serves as the primary training mode for teaching skills in...therapy; 2. the supervisory relationship is one of inherently unequal status, power and expertise; and 3. the relationship possesses therapy-like qualities, insofar as self evaluation and expectations of personal growth are concerned" (p. 168).

Several authors (Bradley, 1989; Hall, 1988a, 1988b; Harrar, VandeCreek & Knapp, 1989; Keith-Spiegel & Koocher, 1985; Kitchener, 1988; Pope, 1988; Stoltenberg & Delworth, 1987; Stout, 1987; Vasquez, 1988) have identified a number of sections of the APA (1981) Ethical Principles of Psychologists (EP) which are directly related to the supervision of professional practice, particularly the practice of health service providers. They specifically cite the following eight principles: 1. Responsibility, 2. Competence, 3. Moral and legal standards, 4. Public statements, 5. Confidentiality, 6. Welfare of the consumer, 7. Professional relationships, 8. Assessment techniques.

The relevant sections of each of these principles will be discussed (Principles 4 and 8 will not be discussed due to their less direct reference to activities of a psychotherapy supervisor) and examples of how they apply to supervision of psychotherapy will be provided in the following sections.

1. Responsibility

> **Case A:** A supervising psychologist submitted to the Board of Examiners a notarized documentation of acceptable supervised hours in support of an applicant for licensing. Just prior to the exam, the Board received a letter in which the supervisor attempted to withdraw his documentation of supervision, alleging that his former supervisee had engaged in unethical and unprofessional behavior at the supervision site following completion of the internship. Upon investigation, the Board determined that the supervisor had come under pressure to withdraw his endorsement when the applicant, his former supervisee, had engaged in "whistle-blowing" regarding the actions of the head of the agency.

The preamble of Principle 1 states, "In providing services, psychologists maintain the highest standards of their profession. They accept responsibility for the consequences of their acts and make every effort to ensure that their services are used appropriately" (EP:1). Paragraph 1f notes that psychologists bear a "heavy responsibility because their professional actions, including recommendations, may alter the lives of others and they need to be cognizant of a variety of pressures that might lead them to misuse their influence" (EP:1f).

Although a number of ethical principles are involved in Case A, particularly relevant to Principle 1 is the fact that the supervisor attempted to avoid responsibility for his acts. He attempted to withhold documentation of having delivered acceptable supervision on the basis of alleged acts that occured subsequent to the supervised experience. Further, he attempted to misuse his influence in a way that could have altered the professional life of another. The appropriate course of action for the supervisor with regard to the Board of Examiners would have been the filing of a formal complaint against his former supervisee.

2. Competence

> **Case B:** A psychologist came to the attention of a licensing board as a result of a complaint brought by an insurance company. Investigation revealed that in the course of conducting sex therapy, an unlicensed supervisee showed the movie "Deep Throat". The licensee, though aware of his supervisee's actions, was unable to provide a rationale for this intervention. He demonstrated no knowledge of sex therapy, had no training as a supervisor and displayed limited knowledge of the practice of supervision.

Case B illustrates the importance of supervisors having competence both in clinical areas and in the practice of supervision.

The preamble of Principle 2 states, "Psychologists recognize the boundaries of their competence.... They only provide services and only use techniques for which they are qualified by training and experience." To date, the attention regarding supervisors' competency has focused on the supervisor's competency in the *clinical* areas in which the supervisee is practicing. This is evident in the various statutes and definitions cited in the previous section of this chapter and Hall's (1988a) discussion of Competence to Supervise.

Several segments of our society, e.g., government, health provider organizations, consumers of health services, sanction the delivery of health services by persons who are not fully trained, i.e., interns, trainees, assistants, etc. This sanction is given "on the theory that supervision will remedy any deficiencies" (Slovenko, 1980, p. 467), thus underscoring the heavy burden which supervisors carry. Slovenko is also concerned about the potential for a variety of litigations related to the supervisory role. He considers the vulnerable areas to be 1. the service areas being supervised and 2. the supervisor's demonstrable competence in the practice of supervision. As Stoltenberg and Delworth (1987) point out, "Given the current lack of training in supervision..., there appears to be a serious ethical issue in regard to competency to supervise. Just as we now consider it unethical to [deliver psychotherapy] without prior training, we may soon apply the idea to supervision" (p. 171).

Case C: A first year graduate student in psychology was assigned a supervisor, who was also a faculty member, for her initial placement. This supervisor/professor had recently been rejected by his lover for whom he had arranged admittance to the same graduate department. When the supervisor began to make sexual advances toward his new supervisee, she clearly indicated her lack of interest. For the remainder of the academic year, based on information gained from and observations made during supervision, the supervisor/professor continually made negative comments about his supervisee in supervision sessions as well as in classes which he taught. The student became increasingly distressed and withdrew from the doctoral program at the end of her first academic year.

Case C illustrates the relevance of the following section of Principle 2: "Psychologists recognize that personal problems and conflicts may interfere with professional effectiveness...they refrain from undertaking any activity...[which is] likely to lead to inadequate performance or harm...as a consequence of their personal problems" (EP: 2f).

3. *Moral and legal standards*

Case D: As a consequence of a contractual breach, a psychologist was suspended from participation as a provider by a third-party carrier. Following her suspension, the psychologist "convinced" her supervisee, also a licensed psychologist, to submit insurance claims for patients the suspended psychologist continued to treat.

The responsibility of psychologists to uphold legal and moral standards extends beyond the responsibilities of other citizens. Psychologists must avoid actions that "compromise the fulfillment of their professional responsibilities or reduce the public trust in psychology and psychologists" (EP:3). In further specification of this Principle, psychologists as employers do not engage in or condone practices which result in illegal or unjustifiable actions (EP:3b); they avoid actions which may diminish the legal and civil rights of clients and others (EP:3c).

The sequence of events described in Case D is an example of unethical, illegal and unjustifiable actions. As a result of the undue influence exerted upon the supervisee, a fraud was committed. Upon discovery of the fraud, the insurance company disallowed payment of the claims in question, thus depriving the insured of monetary benefits for which they had paid and thereby their legal rights were diminished.

5. *Confidentiality*

Psychologists have an obligation to respect the confidentiality of information obtained from persons during their work in clinical and consulting relationships. This information "is discussed only for professional purposes..." (EP:5a). Supervisors have an evaluative as well as an educative function. In the former role, some confidential information about the supervisee will be shared with others who have an appropriate professional interest, e.g., faculty members, directors of training. As part of the supervisory contract, "the supervisor should be explicit regarding what information about the supervisee she or he will share, with whom, and with what process" (Stoltenberg & Delworth, 1987, p. 172). This standard is also specified by Keith-Spiegel and Koocher (1985) in concluding their discussions of issues related to supervisees (p. 306). The case of the graduate student (Case C) contained in the section on *Competence* illustrates a supervisor's abuse of a confidential relationship with a supervisee and how this abuse can harm the supervisee.

6. *Welfare of the consumer*

Case E: The Board of Examiners received a formal complaint from the group practice partners of Dr. F. The partners alleged that Dr. F was engaged in a sexual relationship with a patient. In an informal hearing before the Board of Examiners, Dr. F not only denied any impropriety with the patient, but he impugned the integrity of his former partners. Following additional investigation and confrontation with "hard evidence", Dr. F did admit having had a sexual relationship with the patient for a period in excess of 18 months. Dr. F also stated that his therapist had counseled him to "tough it out" with the Board as part of his therapeutic work on assertiveness.

The Board subsequently learned the therapist's identity when it received a letter from Dr. C indicating that Dr. F would be joining his practice under his supervision. Dr. C also indicated that he would continue psychotherapeutic treatment of his "new" supervisee, Dr. F.

> In an informal hearing, Dr. C admitted advising Dr. F to circumvent the Board and also admitted having had knowledge for some time of Dr. F's sexual relationship with a patient.

Particularly relevant to the practice of supervision is Principle 6a which addresses the issue of dual relationships. Psychologists are advised to "make every effort to avoid dual relationships that could impair their professional judgment or increase the risk of exploitation" (EP: 6a). There are a number of opportunities for supervisors to become enmeshed in dual relationships with supervisees (Keith-Spiegel & Koocher, 1985; Stoltenberg & Delworth, 1987), including: professor and supervisor, supervisor and sexual intimate, supervisor and therapist, supervisor and close personal friend, supervisor and family member. The danger in such dual relationships is directly related to the inherently uneven distribution of power and potential for a lack of objectivity. In these cases, the supervisor's potential for abuse of power, be it intentional or unintentional, is great and requires constant vigilance on the supervisor's part.

Trust and dependency are significant facets of the supervisory relationship and can easily become compromised as a dual relationship develops. The compromise can frequently result in harm to the supervisor, supervisee and potentially to patients.

The concept of modeling by supervisors is particularly important in the area of ethics training. A supervisor's teaching of ethics is implicitly communicated through modeling behavior and the behaviors carry more weight than overt directions. How the supervisor behaves, what s/he overlooks and what behaviors are encouraged, are more influential than what is communicated in words.

For many years, Pope (Ethics Committee, 1988a) has been engaged in researching the prevalency of sexual behavior between trainers and students. The data gathered by Pope, Schover and Levenson (1980) indicate that 15% of psychologists in training report having had a sexual relationship with a professor/trainer. This proportion in and of itself is significant and has important implications. That is, not only does such a relationship compromise and undermine the obligation of supervisors to provide fair and accurate evaluations of their supervisees (Keith-Spiegel & Koocher, 1985; Pope et al., 1980), it is reasonable to expect that those supervisees, having suffered the transgressions of their supervisors, are more likely to engage in sexual relationships with their supervisees and clients. Indeed, Pope (1988) has noted that this sample of students, when they become supervisors or administrators, tend to collude with the sexually acting-out supervisee by "sweeping the matter under the rug".

The APA Ethical Principles states, "Sexual intimacies with clients are unethical" (6a). The "supervisee holds a special 'dual role' as both a provider [of clinical services] and as a consumer [of supervisory guidance]" (Stout, 1987, p.91). Though the Ethical Principles did not specifically refer to supervisees as clients, it is plausible to equate supervisee with client. Indeed, Stout makes the flat statement "that any [sexual] contact between a supervisor and a supervisee...is considered unethical conduct..." (p. 94). Keith-Spiegel and Koocher (1985) say "that although the [Ethical Principles] does not ban sexual intimacies with [supervisees] outright, aggrieved...supervisees have sufficient avenues of recourse..." (p. 266) in areas of the Principles which address responsibility for professional development (7c) and exploitation (7d). The National Register of Health Service Providers in Psychology has recognized the possibility of impaired judgment and risk of exploitation by supervisors in a dual relationship (Hall, 1988b) by including the following statement under Supervisor Qualifications: "4. Supervisor, at the time of supervision, must not be in a dual relationship with the supervisee; e.g., spouse or other close relative, therapist." This standard has been adopted by a number of the individual regulatory boards.

In the fall of 1988 the APA Ethics Committee recognized the persuasive arguments cited above and issued a policy statement which further clarifies Principle 6a: "Principle 6a clearly prohibits dual relationships that could impair professional judgment or increase the risk of exploitation. Romantic or sexually intimate relationships between clinical supervisors and supervisees constitute, by fact and definition, dual relationships. Psychologists make every effort to avoid such dual relationships." (Ethics Committee, 1988b). Though stopping short of defining such relationships as clearly unethical, as Principle 6a does in the matter of clients, this new policy sends a significant signal to psychotherapy supervisors.

An additional, frequent instance of a dual relationship concerns the situations in which the supervisor is also the supervisee's therapist, e.g., Case E. The potential for abuse and exploitation is high as the supervisor must juggle the functions of educator and evaluator with the intimacy of a therapeutic relationship, while maintaining clear boundaries. In a survey conducted by Pope, Tabachnick and Keith-Spiegel (1987), "about one-fourth of the [APA Division of Psychotherapy] members reported providing therapy to their supervisees... It is reasonable to assume [such] dual relationships would be found to be unethical" (Ethics Committee, 1988a, p. 568).

7. *Professional relationships*

It is apparent from the material presented in the preceding section that supervisors who become involved in sexual or other intimate relationships with their supervisees have the potential for exploiting the relationship and compromising the supervisee's professional development. Principle 7c states, "Psychologists who...supervise...accept the obligation to facilitate the further professional development of these individuals." 7d adds, "Psychologists do not exploit their professional relationships with...supervisees...sexually or otherwise."

Just as a therapist in relationship with patients, the supervisor, in relationship with supervisees, has the burden of responsibility to establish and maintain appropriate boundaries. The supervisor's hierarchical position in the profession, combined with his/her key role as evaluator, places the supervisee in a dependent, vulnerable position and can lead to various forms of abuse. For example, supervisors may distort evaluations, fail to provide timely feedback, provide the supervisee with favorable or unfavorable recommendations according to sexual favors granted or denied [see Case C].

Other relevant principles

Although Principle 4, Public Statements, and Principle 8, Assessment Techniques, have not been discussed, it should be noted that supervisors [with the exception of SITs] assume professional and ethical responsibility for their unlicensed supervisees and are therefore accountable for ethical breaches committed by their supervisees. Therefore, it follows that all sections of the Ethical Principles are ultimately relevant in the supervisory relationship.

Gatekeeper Accountability

Included among the responsibilities of psychotherapy supervisors is the ongoing evaluation of their supervisees. The supervisee's ethical behavior is one of the foci of the ongoing evaluation. Instructors of psychotherapy supervision should be no less involved in the ongoing evaluations of their SITs' ethical behavior.

Supervisors and faculty members are key gatekeepers for the profession of psychotherapy and bear a heavy responsibility when they become aware of a supervisee/student who behaves unethically, functions with insufficient competence, or is otherwise impaired.

It is not uncommon to hear stories of students and supervisees having their unprofessional or difficult behavior overlooked, excused, or swept under the rug. Fear of litigation and the desire to avoid conflict are probably major contributors to the failure of supervisors and faculty members in confronting these difficult issues. Kitchener (1988), a former APA Ethics Committee Chair, notes that unethical psychologists were trained somewhere and it is likely that they displayed symptoms of future problems during their graduate training. Thus, not only is the student/supervisee to be held accountable for not complying with ethical standards, the trainers (supervisors, faculty) are also accountable for treating the trainee (supervisee/student) in an ethical manner by "ensuring remedial action is taken, or engage in a process of assessing remediation" (Kitchener, 1988, p. 4).

There are instances in which supervisees are unable or unwilling to remediate unacceptable behavior as a result of their failure to cooperate, lack of motivation or psychological impairment. These supervisees must not be allowed to pass through, eventually become credentialed and thereby place the public at risk while simultaneously undermining the profession as a whole (Kitchener, 1988).

While there are no simple or easy ways of dealing with the complexities of a supervisee/student who is presenting questionable or unethical behavior, Kitchener (1988) and Vasquez (1988) do provide guidance for supervisors and faculty members. The following five points are critical:

1. Face the problem.

2. Provide clear guidance in the area of ethics, modeling by supervisors/faculty is considered a vital component.

3. Have a formal statement which addresses the issues of the supervisee's/student's rights and responsibilities and contains a procedure which ensures due process.[10]

4. Differentiate between problems and impairment; often this involves assessment by an independent consultant.

5. Provide remediation opportunities and be prepared to dismiss the student or fail the supervisee if s/he is unable to meet a minimal standard.

A perplexing circumstance

Case F: A female member of a therapy group filed a complaint against her therapist, who was unlicensed, for a. having administered a designer drug during sessions and b. for involving her in sexual behavior both during and outside therapy sessions. The therapist was supervised weekly by a licensed psychologist. The supervisor professed no knowledge of the illegal and unethical behavior until after the complaint was filed.

10. A document which could serve as a model is, Rights and Responsibilities of Trainees. Counseling and Mental Health Center. The University of Texas at Austin. (Vasquez, 1988, Appendix A, 10-19.)

This case presents a particularly difficult and perplexing situation for supervisors–and regulators, i.e., the instance in which a supervisee, intentionally or otherwise, withholds critical information or misrepresents material that has ethical and/or legal implications. Often this information initially comes to the supervisor's attention following a patient's complaint.

Case F is very similar to one described by Keith-Spiegel and Koocher (1985, p. 306) and probably is representative of an occurence which happens more frequently than any supervisor would like to imagine.

While the supervisor will maintain that s/he is not to blame, there is no way for the supervisor to avoid legal and ethical responsibility, and apparently there are no absolute safeguards in such situations (Hassenfeld & Sarris, 1978). Usually this type of situation occurs when either the supervisor is not assiduous in supervising, develops a special relationship or close friendship with the supervisee which influences his/her judgment, or colludes in a *pro forma* supervision for purposes of third-party reimbursement of the supervisee's services.

Legal Issues

The preceding section, while focused on ethical issues, clearly included legal issues as well. Every licensing or certification law governing psychologists contains an ethics and/or a code of conduct section which either incorporates or derives from the APA Ethical Principles. Thus, for the licensed psychologist a breach of ethics may also be a violation of state law (Harrar et al., 1990).

Vicarious Liability

The information covered in this section is important to the SITs' instruction, however, based on the parameters of their role as trainees, the SITs are exempt from "vicarious liability."

The example presented in the preceding section (Case F) which described a supervisee engaged in unethical acts without the supervisor's knowledge (or perhaps even with it) has both ethical and legal consequences for the supervisor. The legal doctrine of "vicarious liability" or "imputed negligence" holds that in certain relationships the negligence of one party [supervisee] may be charged against the other party [supervisor] even though "the latter [supervisor] has played no part in it, has done nothing whatever to aid or encourage it, and in fact has done all that he possibly can to prevent it (Prosser, 1971, p. 458)" (Slovenko, 1980, p. 453). Hall (1988b) cites Mariano and Cohen (1982) as noting that practitioners have been held liable for the conduct of their agents, i.e., supervisees, in malpractice actions. "As pointed out by

[Cohen and Mariano], psychotherapy supervision...may be carried out in a pro forma fashion with little attention to the needs of the individual supervisee or the clients served by that individual" (p. 3). This type of inadequate supervision is not uncommon in large fee-for-service organizations or practices.

Difficulties related to health insurance reimbursement

Supervisors do get into ethical and legal difficulty in situations involving third-party reimbursement by insurance carriers. Some of the more frequent infractions involve fraud or misrepresentation to the insurers. Usually this takes the form of a supervisor representing work performed by supervisees as personally delivered by him/her. Case D is a blatant example of such an infraction.

The above points are amplified by the Ethics Committee (1988a) with the warning that "billing for services that have not been rendered by the psychologist signing the [insurance] form" must be avoided. "This includes signing forms for supervisees without the supervisee's cosignature. Kovacs (1987) noted that 'such behavior constitues insurance fraud, requires perjury to commit...and if done as part of a plan concocted with...the client may constitute conspiracy as well' (p. 22)" (p. 569).

Exposure to financial liability is further compounded for the supervisor who employs assistants. "A judgment arising out of an activity carried out by an unlicensed or otherwise incompetent employee might not be covered by the employer-physician's malpractice insurance, since most policies provide coverage only for negligence of 'duly qualified' assistants (Holder, 1975, p. 201)" (Slovenko, 1980, p. 454). In this context, a recent letter to all professional liability insureds from the Chair of the American Psychological Association Insurance Trust (APAIT) lists "failure to supervise properly," which likely includes many of the practices described in the preceding cases, as a reason for suit based on APAIT's experience (Bennett, 1987).

The increasing proliferation of various health care models primarily designed for cost containment, e.g. health maintenance organizations, which rely on a structure of lower paid service deliverers under the supervision of a qualified professional, may lead to the "suit of the future," i.e., malpractice litigation involving supervisors (Slovenko, 1980). Slovenko cites three cases, including *Tarasoff v Regents of University of California* (1974), in which supervisors were sued as a result of supervisees' actions. He identifies thirteen circumstances in which it can be assumed that the actions of the supervisor or supervisee proximately caused damage or injury to the patient and are therefore potential areas of malpractice (p. 463).

How then can the supervisor of psychotherapy discharge his/her responsibilities for training psychotherapists, being professionally, ethically and legally responsible for his/her supervisees, while simultaneously reducing his/her vulnerability to malpractice suits and disciplinary actions? Keith-Spiegel and Koocher (1985), Slovenko (1980) and Stoltenberg and Delworth (1987) do offer some guidelines which, though not complete safeguards, protect the prudent supervisor. Included among their recommendations are careful documentation of supervision, exercise of "due care", i.e., "the degree of diligence, care and skill that ordinarily prudent men would exercise under similar circumstances in like position", personally assessing very disturbed or possibly dangerous patients, following relevant laws and accepted standards of practice. "Most important, *it is vital that the supervisor be well trained, knowledgeable and skilled in the practice of clinical supervision* [italics added]. The supervisor should be cognizant of crucial legal issues and should examine his or her work with these questions in mind" (Stoltenberg & Delworth, 1987, p. 175).

In summary, ethical and legal considerations for supervisors and supervisees have been discussed and their importance in education and practice underscored. It is in this context, and the context of the training program, that we endorse Harrar, et al.'s (1990) encouragement of "training facilities, licensure and credentialing boards, and the the APA to reconsider the assumption that knowledge about ethical and legal guidelines for supervision can be obtained informally" (p. 40). Further, the issue of identifying supervisors' qualifications and competence has been explored.

Trainees and others, i.e., service extenders, not sanctioned to function at the independent practice level are allowed to deliver psychotherapeutic services on the premise that supervision safeguards or improves the standard of care (Bell, 1978; Kapp, 1984; Slovenko, 1980). Thus, the supervisor is placed in the role of an educator, a role for which s/he may or may not be prepared (Slovenko, 1980).

It is in the public's and profession's best interest to heed Stoltenberg and Delworth's (1987) charge: "...there is a need, perhaps even an ethical imperative for training programs and service settings to offer education...about supervision and what we need to know. If we agree on the necessity of training for the role [psychotherapist] perhaps we are ready to admit that such training is needed for the supervisory role as well" (p. 179).

The contents of this volume constitute one tool for meeting that training need.

Appendix
Reading List

Books

Alonso, A. (1985). *The quiet profession.* NY: Macmillan Publishing Co.

Ekstein, R. & Wallerstein, R.S. (1978). *The teaching and learning of psychotherapy.* NY: International Universities Press.

Fleming, J. & Benedek, T.F. (1966). *Psychoanalytic supervision: A method of clinical teaching.* NY: Grune & Stratton.

Hart, G. (1982). *The process of clinical supervision.* Baltimore, MD:University Publishing Press.

Hess, A.K. (Ed.). (1982). *Psychotherapy supervision: Theory, research and practice.* NY: Wiley. [Especially Parts I-III, Chapter 16, and Parts VII-IX.]

Langs, R.J. (1976). *The bipersonal field.* NY: Jason Aronson, Inc.

Stoltenberg, C. & Delworth, U. (1987). *Supervising counselors and therapists: A developmental approach.* San Francisco, CA: Jossey-Bass & Co.

Reprints

Alonso, A. & Rutan, J. (1978). Cross-sex supervision for cross-sex therapy. *American Journal of Psychiatry,* 135, 928-931.

Arlow, J. (1963). The supervisory situation. *Journal of the American Psychoanalytic Association,* 11, 576-594.

Markowitz, M. (1958). A supervisor supervised: A subjective, eclectic experience. *American Journal of Psychotherapy,* 12, 488-492.

Van Buskirk, D. (undated). *Professional transitions and institutional issues in the supervisory process.* Unpublished manuscript.

Resources

Books:

Bradley, L. (1989). *Counselor supervision: Principles, process and practice* (2nd Ed.). Muncie, IN: Accelerated Development.

Gambrill, E. & Stein, T.S. (1983). *Supervision: A decision making approach.* Beverly Hills, CA: Sage Publications.

Journals:

The Clinical Supervisor

Counselor Education and Supervision

References

Akamatsu, J.T. (1980). The use of role play and simulation technique in the training of psychotherapy. In A.K. Hess (Ed.), *Psychotherapy supervision: Theory, research and practice* (pp. 209-225). NY: Wiley.

Albott, W. (1984). Supervisory characteristics and other sources of supervision variance. *The Clinical Supervisor, 2,* 27-41.

Aldrich, L. (1981). *Construction of mixed standard scales for the rating of psychotherapy supervisors.* Unpublished master's thesis, Auburn University.

Aldrich, L. (1982). *Construction of a scale for the rating of supervisors of psychology.* Unpublished master's thesis, Auburn University.

Aldrich, L. & Hess, A.K. (1983, March). *The parallel process in psychotherapy supervision.* Paper presented at the annual Southeastern Psychological Association Convention, Atlanta, GA.

Allen, G., Szollos, S. & Williams, B. (1986). Doctoral students' comparative evaluations of best and worst psychotherapy supervision. *Professional Psychology: Research and Practice, 17,* 91-99.

Alonso, A. (1985). *The quiet profession.* NY: Macmillan Publishing Company.

Alonso, A. & Rutan, J. (1978). Cross-sex supervision for cross-sex therapy. *American Journal of Psychiatry, 135,* 928-931.

Altucher, N. (1967). Constructive use of the supervisory relationship. *Journal of Counseling Psychology, 14,* 165-170.

American Association of State Psychology Boards (1980). *Guidelines for the employment and supervision of uncredentialed persons providing psychological services.* Montgomery, AL: Author.

American Association of State Psychology Boards (1986). *Guidelines for defining supervised experience in an organized psychological internship training program.* Montgomery, AL: Author.

American Psychological Association, Division of Psychotherapy (1971). Recommended standards for psychotherapy education in psychology doctoral programs. *Professional Psychology, 2,* 148-154.

American Psychological Association. (1972). *Ethical standards of psychologists.* Washington, D.C: Author.

American Psychological Association (1977). *Standards for providers of psychological services.* Washington, DC: Author.

American Psychological Association (1981). *Ethical principles of psychologists.* Washington, DC: Author.

American Psychological Association (1987). General guidelines for providers of psychological services. *American Psychologist, 42,* 712-723.

Arbuckle, D.S. (1963). The learning of counseling: Process not product. *Journal of Counseling Psychology, 10,* 163-168.

Arbuckle, D.S. (1965). Supervision: Learning, not counseling. *Journal of Counseling Psychology, 12,* 90-94.

Archer, R. & Peake, T. (1984). Learning and teaching psychotherapy: Sign posts and growth stages. *The Clinical Supervisor, 2,* 61-74.

Arlow, J. The supervisory situation. *Journal of the American Psychoanalytic Association, 11,* 576-594.

Banikiotis, P. (1975). Personal growth and professional training. *Counselor Education and Supervision, 15,* 163-168.

Baranger, M. & Baranger, W. (1966). Insight in analytic situation. In Riditman (Ed.), *Psychoanalysis in the Americas.* NY: International Universities Press.

Bartlett, W.E. (1983). A multidimensional framework for the analysis of supervision of counseling. *The Counseling Psychologist, 11,* 9-17.

Barth, R. & Gambrill, E. (1984). Learning to interview: The quality of training opportunities. *The Clinical Supervisor, 2,* 3-14.

Bell, W.S. (1978). Medico-legal implications of recent legislation concerning allied health practitioners. *Loyola of Los Angeles Law Review, 11,* 379-398.

Bennett, B. (1987, Dec. 15). *Letter to all professional liability insureds.* (Available from APAIT, 910 17th St. NW, Washington, DC.)

Bernard, J.M. (1979). Supervisory training: A discrimination model. *Counselor Education and Supervision, 19,* 60-68.

Bernard, J. M. (1981). In-service training for clinical supervisors. *Professional Psychology, 12,* 740-748.

Bernard, J. M. (1989). Training supervisors to examine relationship variables using ISR. *Clinical Supervisor, 1,* 103-112.

Bernstein, B.L. & Lecomte, C. (1979). Supervisory-type feedback effects: Feedback discrepancy level, trainee psychological differentiation, and immediate responses. *Journal of Counseling Psychology, 26,* 295-303.

Blocker, D.H. (1983). Toward a cognitive developmental approach to counseling supervision. *The Counseling Psychologist, 11,* 27-34.

Borders, L.D. (1989, August). Learning to think like a supervisor. In M.V. Ellis (Chair), *Training psychotherapy and counseling supervisors: A diversity of approaches.* Symposium conducted at the 97th Annual Convention of the American Psychological Association, New Orleans.

Bourg, J. (1988, August). Discussant. In A.R. Nurse (Chair), *New developments and controversies in the education of professional psychologists.* Symposium conducted at the 96th Annual Meeting of the American Psychological Association, Atlanta, GA.

Boyd, J.D. (1978). The behavioral approach to counselor supervision. In J.D. Boyd (Ed.), *Counselor supervision: Approaches, preparation, practices,* (pp. 87-132). Muncie, IN: Accelerated Development.

Bradley, L. (1989). *Counselor supervision: Principles, process and practice (2nd Ed.).* Muncie, IN: Accelerated Development.

Brameld, T. (1959). *The remaking of a culture: Life and education in Puerto Rico.* NY: Harper.

Brammer, L.M. & Wassner, A.C. (1977). Supervision in counseling and psychotherapy. In D.J. Kurpius, R.D. Baker & I .D. Thomas (Eds.), *Supervision of applied training: A comparative review* (43-82). Westport, CN: Greenwood Press.

Brannon, D. (1985). Adult learning principles and methods for enhancing the training role of supervisors. *The Clinical Supervisor, 3,* 27-41.

Brodsky, A. (1980). Sex role issues in the supervision of therapy. In A.K. Hess (Ed.), *Psychotherapy supervision: Theory, research and practice,* (pp. 509-522). NY: Wiley.

Brown, G.I. (1972). *Human teaching for human learning.* NY:Viking.

Bruch, H. (1974). *Learning psychotherapy: Rationale and ground rules.* Cambridge, MA: Harvard University Press.

Bruner, J. (1957). Going beyond the information given. In *Contemporary approaches to cognition.* Cambridge, MA: Harvard University Press.

Buber, M. (1970). *I and thou.* NY: Scribner's.

Burns, C. & Holloway, E. (1989). Therapy in supervision: An unresolved issue. *The Clinical Supervisor, 7 (4),* 47-60.

Butler, E.R. & Hansen, J.C. (1973). Facilitative training: Acquisition, retention, and modes of assessments. *Journal of Counseling Psychology, 20,* 60-65.

Carifio, M.S. & Hess, A.K. (1987). Who is the ideal supervisor? *Professional Psychology, 18,* 244-250.

Cohen, L. (1980). The new supervisee views supervision. In A.K. Hess (Ed.), *Psychotherapy supervision: Theory, research and practice* (pp. 78-84). NY: Wiley.

Cohen, R.J. & DeBetz, B. (1977). Responsive supervision of the psychiatric resident and the clinical psychology intern. *American Journal of Psychoanalysis, 37,* 51-64.

Collins, E.R. (1962). Teaching and learning in medical education. *Journal of Medical Education, 37,* 671-686.

Connecticut (1986). *Regulation of Department of Health Services.* 20-188-1.

Delaney, D.J. (1972). A behavioral model for the supervision of counselor candidates. *Counselor Education and Supervision, 12,* 40-50.

Delaney, D.J. (1978). Supervising counselors in preparation. In D.J. Boyd (Ed.), *Counselor supervision: Approaches, preparation, practices,* (pp. 339-374). Muncie, IN: Accelerated Development.

Delaware (1982). *The Delaware Psychology Rules and Regulations.*

Dewald, P.A. (1969). Learning problems in psychoanalytic supervision: Diagnosis and management. *Comprehensive Psychiatry, 10,* 107-121.

Dewey, J. (1916). *Democracy and education.* NY: Macmillan.

Doehrman, M.J.G. (1976). Parallel processes in supervision and psychotherapy. *Bulletin of the Menninger Clinic, 40,* 9-84.

D'Zmura, T.L. (1964). Teaching of psychotherapy. The function of individual supervision in teaching of psychotherapy. *International Psychiatry Clinics, 1,* 337-387.

Ekstein, R. (1965). Working through and termination. *Journal of American Psychoanalysis, 13,* 57-78.

Ekstein, R. & Wallerstein, R.S. (1978). *The teaching and learning of psychotherapy* (3rd. ed.). NY: International Universities Press.

Ethics Committee of the American Psychological Association. (1988a). Trends in ethics cases, common pitfalls, and published resources. *American Psychologist, 43,* (7), 564-572.

Ethics Committee of the American Psychological Association. (1988b). Policy Statement, October 5-7.

Fisher, R. & Ury, W . (1984). *Getting to yes.* New York: Penguin Books.

Fleming, J. & Benedek, T.F. (1966). *Psychoanalytic supervision: A method of clinical teaching.* NY: Grune & Stratton.

Florida (1982). *Rules of the Department of Professional Regulation, Board of Psychological Examiners.* Chapter 21 U-10.

Fox, R. (1983). Contracting in supervision: A goal oriented process. *The Clinical Supervisor, 1*, (1), 37-49.

Fox, R. & Guild, P. (1987). Learning styles: Their relevance to clinical supervision. *The Clinical Supervisor, 5,* (3), 65-77.

Freeman, E. (1985). The importance of the feedback in clinical supervision. Implications for direct practices. *The Clinical Supervisor, 3,* 5-26.

Friedman, M. (1988, August). Elements of a new humanistic psychology. In A.R. Mahrer (Chair), *After Maslow and Rogers—A new humanistic psychology?* Symposium conducted at the 96th Annual Meeting of the American Psychological Association, Atlanta, GA.

French, J. & Raven, B. (1960). The basis of social power. In D. Cartwright & H. Zander (Eds.), *Group Dynamics.* Evanston, IL: Row & Peterson.

Gale, M.S. (1976). Resident perception of psychotherapy supervision. *Comprehensive Psychiatry, 17,* 191-194.

Gardner, L.H. (1980). Racial, ethnic, and social class considerations in psychotherapy supervision. In Hess (Ed.), *Psychotherapy supervision: Theory, research and practice* (pp. 474-508). NY: Wiley.

Gilligan, C. (1982). *In a different voice. Psychological theory and women's development.* Cambridge, MA: Harvard University Press.

Gitterman, A. & Miller, I. (1977). Supervisors as educators. In F.W. Kaslow (Ed.), *Supervision, consultation and staff training in the helping professions* (pp. 100-114). San Francisco: Jossey-Bass.

Goin, M.K. & Kline, F.M. (1974). Supervision observed. *Journal of Nervous and Mental Disease, 158,* 208-213.

Goldfarb, N. (1978). Effect of supervisory style on counselor effectiveness and facilitative responding. *Journal of Counseling Psychology, 25,* 454-460.

Goodyear, R.K. & Robyak, J.E. (1982). Supervisor's theory and experience in supervisory focus. *Psychological Reports, 51,* 978.

Grater, Hany, A. (1985). Stages in psychotherapy supervision: From therapy skills to skilled therapist. *Professional Psychology 16,* 605-610.

Gregoc, A.F. (1979). Learning/Teaching styles: potent forces behind them. *Educational Leadership, 36,* 234-236.

Haley, J. (1986). The art of being a failure as a therapist. In Haley, J., *The power tactics of Jesus Christ and other essays, (2nd ed.)* Rockville, MD: Triangle Press.

Hall, J. (1988a). Protection in supervision. *Register Report*, *14*, (4), 3-4.

Hall, J. (1988b). Dual relationships in supervision. *Register Report, 15, 5-6.*

Harrar, W.R., VandeCreek, L. & Knapp, S. (1990). Ethical and legal aspects of clinical supervision. *Professional Psychology, 21,* 37-41.

Hart, G. (1982). *The process of clinical supervision.* Baltimore, MD: University Publishing Press.

Hassenfeld, I.N. & Sarris, J.G. (1978). Hazards and horizons of psychotherapy supervision. *American Journal of Psychotherapy, 32,* 393-401.

Heath, A.W. & Storm, C.L. (1983). Answering the call: A manual for beginning supervisors. *The Family Therapy Networker, 7,* (2), 36-37, 66.

Heisenberg, W. (1974). *Across the frontiers,* (P. Heath, Translator). NY: Harper & Row.

Hendrickson, D.E. & Krause, F.H. (1972) (Eds.), *Counseling and psychotherapy: Training and supervision.* Ohio: Merrill.

Henessey, T.C. (1982). Part I: A background and a basis for a reaction. *The Counseling Psychologist, 10,* 49-52.

Heppner, P.P. & Roehlke, H.J. (1984). Differences among supervisees at different levels of training: Implications for a developmental model of supervision. *Journal of Counseling Psychology, 31*, 76-90.

Hess, A.K. (1980a). *Psychotherapy supervision: Theory, research and practice.* NY: Wiley.

Hess, A.K. (1980b). Training models and the nature of psychotherapy supervision. In A.K. Hess (Ed.), *Psychotherapy supervision: Theory, research and practice* (pp. 15-25). NY: Wiley.

Hess, A.K. (1986). Growth in supervision: Stages of supervisee and supervisor development. In F. W. Kaslow (Ed.), *Supervision and training: Models, dilemmas, and challenges* (pp. 51-67). NY: Haworth.

Hess, A.K. (1987a). Psychotherapy supervision: Stages, Buber and a theory of relationship. *Professional Psychology, 18,* 251-259.

Hess, A.K. (1987b). Advances in psychotherapy supervision: Introduction. *Professional Psychology, 18*, 187-188.

Hess, A.K. & Hess, K.A. (1983). Psychotherapy supervision: A survey of internship training practices. *Professional Psychology, 14,* 504-513.

Hester, R., Weitz, L.J., Anchor, K.N. & Robach, H.B. (1976). Supervisor attraction as a function of supervisor skillfulness and supervisee's perceived similarity. *Journal of Counseling Psychology, 23*, 254-258.

Hill, C.E., Charles, D., & Reed, K.G. (1981). A longitudinal analysis of changes in counseling skills during doctoral training in counseling psychology. *Journal of Counseling Psychology, 28*, 428-436.

Hogan, R.A. (1964). Issues and approaches in supervision. *Psychotherapy: Theory, Research and Practice, 1*, 139-141.

Hora, T. (1957). Contributions to the phenomenology of the supervisory process. *American Journal of Psychotherapy, 11*, 769-773.

Idaho (1985). *Board of Psychologist Examiners, Rules and Regulations.*

Jacobson, N.S. (1988, August). *Efficacy of psychotherapy: Fact or fiction?* Presidential address at the 96th Annual Meeting of the American Psychological Association, Atlanta, GA.

Kadushin, A. (1974). A supervisor-supervisee. *Social Work, 19*, 288-298.

Kadushin, A. (1976). *Supervision in social work.* NY: Columbia University Press.

Kaplowitz, D. (1967). Teaching empathic responsiveness in the supervisory process of psychotherapy. *American Journal of Psychotherapy, 21*, 774-781.

Kapp, M.B. (1984). Supervising professional trainees: Legal implications for mental health institutions and practitioners. *Hospital and Community Psychiatry, 35*, 143-147.

Karr, J. & Geist, G. (1977). Facilitation in supervision as related to facilitation in therapy. *Counselor Education and Supervision, 16*, 263-267.

Keith-Spiegel, P. & Koocher, G. R. (1985). *Ethics in psychology.* NY: Random House.

Kell, B.L. & Mueller, W.J. (1966). *Impact and change: A study of counseling relationships.* Englewood Cliffs, NJ: Prentice-Hall.

Kennard, B.D., Stewart, S.M., & Gluck, M.R. (1987). The supervision relationship: Variables contributing to positive versus negative experiences. *Professional Psychology, 18*, 172-175.

Kitchener, K.S. (1988, August). Training and ethics: What are our obligations when students are unethical? In K.S. Pope (Chair) *Ethics in academic and training settings.* Symposium conducted at the 96th Annual Meeting of the American Psychological Association, Atlanta, GA.

Knowles, M.S. (1970). *The modern practice of adult education.* NY: Association Press.

Kolb, D.A., Rubin, I.M., & McIntyre, J.M. (Eds.) (1974). *Organizational psychology: A book of readings (2nd Ed.).* Englewood Cliffs, NJ: Prentice-Hall.

Krishnamurti, J. (1976). *Bulletin, Krishnamurti Foundation of America, 30.*

Krumbetz, J.D. (1967). Changing the behavior of behavior changes. *Counselor Education and Supervision, 6,* 222-229.

Kubie, L. (1958). Research into the process or supervision in psychoanalysis. *Psychoanalytic Quarterly, 27,* 226-236.

Kurpius, D.J., Baher, R.D. & Thomas, I.D. (1977). The supervisory process: Analysis and synthesis. In D.J. Kurpius, R.D. Baher & I.D. Thomas (Eds.), *Supervision of applied training: A comparative review (224).* Westport, CN: Greenwood Press.

Kutzik, A.J. (1977). The medical field. In F.W. Kaslow (Ed.), *Supervision, consultation, and staff training in helping professions* (pp. 25-60). San Francisco: Jossey-Bass.

Lambert, M.J. (1974). Supervisory and counseling process: A comparative study. *Counselor Education and Supervision, 14,* 54-60.

Lambert, M.J. (1980). Research and the supervisory process. In A.K. Hess (Ed.), *Psychotherapy supervision: Theory, research and practice* (pp. 423-452). NY: Wiley.

Langs, R.J. (1976). *The bipersonal field.* NY: Jason Aronson, Inc.

Leddick, G.R. & Bernard, J.M. (1980). The history of supervision: A critical review. *Counselor Education and Supervision, 19,* 186-19.

Lister, J.L. (1966a). Counselor experiencing: Its implications for supervision. *Counselor Education and Supervision, 5,* 55-60.

Lister, J.L. (1966b). Supervised counseling experiences, some comments. *Counselor Education and Supervision, 6,* 69-72.

Litrell, J.M., Lee-Borden, N. & Lorenz, J.A. (1979). A developmental framework for counseling supervision. *Counselor Education and Supervision, 19,* 129-136.

Loewald, H.W. (1960). On the therapeutic action of psychoanalysis. *International Journal of Psychoanalysis, 41,* 16-33.

Loganbill, C., Hardy, E. & Delworth, U. (1982). Supervision: A conceptual model. *The Counseling Psychologist, 10,* 3-42.

Loganbill, C. & Hardy, E. (1983). In defense of eclecticism. *The Counseling Psychologist, 11* (1),79..

Maine, (1986). *Board of Examiners of Psychologists, Rules and Regulations.*

Mariano, W.E. & Cohen, R.J. (1982). *Legal guidebook in mental health.* NY: Free Press.

Markowitz, M. (1958). A supervisor supervised: A subjective eclectic experience. *American Journal of Psychotherapy, 12,* 488-492.

Marshall, W.R. & Confer, W.N. (1980). Psychotherapy supervision: Supervisee's perspective. A.K. Hess (Ed.), *Psychotherapy supervision: Theory, research and practice* (pp. 92-100). NY: Wiley.

Massachusetts, (1988). *Board of Registration of Psychologists, Rules and Regulations.* 251-CMR.

Mathews, W.M. & Wineman, D. (1953). Problems of supervision and training in clinical psychology. The supervision of clinical diagnostic work. *American Journal of Psychiatry, 23,* 293-300.

McColley, S.H. & Baker, E. (1982). Training activities and styles of beginning supervisors: A survey. *Professional Psychology, 13,* 283-292.

McNeill, B.W., Stoltenberg, C.D., & Pierce, R.A. (1985). Supervisee's perceptions of their development: A test of the counselor complexity model. *Journal of Counseling Psychology, 32,* 630-633.

McNeill, B.W. & Worthen, V. (1989). The parallel process in psychotherapy supervision. *Professional Psychology: Research and Practice, 20,* 329-333.

Melchiode, G.A. (1977). Psychoanalytically oriented individual therapy. In F.W. Kaslow (Ed.), *Supervision, consultation, and staff in the helping professions* (pp. 155-174). San Francisco: Jossey-Boss.

Miars, R.D., Tracey, T.J., Ray, P.B., Cornfeld, J.L., O'Farrell, M. & Gelso, C.J. (1983). Variation in supervision process across trainee experience levels. *Journal of Counseling Psychology, 30,* 403-412.

Moskowitz, S.A. & Rupert, P.A. (1983). Conflict resolution within the supervisory relationship. *Professional Psychology: Research and Practice, 14,* 632-641.

Moustakas, C. (1981). *Rhythms, rituals and relationships.* Detroit, MI: Center for Humanistic Studies.

Mueller, W.J. & Kell, B.L. (1972). *Coping with conflict: Supervising counselors and psychotherapists.* NY: Appleton-Century-Crofts.

Myers, I.B. (1976). *Introduction to type.* Gainsville, FL: Center for Applications of Psychological Type.

Netzky, W., Davidson, J., & Crunkleton, A. (1982). Pertinent consumer issues in choosing a counseling professional. *Journal of Counseling Psychology, 29,* 406-413.

Nevis, E.C. (1987). *Organizational consulting: A gestalt approach.* NY: Gardner Press, Inc.

New Hampshire, (1984). *Board of Examiners of Psychologists, Code of Administrative Rules,* Chapter Psy 100-1000.

New Jersey, (1978). *Board of Psychological Examiners Regulations.* 13: 41-1.1-5.1.

Newman, A.S. (1981). Ethical issues in the supervision of psychotherapy. *Professional Psychology, 12,* 690-695.

Ohio, (1981). *Rules Governing Psychologists.* Chapter 4732 of the Admin. Code.
Olmstead, J. & Christensen, H.E. (1973). *Effects of agency work contexts: An intensive field study,* (Research Report no.2). Washington, DC: Department of Health, Education and Welfare.

Patterson, C.H. (1964). Supervising students in the counseling practicum. *Journal of Counseling Psychology, 11,* 47-53.

Payne, P.A. & Gralinski, D.M. (1968). Effects of supervisor style and empathy upon counselor learning. *Journal of Counseling Psychology, 15,* 517-521.

Payne, P.A., Weiss, S.D. & Kapp, R.A. (1972). Didactic, experimental and modeling factors in the learning of empathy. *Journal of Counseling Psychology, 19,* 425-429.

Payne, P.A., Winter, D.E. & Ball, G.E. (1972). Effects of supervisor style on the learning of empathy in a supervision analogue. *Counselor Education and Supervision, 11,* 262-269.

Pierce, R.A. Carkhuff, R. & Berenson, B. (1967). The effects of high and low funtioning supervisors upon counselors in training. *Journal of Clinical Psychology, 23,* 212-215.

Peter, L.F. & Hull, R. (1969). *The Peter principle.* NY: Morrow.

Petty, M. & Odewahn, C. (1983). Supervisory behavior and sex role stereotypes in human service organizations. *Clinical Supervisor, 1,* (2), 13-20.

Pope, K.S. (1988, August). Student-teacher sexual relations. In K. Pope (Chair), *Ethics in academic and training settings.* Symposium conducted at the 96th Annual Convention of the American Psychological Association, Atlanta, GA.

Pope, K.S., Schover, L.R. & Levenson, H. (1980). Sexual behavior between clinical supervisors and trainees: Implications for professional standards. *Professional Psychology, 11,* 157-162.

Pope, K.S., Tabachnick, B.G., & Keith-Spiegel, P. (1987). Ethics of practice: The beliefs and behaviors of psychologists as therapists. *American Psychologist, 42,* 993-1006.

Ralph, N.B. (1980). Learning psychotherapy: A developmental perspective. *Psychiatry, 43,* 243-250.

Reising, G.N. & Daniels, M.H. (1983). A study of Hogan's model of counselor development and supervision. *Journal of Counseling Psychology, 30,* 235-244.

Rhode Island, (1981). *Rules and Regulations Pertaining to the Certification of Psychologists.* R5-44-PSY.

Rioch, M.J. (1980). The dilemmas of supervision in dynamic psychotherapy. In A.K. Hess (Ed.), *Psychotherapy supervision: Theory, research and practice* (pp. 68-77). NY: Wiley.

Rosenblatt, A. & Mayer, J. (1975). Objectionable supervising styles: Student's views. *Social Work, 18,* 184-189.

Rotholtz, T. & Werk, A. (1984). Student supervision: An educational process. *The Clinical Supervisor, 2,* 15-27.

Russell, R., Grimmings, A. & Lent, A. (1984). Counselor training and supervision: Theory and research. In S.D. Brown & R.W. Lent (Eds.), *Handbook of counseling psychology.* NY: Wiley.

Sager, C. (1976). *Marital contracts.* NY:Brunner/Mazel.

Satir, V. (1972). *Peoplemaking.* Palo Alto, CA: Science and Behavior Books.

Schafer, R. (1973). The termination of brief psychoanalytic psychotherapy. *International Journal of Psychoanalytic Psychotherapy, 2,* 135-148.

Searles, H.F. (1955). The informational value of supervisor's emotional experiences. *Psychiatry, 18,* 135-146.

Semrad, E.J. & Van Buskirk, D. (Eds.) (1969). *Teaching psychotherapy of psychotic patients.* NY: Grune & Stratton.

Shemberg, K.M. & Leventhal, D.B. (1978). A survey of activities of academic clinicians. *Professional Psychology, 9,* 580-586.

Slovenko, R. (1980). Legal issues in psychotherapy supervision. In A.K. Hess (Ed.), *Psychotherapy supervision: Theory, research and practice* (pp. 453-473). NY: Wiley.

Spiegal, P. & Grunebaum, H. (1977). Training versus treating the psychiatric resident. *American Journal of Psychotherapy, 31,* 618-625.

Stevens, J. (1971). *Awareness.* Lafayette, CA: Real People Press.

Stewart, W. (1963). An inquiry into the concept of working through. Journal of the *American Psychoanalytic Association, 11,* 474-499.

Stoltenberg, C. (1981). Approaching supervision from a developmental perspective: The counselor complexity model. *Journal of Counseling Psychology, 28, 59-65.*

Stoltenberg, S. & Delworth, U. (1987). *Supervising counselors and therapists: A developmental approach.* San Francisco, CA: Jossey-Bass & Co.

Stout, C.E. (1987). The role of ethical standards in the supervision of psychotherapy. *The Clinical Supervisor, 5* (1), 89-97.

Styczynski, L. (1980). The transition from supervisee to supervisor. In A.K. Hess (Ed.), *Psychotherapy supervision: Theory, research and practice* (pp. 29-40). NY: Wiley.

Swain, D. (1981). *Behaviorally anchored rating scale for recipients of psychotherapy supervision: Instrument construction.* Unpublished master's thesis, Auburn University.

Tarachow, S. (1963). *An introduction to psychotherapy.* NY: International Univ. Press.

Tarasoff v Regents of University of California, (1974). 529 P. 2d 342, 118 Cal. Rptr. 129, vacated. 17 Cal. 3d 425, 551 P.2d 334, 131 Cal. Rptr. 14 (1976).

Taub, B.R., Porter, J.E., & Frisch, G.R. (1988). Training for psychotherapy supervisors: A supervision traineeship program. *The Clinical Supervisor,* 6 (2), 75-84.

Tylor, J.D. & Weaver, S.H. (1981). Evaluating the clinical supervisee. *Professional Psychology, 12,* 434-437.

Texas, (1987). *Rule's and regulations of the Texas State Board of Examiners of Psychologists.* 461.1-.16.

Uhlemann, M., Lea, G. & Stone, G. (1976). Effect of instructions and modeling on trainees low in interpersonal communication skills. *Journal of Counseling Psychology, 23,* 509-513.

Udang, E. (1979). In defense of process recording. *Smith College Studies In Social Work, 1,* 1-15.

Van Buskirk, D. (undated). *Professional transitions and institutional issues in the supervisory process.* Unpublished manuscript.

Vasquez, M.J.T. (1988, August). Ethics training and monitoring in internship settings. In K. Pope (Chair), *Ethics in academic and training settings.* Symposium conducted at the American Psychological Association, Atlanta, GA.

Vermont, (1987). *Administrative rule for the Vermont Board of Psychological Examiners.* Part 1-4.

Weiner, I.B. & Kaplan, R.G. (1980). From classroom to clinic: Supervising the first psychotherapy client. In A.K. Hess (Ed.), *Psychotherapy supervision: Theory, research and practice* (pp. 41-50). NY: Wiley.

Windholtz, E. (1970). The theory of supervision in psychoanalytic education. *International Journal of Psychoanalysis, 51,* 393-406.

Winnicott, D.W. (1965). *The maturational processes and the facilitating environment.* London: Hogarth Press.

Witkin, H.A. (1977). Cognitive styles in the educational setting. *New York University Education Quarterly, 8* (3), 14-20.

Worthington, E. (1984). An empirical investigation of supervision of counselors as they gain experience. *Journal of Counseling Psychology, 31,* 63-75.

Worthington, E. (1987). Changes in supervision as counselors and supervisors gain experience: A review. *Professional Psychology, 18,* 189-208.

Zinker, J. & Nevis, S.M. (1981). The gestalt theory of couple and family interactions. *Working paper,* Center for study of intimate systems. Gestalt Institute of Cleveland.

Author's Index

Subject Index

Notes

Notes